MIKHAIL BAKUNIN:

THE PHILOSOPHICAL BASIS OF HIS ANARCHISM

MIKHAIL BAKUNIN:

THE PHILOSOPHICAL BASIS OF HIS ANARCHISM

PAUL MCLAUGHLIN

Algora Publishing
New York

No portion of this book (beyond what is permitted by
Sections 107 or 108 of the United States Copyright Act of 1976)
may be reproduced by any process, stored in a retrieval system,
or transmitted in any form, or by any means, without the
express written permission of the publisher.
ISBN: 1-892941-84-8 (softcover)
ISBN: 1-892941-85-6 (hardcover)

Library of Congress Card Number: 2002-001934

McLaughlin, Paul.
  Mikhail Bakunin : the philosophical basis of his anarchism /
by Paul McLaughlin.
     p. cm.
Includes bibliographical references and index.
  ISBN 1-892941-84-8 (alk. paper)
  1. Bakunin, Mikhail Aleksandrovich, 1814-1876. I. Title.
  HX914.7.B34 M35 2002
  335'.83—dc21

                         2002001934

Printed in the United States

Front Cover: Portrait of Bakunin (1814 - 1876)

TABLE OF CONTENTS

Acknowledgements

I wish to thank the following: Prof. David McLellan for his level-headed advice, welcome encouragement, and lentils; Martin Rodden, Maciej Malolepszy, Philippe Vandendaele, and others for hours of instructive conversation (apologies for endless talk of Bakunin and my work on him); Malgorzata Sulislawska for the motivation to complete this project; Marta Majdecka for having the decency to tolerate me of late; and my family — my brother Eugene (for English transport and beer tokens), my sister Aoife (for prolonged use of her computer), my sister Cara (for book acquisition and Hapkin imports), and, most of all, my mother Maura McLaughlin (for everything that long-suffering Irish mothers are known to put up with, and more besides).

INTRODUCTION

Bakunin as Philosopher?

The primary purpose of this essay, as the title indicates, is to examine the philosophical foundations of Mikhail Bakunin's social thought. Thus it is concerned not so much with the explication of the anarchist position of Bakunin as such as with the basic philosophy which underpins it. This philosophy has, as far as I can determine, two central components: a negative dialectic or revolutionary logic; and a naturalist ontology, a naturalistic account of the structure of being or reality. These two components are analyzed in the two main sections of this essay — but a preliminary question is begged, relating to the very significance of Bakunin as a philosophical thinker, the very significance of this apparent philosophical "non-entity" (Karl Marx's judgment, seemingly confirmed by Bakunin's absence from the philosophical canon). The question might be put in the following way: is Bakunin worthy of philosophical consideration?

The mass of scholarship — or certainly Anglophone scholarship — on Bakunin holds that he is not. Anglophones — not surprisingly, given the ideological order in Anglophone countries — are especially hostile; Bakunin is generally regarded more sympathetically and treated more seriously in Latin countries, for instance. Due to the extent of this hostility, and the sheer orthodoxy by now of this hostile interpretation in the Anglophone world — to say nothing of my own background — it is Anglophone scholarship (and the "foreign" element that it has adopted) that is of utmost concern in what is undeniably a broadly sympathetic (though not uncritical) treatment of Bakunin.[1]

By and large, Bakunin scholarship (if it can be called that) falls into two categories — alas, two ideological categories: Marxist and liberal. Conservative analysis of Bakunin is less conspicuous. Nevertheless Eric Voegelin, whose views will be outlined below, has made a serious contribution from this perspective. What is most noteworthy about the case of Voegelin is that it supports an argument of Bakunin's *Die Reaktion in Deutschland* (*The Reaction in Germany*) (1842): that the conflict between consistent revolutionaries and "consistent reactionaries" is marked by more honesty than the conflict between the former and "mediating reactionaries".

Marxist Analysis

Marxist analysis of Bakunin is, it appears, predetermined by the less than flattering analysis of the master (which will be attended to directly later). Indeed, Marxist arguments *against* Bakunin are clearly identifiable as *arguments from authority* (every possible pun intended). Thus Bakunin emerges as a "voluntarist" with no understanding of political economy or the workings of capital, that is to say, as an impatient and "apolitical" "bandit" and a theoretical "ignoramus" — for the simple reason that he dares to disagree with the historically disputed and, as I will argue, philosophically tenuous doctrine, as he dared to cross Marx in his revolutionary activity.[2] This damning indictment of Bakunin is made in spite of the fact that not one Marxist has actually conducted an in-depth analysis of the theoretical writings of Bakunin. Hence one might accuse Marxist scholars of being, at the very least, uninformed.

Examples of this level of Marxist scholarship are numerous, even excluding the most dubious "Marxist-Leninist" material. A standard example is George Lichtheim. (Lichtheim, like Francis Wheen [see below], is marxist [note the lower-case "m"] at least to the extent that he is generally sympathetic to Marx and that he sides with Marx against Bakunin on the major points of their controversy.) His views on Bakunin encapsulate the Marxist critique[3]: basically, Bakunin is no thinker, no philosopher, no theorist, but a mere "agitator". "He remained, one may fairly say [?], all his life a man of action rather than a thinker". The "all his life" phrase is prevalent among those scholars, both Marxist and liberal (as we will see), who seek to impose a uniform and simplistic account on the complex intellectual biography of Bakunin. Hence, we are told that he "remained all his life" either a mindless revolutionary (the Marxist line) or a hopelessly idealistic intellectual (the liberal line). In either case, however, he has no philosophical merit: on this point liberals and Marxists concur. Thus while the liberal maintains that Bakunin was a thinker — but a poor one — the Marxist maintains that he was not really a thinker at all, but to the extent that he was, he was a poor one. As Lichtheim puts it: "There remains the philosophical aspect, for Bakunin of course had to have a philosophy — as a former Hegelian he could hardly afford to be without one". But, as for this philosophy, it was mere "muddled thinking [which] never rose above the level of the professional agitator with a few fixed ideas and a stock of ready-made phrases". (This notion is echoed in an essay of Isaiah Berlin's, as we will see shortly.)

There are a number of criticisms to be made of Lichtheim's account. Firstly, he misunderstands (or misrepresents) the genesis of Bakunin's thought. Repeating the Marxist orthodoxy, he associates Bakunin as closely as possible with Proudhon, the "petty bourgeois" quasi-liberal. (Indeed, even the detested Proudhon is given more credit than Bakunin; at least he was "a theorist, though a self-made one". "Self-made", a standard Marxist insult with respect to Proudhon, presumably means a hick not educated at the University of Berlin.) While Proudhon was a major influence on Bakunin, to leave it at that, citing (the misrepresented) Proudhon alone, is to obscure the diversity of influences on Bakunin and the complexity of his intellectual development — no doubt with the intention of simplifying his thought.

Secondly, in this context, Lichtheim simply fails to grasp Bakunin's argument. For example, he does not see the "link between his atheism and his anarchism" — the very foundation of Bakunin's social philosophy, as I hope to demonstrate. For Lichtheim, the two elements are attributable to Bakunin's supposed "pan-destructive" lust. Additionally, Lichtheim utterly misreads Bakunin by claiming that "He was after all a Romantic" with "an unshakable faith in the goodness of mankind". Bakunin was no romantic in this or any other respect. Man is not "naturally good" for Bakunin; neither is "naturally bad" or "crooked" as the theologistic argument of his opponents would have it. He is naturally morally-neutral — with the capacity to act morally in a "just" social environment. Thus, "for men to be moralized, their social environment must be moralized".[4] In any case, Bakunin's roots are very much in the Enlightenment tradition and his main philosophical interest is the development of Enlightenment naturalism and "anti-theologism". Romanticism is, for Bakunin, a form of "modern idealism" or anthropocentrism, the very object of his naturalistic critique. In fact, the accusation of romanticism, not confined to Lichtheim's account, has a ring of Marx's unquestioned accusation of "voluntarism" — an accusation to be questioned below.

Lichtheim concludes with a bit of nationalistic gibberish — of the kind that Marx tended to direct Bakunin's way. Needless to say, Bakunin himself was guiltier than most of engaging in nationalistic and racist invective — reciprocating Marx's (and Engels') anti-Slavism with anti-Germanism and, worse still, passionate anti-Semitism. This aspect of Bakunin's writing is, from any standpoint, indefensible. The least that might be asked of Lichtheim, however, would be to raise the tone of the debate by abandoning this nonsense — together with the related forms of class snobbery and intellectual supremacism, which are rarely absent from Marxist discussion of anarchism. But he writes: "Bakunin had translated into words what the Russian peasant — or the landless Italian and Spanish laborer — *dimly felt* about the civilization erected at his expense. Anarchism was destined for a career in these lands".

Lichtheim's final insult is to chastise this peasant ideology for "its inability to come to terms with the modern world". As a marxist criticism of anarchism, this is really too much. While the majority of

"Marxists" stubbornly persist with outmoded and discredited dogma, unwilling to meet the modern demands of ecological crisis for example, or capitulate entirely to liberal capitalism, Blairite-fashion (and in that sense literally "come to terms with the modern world"), anarchism, in the tradition of Bakuninian naturalism, has sought to progress beyond myopic economism and to develop genuinely revolutionary modern ideas and movements (not least in the shape of social ecology). Philosophically, in any event, the fact that Bakunin remains a more progressive influence on the left than Marx has been acknowledged at last in mainstream philosophy (by Peter Singer), as we will see. But this whole debate will be pursued further in the body of this essay.

A recent example of essentially marxist (again, lower-case "m") analysis of Bakunin can be found in Francis Wheen's biography of the master.[5] Aside from the superfluity of this work, the idiocy of its tone, and the poverty of its content overall, its chapter on Bakunin ("The Rogue Elephant", a title which, like the rest, illustrates the public schoolboy wit of Wheen) captures the essence of Marxist critique once again — in other words, it rehashes Marx's original words of abuse, adding only an element of *Private Eye* "humor" in its references to the "fat, toothless giant" etc.[6] (Actually, Marx himself, as Wheen observes approvingly, employed similar terms of "humorous" abuse.) As a contemporary and archetypal marxist critique, and, at that, one with a wide circulation and an unjustifiably authoritative air, it is worth commenting on briefly, though no more than that.

Wheen's argument amounts to the following: Bakunin is no philosopher, but a revolutionary hothead with a taste for intrigue and no understanding of capital. As Wheen himself puts it: Bakunin "bequeathed no great theoretical scripture" (clearly Marx, on the other hand, did bequeath such a "scripture", as handed down by hordes of disciples); "His legacy was the single idea that the state was evil and must be destroyed" (a simple falsehood, as this essay will demonstrate); "Bakunin was . . . a creature of pure emotion who despised Marx's meticulous rationalism and attention to detail. His lack of interest in the complex mechanics of capital was matched or balanced by Marx's contempt for cloak-and-dagger skullduggery"; etc. Astonishingly, Wheen has the temerity to state that "almost everything said and written [thus far] about this battle of the giants is nonsense"; this is not untrue, but the suggestion that *Wheen's* account will clear the water once and for all (despite the best efforts of Bakuninists to defend his honor[7]) — that *his* supposedly original and penetrating account is an exception to the rule of nonsense — is preposterous.[8]

The account offered by Wheen is not original at all: it is, as I have said, Marx's account parroted and an account regurgitated by legions of Marxists before Wheen. Neither is Wheen's account penetrating; indeed, the truth-content of the chapter on Bakunin approaches zero. The contention that Bakunin was "a creature of *pure* emotion", for example, is plainly meaningless — what could it possibly mean? The contention that he lacked "interest in the complex mechanics of capital" is, as a criticism, similarly meaningless; Bakunin just disputed the one-sidedness of Marxian economism and, as Marxists might concede, there is a world of difference between disagreement and disinterest or ignorance. That Wheen's account should be unoriginal and unpenetrating is not surprising in any event since, evidently, he has not read Bakunin and depends entirely on secondary material: there are no first-hand references to original texts of Bakunin in the chapter — never mind references to any philosophical texts which might entitle Wheen to dismiss Bakunin's ideas. Thus Wheen's account lacks any scholarly merit.

Liberal Analysis

We turn now to liberal analysis of Bakunin. Remarkably, this is even more hostile than Marxist analysis. Why this is so is a pressing question. My suspicion is that there are two basic reasons. The first is that Bakunin's critique of liberalism is stinging, a great deal more powerful than he has been credited for, and that it has therefore offended this tradition to no inconsiderable extent. The second is that, from the liberal perspective at least, Bakunin is seen to occupy common ground (on the central concept of liberty in particular), but that he is seen to occupy it much more consistently (embracing negative *and* positive aspects of liberty) and radically (seeking a *meaningful* or *concrete* realization of liberty). The very integrity of Bakunin's theory is a challenge to the malleable and abstract theory of liberals.

As mentioned above, liberals, like Marxists, seem intent on portraying Bakunin as a philosophical non-entity. (An immediate and clear example is Thomas Garrigue Masaryk, who concludes: "In the theoretical field Bakunin did little to further the formulation either of socialism or of anarchism".[9]) Again, however, liberals tend to lack any awareness of Bakunin's theoretical work (or any philosophical acumen when this work receives perfunctory attention); they are preoccupied, as a rule, with his "eccentric" personality and how any depiction of it might downgrade his thought. Thus they proceed from personal slurs to philosophical dismissal, a method which would be repudiated in any other field of scholarship (that is, by genuine scholars). Such an approach to Marx, for example, would be found unacceptable, even among liberals. Hence liberal criticism tends to come from the psychological or psychoanalytic direction, albeit tarted-up in "psycho-historical" form. Brian Morris has summed up the state of Bakunin scholarship accordingly: "Marxists dismiss him as a misguided romantic with a bent for destruction and secret societies . . . . Liberal scholars, on the other hand, continue to find Bakunin fascinating — but only as a subject for studies in utopian or Freudian psychology".[10]

This liberal procedure — the move from the personal to the theoretical — is explained in the manner of Eugene Pyziur: "the contradictoriness of Bakunin's character influenced not only his relations with his companions and his private life, but also his political deeds and their ideological rationalizations". In other words, Bakunin's "character was the basis of *all* that [he] did". This procedure is, of course, grounded on an assumption that Bakunin's theory was developed purely in line with political or even personal needs, independent of general philosophical or ethical considerations — an assumption which is groundless and which would be rebuffed, justly, in the case of anyone else (e.g., Marx or Mill). Pyziur informs us,

He used philosophy in an arbitrary manner for the support of his socio-political premises. These, however, were not usually reached by the means of philosophical cognition. The philosophical superstructure was imposed on top of ready-made ideological and political conclusions. In the revolutionary era of his life, Bakunin's attitude toward philosophy was, on the whole, a utilitarian one, and therefore his extensive variations on philosophical themes contribute little toward an understanding of his political doctrine. [11]

This is a pretty harsh judgment of any writer, and it is difficult to imagine how it might fairly have been arrived at in this case. At any rate, no scholar, Pyziur included, has yet justified such a judgment. It seems to me that critics of Bakunin are a great deal guiltier of what they accuse him of doing: trying to fit factual evidence into some sort of *a priori* (or, if you prefer, ideological) framework, or trying to make the facts accord with their (psycho-) logic. Thus, when Aileen Kelly (who we will discuss below) says the following of Bakunin, she describes herself and those of a similar disposition fittingly:

> As with all explanations of the world which are based on *a priori* assumptions, the formal coherence and symmetry of his abstract structure was much more important to Bakunin than its conformity with empirical data, which could always be interpreted *a posteriori* to fit a given thesis.[12]

Robert M. Cutler, sharing my interpretation, has surmised that Kelly's book "tends less to reconstruct the meaning of the evolution of Bakunin's thought over time than to place his ideas in the mold of a seemingly precast interpretive design".[13]

Others who have undertaken to establish his philosophical stature have observed the broad liberal approach to Bakunin. Richard B. Saltman, for instance, notes that Bakunin scholarship as a whole has tended to marginalize his theoretical achievements, which are said to be "without serious intellectual or political merit", and to concentrate on "his eccentric personality". Indeed, the supposed fact that Bakunin was "psychologically deficient" is the basis of the little theoretical critique of

Bakunin that is put forward from the right. Saltman also agrees that the attempt to deny Bakunin's theoretical caliber is made in spite of "the evident unfamiliarity with Bakunin's actual manuscripts" of most commentators.[14] Paul Avrich has noticed a similar approach in E.H. Carr's biography, the first serious study of Bakunin in English.

> Carr's book, though well-written and still indispensable to anyone interested in Bakunin, places undue emphasis on the more curious and eccentric aspects of Bakunin's personality while paying too little attention to his ideas and their impact on the revolutionary and working-class movements. There is no serious discussion of *The Knouto-Germanic Empire and the Social Revolution*, and *Statehood and Anarchy* is not even mentioned, though these are Bakunin's longest and most important works.[15]

The spiritual leader among liberal critics of Bakunin is Isaiah Berlin. His, in the current context, utterly predictable assessment of Bakunin is that "he is not a serious thinker", that "what is to be looked for in him is not social theory or political doctrine, but an outlook and a temperament". He repeats, "There are no coherent ideas to be extracted from his writings of any period, only fire and imagination, violence and poetry". (Quite where the poetry is in Bakunin's work is anyone's guess. Alexander Herzen, whom Berlin champions, is much more the poet — and Bakunin, despite what he says, much more the political thinker. In this sense, as Morris has pointed out, "Berlin's thesis is back to front".[16]) Again: "Bakunin . . . has not bequeathed a single idea worth considering for its own sake; there is not a fresh thought, not even an authentic emotion" in his writing. In fact, Bakunin was not interested in bequeathing ideas *for their own sake*: his ideas were understood by him to be related to reality as a whole and to have some bearing on at least the socio-political aspect of it. They were not, like a great number of Berlin's essays, intellectual indulgences. As for "authentic emotion": that is something rather difficult to gauge, and beyond my powers if not Berlin's. The "psycho-historians" can speculate on such things to their hearts' content; as far as I am concerned, it has no bearing on philosophical inquiry. "Fresh thought", on the other hand, is a particular obsession of Berlin. Ultimately his comparison of Herzen and Bakunin is that Herzen's thought is "original to an arresting degree", that he "is an original thinker", while Bakunin is "never original". Even if this is true (I will reserve judgment for the time being), so what? Originality in itself is no philosophical endorsement. Berlin's fixation with this matter is, however, easily understood given that he is, by any measure, a profoundly unoriginal thinker himself. This fact in itself would not merit a mention but for the fact that Berlin's most recognized "bequest" — his distinction between two concepts of liberty — had been acknowledged before him by none other than the "never original" Bakunin — who was rather indifferent to whether he was the first, himself.[17] Indeed, what is most amusing about Berlin's account is that what he criticizes (fairly or not) in Bakunin is often much more evident in his own writing. How about the following for a self-portrait: "his positive doctrines . . . turn out to be mere strings of ringing commonplaces, linked together by vague emotional relevance or rhetorical afflatus rather than a coherent structure of genuine ideas"?[18]

Even those who recognize Berlin's "intellectual brilliance" (I have to say I remain unconvinced) deduce that "his portrayal of Bakunin is biased, crude, and unfair".[19] His bias is patently ideological, and his critique a quite fanatical liberal attack on a thinker whose dismissal seemingly warrants only a few pages in an essay that is frankly an ode to a misrepresented Herzen (and a few passing comments elsewhere). Nevertheless, bad as the ideologue may be, there is something worse: the ideologue's lackey. This role is fulfilled by the most rabid in the long list of "scholarly" Bakunin critics, Aileen Kelly.

Kelly's volume receives considerable attention in this essay. This is no mark of respect. The simple and unfortunate fact is that any seemingly substantial work on a subject as rarely treated as Bakunin — particularly when it is the work of an Oxbridge scholar, is published by a reputable and widely-circulated publisher, and says nothing in the least likely to offend those who count — tends to be regarded as definitive (or definitive by default). Indeed, formally, Kelly's work is impressive: it has all the trappings of a scholarly work (extensive notes, a sprinkling of the appropriate terminology, a confident tone) and there is no doubt that it has been well researched. This may account for the book's positive reception by (ideologically sympathetic) reviewers. However, none of this substitutes for scholarly content, and in this respect, as I hope to demonstrate throughout this essay, Kelly's study is quite unimpressive. (Morris has arrived at the same opinion: "Kelly's study is . . . scholastic [but] not a work of scholarship".[20]) Her philosophical ignorance is apparent (and something of a liability given Bakunin's philosophical concerns), her basic "utopian" thesis absurd (see below), and her hostile conclusions obvious to all (as, no doubt, they were to her) at the outset. These criticisms, in any case, will be explained in the main part of this essay.

The liberal procedure, again, is to move from some would-be psychological analysis of Bakunin to a wholesale rejection of his ideas. This procedure is as evident in Kelly's work as anywhere else. Thus her all-round personality assassination makes comic ground out of, for example, Bakunin's alleged sexual deviations (e.g., "his possessive affection for his sister Tatyana which went beyond the bounds of brotherly love") and, more so, his financial misdemeanors (or "his unscrupulousness over matters of money"[21]). About these I am bound to declare that I do not care — for the simple reason that they seem irrelevant to an analysis of Bakunin's thought. I have no more desire to know about these aspects of Bakunin's existence than to discover the intimate details of Kelly's life. Such preoccupations seem to me much more perverse than their objects and, intellectually, far more revealing.

When even this aspect of criticism is shelved in Kelly's Conclusion — and it is hardly powerful enough a slander to leave in the reader's memory — she follows the lead of her liberal predecessors in applying one last slanderous method against Bakunin: dubious association with a subsequent historical nightmare — in this case, the Stalinist nightmare. The message to Bakunin critics seems to be: if you can't disgust your readers, try to terrify them. Hence:

> Bakunin's vision of the unified human personality of the distant future may differ from the Marxist one in its rhetoric and the immediacy of its appeal, but it comes from the same philosophical stable [no, it does not, as we will see] and imposes the same

constraints on the choice of means [clearly not]. Given that the use of force is the only way yet devised of eliminating the tension between the individual and the whole, the proponents of the ideal of the unity of civic and political society [that is not Bakunin's ideal] are constrained by their own logic to propose a dictatorship which submerges the first in the second as a means to the goal of the ideal society. Our century has seen how the means tend to become the immediate end; the goal recedes to a distant future, and eventually the despotism which was to lead to paradise becomes instead a "desperate simulation" ["[the] phrase used by Leszek Kolakowski to characterize the Stalinist state"] of paradise itself.[22]

Fine. Bakunin said all this before Kelly, as we will see, and it is highly respectful of her to repeat it, in utter ignorance, as a criticism of Bakunin himself. What more can one say? Bakunin criticized such "Stalinist" tendencies and must therefore, of necessity (by the constraints of his own logic), be some kind of "Stalinist" himself.

This method is employed even more explicitly by Carr (who associates Bakunin with Italian fascism), Masaryk (who associates him with Bolshevism), Pyziur (who follows Masaryk), and Berlin (who also associates him with fascism[23]). As I see it, such criticism does not warrant much of a response. As tendentious as it is to associate a thinker (like Marx) with subsequent movements that he seems to have advocated, it is completely unjust to associate a thinker with subsequent movements that represent exactly what he unambiguously denounced. In the last analysis, such arguments, such desperate final attempts to disparage, reveal the misdirection, if not the baselessness, of the criticism overall.

Two Further Considerations

Bakunin's writings, as critics have never tired of pointing out, are somewhat chaotic. (Naturally, such a trait is seen to be characteristic of caricatured anarchism.) For example, "his writings are a disconnected series of fragmentary articles, essays, and pamphlets, most of them unfinished, almost all of them poorly composed".[24] This formal flaw — which rapidly metamorphosizes into a substantial flaw in the eyes of critics —

is generally exaggerated: there is plentiful coherent, original, and insightful material in an *oeuvre* that, admittedly, does invite and often requires extensive editing. For the most part, this is the material that I draw on for this essay. I do not think this is too difficult to justify: it does not seem unreasonable to concentrate on the best material of a philosopher when evaluating his contribution. If one were to concentrate, after personal defects and misdeeds, on every philosopher's more embarrassing intellectual efforts, tossing the more worthy achievements onto the garbage heap along with them without serious analysis, then it would appear that there is no philosopher worth reading. It seems only fair that Bakunin should receive the same scholarly treatment as everyone else. The fact that his ideas apparently shock and threaten most scholars does not justify the application of different, or lower, analytical standards. It certainly does not justify, for example, a one paragraph discussion of Bakunin's major work in an "intellectual biography" that concludes, presumably on the basis of evidence, that "His anarchism is intellectually shallow". That kind of analysis would not make the grade in an undergraduate essay — and neither should it.[25]

Those who seek to minimize Bakunin's philosophical accomplishment have also, on occasion, noted his own repudiation of philosophy.[26] They might put it as follows: how could one who denies being a philosopher, and who seems so philosophically inept to experts such as ourselves anyhow, possibly have anything of philosophical interest to say? This is a widely misinterpreted aspect of Bakunin's writing. It is clear, both contextually and extra-contextually, that what Bakunin rejects is a certain kind of philosophy, a kind he associates with figures whom, in part (but in part only), he admires (e.g., Marx and Comte); that is, *systematic* and *theologistic* philosophy and, especially, philosophy which claims to have the future within its *speculative* sight. We will comment on his criticism of these forms later, but two very basic facts need to be mentioned at the outset. First, if Bakunin really thought of himself as a nonphilosopher, it is curious that one of his most important later writings should be entitled *Considérations philosophiques sur le fantôme divin, sur le monde réel et sur l'homme* (*Philosophical Considerations on the Divine Phantom, on the Real World, and on Man*) (1871). Second, it is similarly curious that Bakunin should describe himself as "a passionate seeker of the truth", a highly classical definition of a philosopher, as he would have recognized.[27] The fact is that, by this definition (and what better definition is there?), Bakunin clearly identifies himself as a philosopher, all the while distancing himself from certain philosophical deformations such as deism and romanticism.

In any case, such is the state of Bakunin scholarship — at least in the Anglophone world — to date. For this reason, I am inclined to agree with Morris' assertion that, with some minor exceptions, Bakunin's thought "has not been discussed anywhere with the seriousness it deserves".[28] It is the intention of this study to discuss it in all seriousness, not in the hope of establishing Bakunin as a philosophical great (which I do not believe he is), but in the belief that he is both part of a significant tradition of thought and at least significant in himself. Bakunin's significance is akin to that of Feuerbach — another misunderstood and marginalized thinker. Feuerbach is no philosophical great, either, but in a sense his significance transcends systematic greatness or freewheeling genius. The same can, I think, be said of Bakunin.

The Structure of the Essay

I mentioned in the introductory paragraph that there are, as I see it, two basic elements in Bakunin's philosophy. I divide this essay accordingly. In the first part, I explore Bakunin's revolutionary outlook as conditioned by the negative dialectic he developed during his Left Hegelian period under the influence of Bruno Bauer, among others. Thus I concentrate on Bakunin's Berlin thought and explore its relation to his earlier (presumably) Fichtean period and, in particular, his later anarchist period. I hope to arrive thereby at an understanding of the development of his naturalism, which underpins his later philosophical atheism and, in turn (via the "anti-theologistic" critique of divine authority), his mature anarchism. I analyze Bakunin's naturalistic atheism in the second part, detailing in particular the influence of Feuerbach and Comte. In addition, I attempt to demonstrate how wide the gulf is between Bakunin's naturalism and the anthropocentrism of past and present Kantians, including, controversially, Marx.

The purpose of this essay, then, is twofold. The first purpose is to counter the academic orthodoxy on Bakunin that has been summarized above. The second is to suggest the relevance of Bakunin's thought to contemporary affairs, theoretical and practical. This is a theme that will be taken up, subsequent to the core analysis, in the conclusion.

Notes to Introduction

1. Bakunin scholarship has proliferated in non-English languages over the years. A selection of noteworthy contributions is listed (by language) in the Additional Reading appendix to the Select Bibliography.

2. The main theoretical difference between Bakunin and Marx concerns the "materialist conception of history", as I will argue below. Bakunin, I maintain, sees only relative value in this theory; that is, he sees economic factors as determinants, albeit important ones, *among others*, including more fundamental ones. (When Thomas Garrigue Masaryk says that "Bakunin accepted historical materialism" but that "he is not a consistent historical (economic) materialist", he implies theoretical incoherence. In fact, the "marked *vacillation* between the idea of economic primacy and that of political and religious primacy" (only then, it might be said, from the abstract social or anthropological perspective) is perfectly coherent: certain historical causes are "primary" at particular stages of *human* development, though, from the naturalistic perspective, they are always "secondary" or relative — for example, contingent on the limits of human nature or catastrophic natural events [see *The Spirit of Russia*, Second Edition, I, trans. Eden and Cedar Paul (London: Allen & Unwin, 1955), pp. 461-69; emphasis added]. Furthermore there are, as we will see, grounds to believe that Bakunin was skeptical about the whole economic-political causal distinction.)

    Bakunin disputes Marxian economism on the grounds that it comes into conflict with his naturalism. Thus Marxists characterize his opposition to the true "materialism" as idealism, though, unlike Proudhon's idealism, idealism qualified by a partial (and "reluctant", according to George Lichtheim [see below]) recognition of the "truth". As Georgii Plekhanov expresses it, Bakunin "did not understand the materialist conception of history; he was only 'adulterated' by it"; or, Bakunin "is a Proudhonian adulterated with 'detestable' Communism, nay even by 'Marxism'" [see *Anarchism and Socialism*, trans. Eleanor Marx-Aveling (Chicago: Charles H. Kerr & Co., 1909), pp. 78-88]. The exposition of Bakunin's thought offered here attempts to show that Plekhanov and Marxists generally have it the wrong way round: Bakunin is a consistent materialist and Marx is some kind of materialist adulterated by (Kantian) idealism.

3. *A Short History of Socialism* (London: Weidenfeld & Nicolson, 1970), pp. 119-36. All

quotes, below, are from these pages. Emphasis added.

4. *L'Instruction intégrale* (*Integral Education*) (1869), *Le Socialisme libertaire*, ed. Fernand Rude (Paris: Editions Denoël, 1973), p. 137.

5. *Karl Marx* (London: Fourth Estate, 1999).

6. *Ibid.*, p. 318.

7. Wheen notes that "It is remarkable how many of [Bakunin's disciples] there are" [ibid., p. 316]. Obvious question: Who? Or, obvious rejoinder: It is truly remarkable how many more of Marx's disciples there *still* are.

8. *Ibid.*, pp. 315-16.

9. *Op. cit.*, p. 470.

10. *Bakunin: The Philosophy of Freedom* (Montréal: Black Rose Books, 1993), p. vii.

11. *The Doctrine of Anarchism of Michael A. Bakunin* (Milwaukee: Marquette University Press, 1955), pp. 5, 12, 19. Emphasis added.

12. *Mikhail Bakunin: A Study in the Psychology and Politics of Utopianism* (Oxford: Clarendon Press, 1982), p. 220.

13. *The Basic Bakunin: Writings 1869-1871* (Buffalo: Prometheus Books, 1992), p. 234.

14. *The Social and Political Thought of Michael Bakunin* (Westport: Greenwood Press, 1983), pp. 7-15.

15. "Bakunin and His Writings", *Canadian-American Slavic Studies*, X (1976), p. 591.

16. *Op. cit.*, p. 73.

17. See, for example, *Integral Education*, p. 138, note: "by freedom we mean, on the one hand, the fullest possible development of all the natural faculties of each individual, and, on the other, [the individual's] independence — not vis-à-vis natural and social laws, but vis-à-vis all the laws imposed by other human wills, whether collective or isolated". He refers to these two aspects as "the positive condition of freedom" and "the negative condition of freedom" in *Trois Conférences faites aux Ouvriers du Val de Saint-Imier* (*Three Lectures Delivered to the Workers of Val de Saint-Imier*) (1871) (see *Archives Bakounine*, VI, ed. Arthur Lehning (Leiden: E.J. Brill, 1974), pp. 217-45). Obviously Berlin would dispute the former condition of, in his terms, "self-realization". Nevertheless, the point is that Bakunin is well aware that there are two concepts of liberty — though, for him, they are only separable in abstraction; the meaningful concretion of freedom ("its reality") requires the fulfillment of both conditions as well as the achievement of equality. Anything less is the "phantom" of freedom and justice for Bakunin. We will comment further on this below.

    Christopher Hitchens has also referred to such a "want of originality" in his ruthless critique of Berlin ["Moderation or Death", *London Review of Books*, 26/11/1998, pp. 3-11]. He contends, and I concur, that Berlin "never broke any really original ground in the field of ideas", though "he turned over some mental baggage". Thus, for instance, his "favorite, Benjamin Constant, proposed a distinction between the 'liberty of the ancients' and the 'liberty of the moderns'; T.H. Green spoke of liberty in the 'positive' and the 'negative', and the same antithesis is strongly present in Hayek's *Road to Serfdom* — the title page of which quoted Lord Acton saying that 'few discoveries are more irritating than those which expose the pedigree of ideas'". Hitchens also exposes the intellectual hypocrisy of this "lion" of liberalism — preaching negative liberty, moderation, and the like while "seconding the efforts of unscrupulous power-brokers in [Vietnam-period] Washington". Thus critics of Bakunin might observe that Berlin is a more appropriate subject for studies of political intrigue, not to mention intellectual love for liberty giving way to practical tyranny.

Of course, Berlin's toadies have leapt to his defense. Michael Ignatieff responded with something of a tantrum ["The Devil and the Deep Red Sea", *The Guardian*, 22/1/2000]. He is utterly devastated to find that "the great old man", "a man [he] loved", "a figure of real stature", "a skeptical, moderate, and wise old Russian Jew", a man whose "essays . . . will be read long after the quarrels about his reputation cease to make any sense", a man whose misdeeds were merely the result of having "occasionally to betray one set of liberal values for the sake of another" (how difficult to be a liberal!), should be attacked by "such pygmies and their poison darts". This sort of empty adulation — coupled with puerile abuse — says much about Berlin's advocates. Hitchens' critique, however, stands firm.

18.   All quotes from "Herzen and Bakunin on Individual Liberty", *Russian Thinkers*, ed. Henry Hardy and Aileen Kelly (Harmondsworth: Penguin Books, 1978), pp. 82-113.

19.   Morris, *op. cit.*, p. 71.

20.   *Ibid.*, p. 3.

21.   *Op. cit.*, pp. 43, 62. The latter phrase is taken from Herzen.

22.   *Ibid.*, pp. 291-92.

23.   E.H. Carr, *Michael Bakunin* (New York: Octagon Books, 1975) [originally published London: Macmillan, 1937], p. 456; Pyziur, *op. cit.*, p. 111, 147 (Masaryk is quoted by Pyziur on the latter page); Berlin, *op. cit.*, p. 113.

24.   Pyziur, *op. cit.*, p. 18. There is, of course, a certain appeal to the belief in Bakunin's incapacity for formal structure on the one hand and theoretical coherence on the other. (Of the latter, Pyziur says: "Nearly all [Bakunin's writings] contain inconsistencies, obscurities, and striking contradictions . . . Bakunin's philosophical digressions [sic] cover almost all conceivable problems, and in them he does not seem to have had the gift of clarity". Bakunin's philosophical contradictions are, in fact, few, as I will argue below, and, unlike many more reputable philosophers, including numerous contemporaries, Bakunin expresses himself quite clearly.) The appeal is that the scholar has the pleasure of "reconstructing" Bakunin's thinking *for him*. At least Pyziur thinks this is a worthwhile enterprise, and acknowledges that biography, which has, "rather than critical analysis[,] been the chief manner of treatment", is "only a partial substitute for an evaluation of [this] doctrine". Pyziur himself writes, then: "Nowhere do we find a consecutive exposition of Bakunin's views as a whole. [Actually, few philosophers, even among the greats, have left such a convenient exposition of their thinking.] Instead, we have a series of isolated pronouncements on the problem of anarchism scattered throughout Bakunin's essays, pamphlets, and articles, as well as in his letters and in the statutes of his secret societies. The only way to reconstruct Bakunin's political doctrine of anarchism is to disentangle these statements from the jungle of his reasoning" [*ibid.*, pp. 19-20].

Incidentally, I do not deny that this essay itself involves some level of reconstruction. All scholarly work does. What I do deny is that this is any more necessary or troublesome in Bakunin's case than that of any other philosopher whom we seek to understand. At any rate, I do not feel that I am reconstructing in the absence of any original structure *for Bakunin himself*.

25.   Kelly, *op. cit.*, pp. 186, 193. Kelly, applying the strictest scholarly standards, concludes in the paragraph in question — quite independently of any argument, lame or otherwise

— that Bakunin's argument in *L'Empire knouto-germanique et la Révolution sociale* (*The Knouto-Germanic Empire and the Social Revolution*) (1870-1871), as she misrepresents it, is "lame". The undergraduate tutor would reasonably ask her: "Why?" Saying it, need we remind ourselves, does not make it so.

26.   Pyziur quotes two good examples of Bakunin saying "I am not a philosopher" [*op. cit.*, pp. 16-17].

27.   *Préambule pour la seconde livraison de l'Empire Knouto-Germanique et la Révolution sociale* (*Preamble to the Second Part of the Knouto-Germanic Revolution and the Social Revolution*) (1871) [also known as *La Commune de Paris et la notion de l'état* (*The Paris Commune and the Idea of State*)], *Archives Bakounine*, VII, ed. Arthur Lehning (Leiden: E.J. Brill, 1981), p. 291.

28.   *Op. cit.*, pp. 73-74.

PART ONE

BAKUNIN'S DIALECTIC AND THE CRITIQUE OF SPECULATION

> Oh, away with these modern notions, these wordy ex-
> changes and worrisome give and take, they all rest
> upon one principle — that truth and error can be rec-
> onciled. Away with this rage of reconciliation, with
> this sentimental slop, with this slimy and lying secu-
> larism.[1]

1.1 *The Reaction in Germany*: Freedom and its Opponents.

A major task of Bakunin's philosophy is to express the principle of freedom, the democratic principle, adequately. This principle and its re-alization, understood as an historical process, undeniably stand "at the head of the agenda of history". Consequently, "no one dares openly and fearlessly to profess that he is an enemy of freedom". Nevertheless, there remain those who are not true believers in freedom, and it is these people to whom Bakunin addresses himself in his seminal 1842 article, *The Reaction in Germany*.[2] Though we run the risk of losing ourselves in Hegelian jargon, we are compelled to examine this article in detail for, as Arthur Lehning writes, in it "lies the quintessence of the philosophy of history, and the conception of revolution, which determined Bakunin's thought and activity for the next three decades".[3]

According to Bakunin, the tacit enemies of freedom are of three kinds. Firstly, there are those "high-placed [and] aged" individuals who, having ostensibly embraced the principle of freedom in their youth (at least as a "piquant pleasure" that "makes [them] twice as interesting in business"), rather patronizingly claim *experience* as a justification for their lethargic repudiation of it in later life. (Bakunin's talk of "that much abused word, 'experience'" brings to mind a passage from Sartre's *La Nausée* (*Nausea*) (1938). Sartre writes there of those figures who hit "about the age of forty" and begin to "baptize their stubborn little ideas . . . with the name of experience" and utter the likes of "'Believe me, I'm talking from experience, I've learnt everything I know from life'". Bakunin himself might well have asked Roquentin's question in the novel: "Are we to understand that Life [or bare "experience" in itself] has undertaken to think for them?"[4]) Dialogue with these people is worthless since "they were never serious about freedom" to begin with, that is to say, since "freedom was never for them a religion" [15-16/37]. (In Bakunin's later writings, as we will see, freedom and religion become completely antithetical.)

Secondly, there are the apathetic aristocratic and bourgeois youths who lack any passion for the principle of freedom. Their concerns are limited, on the contrary, to "their paltry, vain, or monetary interests"; consequently, "they have not even the slightest conception of life and of what goes on around them". Indeed, had they not been assured otherwise, "they would apparently believe that nothing in the world had ever been different to the way it is now" (and, perhaps, that nothing will ever be significantly different in the future). Unlike their elder counterparts, who "had at least a glimmer of life", these individuals are "lifeless from the beginning" and, as such, offer no real challenge to the principle of freedom, since "only that which is alive can be effective" [16-17/38]. Hence, dialogue with them is pointless.

Thirdly, and most importantly, there is the *Reactionary Party*, which is manifest, for example, as conservatism, the historical school, and Schellingian (not Comtean, as the standard misreading has it) positivism in politics, law, and philosophy respectively. Dialogue with this party is essential because of its dominance. It is imperative that advocates of the democratic principle (the Democratic Party) recognize the strength of this opponent and, correlatively, the full extent of their own party's weakness. "Through this recognition the Democratic Party first steps out of the uncertainty of fantasy and into the reality in which it must live, *suffer*, and, in the end, conquer". Within this process, Bakunin argues, the

Democratic Party recognizes both that its enemy is as much within itself as outside itself, and that the need is to conquer the *enemy within* first. It also recognizes that democracy is not merely the enemy of *the* government, but of government as such, and that it represents, beyond all governmental forms, and beyond all "constitutional or politico-economic change", "a *total transformation* [*eine totale Umwandlung*]" of the world, heralding "an original, new life which has not yet existed in history". And, furthermore, it recognizes that democracy itself constitutes a *religion* and that democrats must therefore become truly religious, that the democratic principle must infuse every facet of their lives, practical as well as theoretical, if their party is to "conquer the world" [18-19/39].

1.2 *The Reaction* in Context

We see here three features which, according to Aileen Kelly, characterize Bakunin's early philosophical thought — three features which, again according to Kelly, illustrate its fundamentally Fichtean nature. This is Kelly's main contention with regard to Bakunin's philosophy: that it remains, even under Hegel's influence and that of the Left Hegelians, once again, fundamentally Fichtean. Put simply, her view is that Bakunin is "*particularly* attracted to Fichte's vision of absolute liberty as an earthly ideal to be attained through a protean feat of will".[5] She is therefore obliged to distinguish her view from that of a long list of scholars who disagree with her ("These authors offer differing views on the question of the degree to which Fichte influenced Bakunin's approach to Hegel; in the view of the present study, they *all* underestimate Fichte's importance in this regard"[6]; but of course), in spite of the fact that her views are largely parasitic upon theirs. Her knowledge of German Idealism and Left Hegelianism seems almost entirely second-hand and is appropriately flimsy (though — pretentiously — she still offers "Focuses on the influence of idealist philosophy on [Bakunin's] thought" as a one-line description of her own book[7]). As for her knowledge of subsequent influences on Bakunin's ideas (notably Feuerbach and Comte), in other words, as for her knowledge of the explicitly non-Fichtean influences on Bakunin (assuming — as she does with her profound knowledge of these things — that Hegel is not explicitly so): well, it is apparently non-existent. One is inclined to speculate that Kelly, approaching her study at the outset with little if any knowledge of the philosophical tradition, but an axe to grind (that of Berlin), became fixated upon the earliest discernible influence on Bakunin's philosophy and was unwilling, or simply intellectually unable, to admit that Bakunin's Fichtean phase passed. (Saltman has stated that Kelly is not alone in this. "Commentators like Carr and Pyziur drew upon Bakunin's early attraction to Fichte . . . to confirm their own contention that the only consistency within Bakunin's work lay within his own unfettered will".[8] This is not altogether true since, for example, Pyziur admits that "Bakunin's exaltation of Fichte did not . . . last very long" and emphasizes Bakunin's socialism or "equalitarianism" throughout.[9] In any case, there is little doubt that Kelly is the most fanatical proponent of the "Fichtean thesis".) It is altogether too convenient for Kelly's psychological account to focus on Fichte-the-egoist; it is also contemptuous of the facts. Thus we will demonstrate below that Bakunin's Fichtean phase did pass, and indeed, that his later philosophy is inspired by the Hegelian reaction to the Kantian tradition, including Fichte. But let us humor Kelly for the time being.

Firstly, we see in these passages of *The Reaction*, in common with Bakunin's early philosophical thought, the "urge for self-surrender" (Kelly) or self-denial, motivated by the perceived need to conquer the "enemy within". All men "have the right to their divine inheritance but they alone exclude themselves from it". Consequently, they can be said to be their own worst enemies; hence, they must deny themselves as limited, finite, terrestrial egos. Secondly, and paradoxically, there is an equally strong "yearning for self-affirmation" (Kelly again), for affirmation of the absolute ego, i.e., God, or the "divine nature" of man, for "God is within us". This yearning is expressed in religion, a willing of the divine, which must "become the basis and reality of our lives and our actions". Thirdly, there is the necessary mediating act of suffering. Suffering reconciles the limited ego, or man as such, with the absolute ego, or

God. As a result it is exemplified by Christ — divine man — and specifically by the mystery of the Passion, which demonstrates that "His suffering was indeed bliss". Christ's suffering, then, ought to become our model, and, in acting in accordance with it, we show ourselves to be entirely "penetrated by the religion of Christ" and affirm the divine in man.[10]

More importantly, however, and regardless of Kelly's contention (assuming that it is as accurate and interesting as she believes it to be), we see in these passages of *The Reaction* something that is distinct from Bakunin's early philosophical thought, something distinctly non-Fichtean (compare it with a work known by Bakunin, *Reden an die deutsche Nation* (*Addresses to the German Nation*) (1807-08), for example); something which marks a crucial, in broad terms Left Hegelian, transition. We see a genuinely radical streak both in his (philosophical) opposition (not only to all forms of alien religion but also) to *all* forms of government, and in his (philosophical) espousal of revolutionary change (as the reappropriation of the human from alien *political* as well as religious forms). We witness, that is to say, the *genesis* of his *philosophical* anarchism.

The extent to which the atheistic aspect of the Left Hegelian analysis of religion (somewhat understated but implied in Bakunin's account here) is Hegelian is well documented and will be examined here later. However, the extent to which the anarchistic aspect of the Left Hegelian analysis of politics is Hegelian is less well documented. It may be that Hegel is "implicitly" more atheistic than anarchistic, but there is undoubtedly room for the kind of critique that the Left Hegelians engage in on this subject. Hegel certainly idealizes the State[11]; but, then again, he also idealizes God. And, as it is the idealization of God in terms of the Absolute that exposes the religious contradiction, it may also be that it is the idealization of the State in terms of Freedom that exposes the political contradiction.

Therefore, it would seem to be as legitimate to critique Hegel's "State" (defined as "the actuality of concrete freedom") as it is to critique his "God" (as the Absolute which "it may be expedient" not to name as such).[12] To do so in a convincing way would require a separate study in which, as one might attempt to demonstrate a contradiction between "God" (the object of religion) and the Absolute, one attempts to demonstrate a contradiction between the State (the object of politics) and Freedom. It may be that the State is Freedom that it is expedient not to name as such. Perhaps this brings Left Hegelianism to another level, but there is the tiniest encouragement in Hegel's writings when he argues — not as an anarchist, but in the spirit of anarchism — that the State is not an ethical community, but a merely political "mechanism" which is completely antithetical to freedom. (Later he seeks something non-political in this sense within the State, and Karl Marx follows his lead[13]; but even by 1842 Bakunin holds that the State is entirely political (or "partial"), and that freedom must be sought outside it, in the realm of "religion".) As an example of Hegel's encouragement, consider the following, written in 1796:

> . . . just as there is no idea of a machine, there is no idea of the State, for the State is something mechanical. Only that which is an object of freedom may be called an idea. We must, therefore, transcend the State. For every State is bound to treat free men as cogs in a machine. And this is precisely what it should not do; hence the State must perish.[14]

The crucial point of Bakunin's proto-anarchism in *The Reaction* is that the political is subordinated to the religious, in the Hegelian sense to be discussed further below. This subordination is, as Bakunin sees it at this point, necessary for the realization of democracy, which is essentially a religious rather than a political principle. (The following year, the subordination is said to be necessary for the realization of "true communism": "We are on the eve of a great revolution . . . which will not be merely political in character, but concerned with principles and religion".[15]) Thus, in *The Reaction* the critique of the political *as such* (that is, in *all* forms) oversteps the critique of the religious (which is confined, as yet, to *alien* forms as opposed to the supposedly true "Democratic" form).

This contrasts, as we will see below, with Bakunin's earlier attempt, in *Predislovie perevodchika: Gimnazicheskie rechi Gegelia* (*Preface to Hegel's Gymnasial Lectures*) (1838), to reconcile the religious (as a form of "the reason that is conscious of itself") with the political (in its actuality, as the State, "the reason that is"). At this stage, prior to any anti-political or anarchist sentiment, Bakunin had developed no critique of the political as such (as being an inadequate form of freedom), any more than he had of the religious as such (as being an inadequate form of reason). However, this does not mean that the attempted reconciliation with actuality is conservative.[16] Bakunin recognizes that a tension exists between rationality in its present inadequate form and political actuality. The reconciliation he proposes is an attempt to overcome this tension — or the alienation (*Entfrendung*) of the former from the latter — by developing the rational form (currently more or less "subjectivist") in line with the *implicit*, but not yet *explicit*, political content (freedom). Martine Del Giudice comments: "when Bakunin refers to the 'rationality of the actual' or stresses the importance of a 'reconciliation with actuality', it is clear that he is thereby not committed to condoning the existing forms of social life, which involve historical contingency (i.e., Russian society as it was)".[17] So, again, while there is an attempted reconciliation between the religious and political actuality (to be achieved by the process of "education" [*Bildung* in German or *obrazovanie* in Russian]) in the *Preface*, in *The Reaction* the ultimate aim is to negate the political *form* of freedom and to realize the religious essence (now represented as the democratic principle) beyond it. The political is seen henceforth as inadequate to human needs, as a form inadequate to historical content: as irreconcilable with freedom.

In Bakunin's later writings, the religious itself is seen as inadequate to human needs — to human liberation. The religion of democracy is then replaced, as a result of the critique of the religious *as such*, as the ultimate ground of the right of political authority, by the anti-theologistic philosophy and praxis of anarchism. (Bakunin's unequivocal anti-theologism or atheism is affirmed by the mid-1860s. In 1865, anticipating a more famous statement of 1871, he writes: "God exists, therefore man is a slave. Man is free, therefore there is no God. I defy anyone to escape this circle".[18] Bakunin's anarchism is expressed as such for the first time in *La questione slava* (*The Slavic Question*) of 1867.[19]) Nevertheless, from Bakunin's 1838 *Preface* to his writings of the 1860s and 1870s, a fundamental relation between the religious and the political is maintained. Thus, in 1838 Bakunin could declare "Where there is no religion, there can be no State"; in 1842 he declares "without religion . . . the State is impossible" [48-49/57] (and his conviction now is that the State is precisely that, since it is incompatible with the true or universal religion of freedom); and in 1871, almost identically, he declares "There is not [and] there cannot be a State without religion" (that is to say, the religious falsehood is responsible for political authority — insofar as it is conceived as a right).[20] The theologistic and statist motivation for reconciliation in 1838 disappears in the later writings (the statist motivation having disappeared, philosophically at least, by 1842), where atheism (understood as anti-theologism) and anarchism (understood as anti-statism) — where these two inseparable aspects of the ultimate social revolutionary project — are established.

In fact, the *active* reconciliatory element in 1838 later becomes a fundamental means of overcoming both the religious and the political (though secondary to social revolution as such, without which education remains partial). That is to say, Bakunin comes to see education as a *practico-revolutionary* means (hence he declares that "the workers [should] do everything possible to obtain all the education they can in the material conditions in which they presently find themselves"), but "integral [or complete] education" ("*l'instruction intégrale*", a phrase from Charles Fourier) itself as possible only after social revolution (hence he declares, "Let them emancipate themselves [i.e., create the necessary conditions for their education] first, and [then] they will educate themselves" more adequately — freeing themselves from the oppressive and stupefying influence of "religious, historical, political, juridical, and economic prejudices").[21] Having placed *The Reaction* in context, let us now return to the question at hand: the conflict between democracy and reaction in *The Reaction in Germany*.

1.3 Democracy and Revolution

The strength of the Reactionary Party is, Bakunin assures us, in no way due to the weakness or inadequacy of the democratic principle, the *essence* of the Democratic Party, which is the most "universal and all-embracing" of principles and therefore the very "essence of Spirit". Rather, it is due to the (political) *existence* of the Democratic Party in its state of partial self-consciousness. The Democratic Party has grasped the *merely* negative or *revolutionary* aspect of the democratic principle only, and, as such, "the whole fullness of life is necessarily external to it". So:

> With respect to its essence, its principle, the Democratic party is the universal, all-embracing one, but, with respect to its existence, it is only a particular one, the Negative, against which stands another particular one, the Positive [19-20/40].[22]

The Negative is devoted to the destruction of the Positive within this contradiction. Its whole existence, that is to say, is negation or revolution. But, in what amounts to the same thing as we will see, the Negative is also devoted to the destruction of itself as merely negative, as merely revolutionary and merely (anti-) political; "as this evil, particular existence [or *form*] which is inadequate to its essence [or *content*]". Democracy is therefore devoted to destroying not only its antithesis, but also itself insofar as it is dependent on its antithesis — insofar as it is a mere antithetical political existence or anti-political existence — in order to establish itself "in its affirmative abundance [*in seinem affirmativen Reichtum*]", that is, "as its own living fullness". This can only be achieved with a radical "self-change" which cannot be merely *quantitative*: it must constitute a "*qualitative* transformation [*qualitative Umwandlung*]" (from the political to the religious, from the revolutionary to the affirmative) which will usher in "a new heaven and a new earth, a young and magnificent world in which all present discords [*Dissonanzen*] will resolve themselves into harmonious unity [*harmonischen Einheit*]" [20-21/40].

1.4 Revolution and Metaphysics

Bakunin, as a naturalist, will later reject any such notion of qualitative transformation, even at the socio-historical level, where all changes are changes in the *degree* of (dialectically unfolding) freedom. The religious and the political then represent consecutive forms of unfreedom or, more exactly, partial freedom. In other words, as stated above, religion is seen as an inadequate form of human freedom, not its realization. Therefore, Bakunin, as a more consistent Left Hegelian, later discovers the principle of the formal inadequacy of religion, its limitations with respect to spiritual content or freedom.

What of the qualitative transformation from the revolutionary to the affirmative? This is expressed in the so often woefully misunderstood final line of *The Reaction*: "The passion for destruction [the revolutionary passion, the negative side of democracy, the politics of revolution] is a creative passion [an affirmative passion for democratic order], too" [51/58]. Hardly the pan-destructive or nihilistic proclamation many would have us believe. (In any case, the violent tone in Bakunin's writings, especially the later writings — which many attribute to certain personal quirks or "pathological traits"[23] (as their "psycho-historical" accounts require) — is inspired by very real and bitter personal experience of authority (which his critics tend to ignore) and a certain realism about the strength of that authority (which his critics generally support without serious consideration, which is the very least that might be demanded of it). This realism (as appropriate, as I write, as it ever was) is illustrated, for instance, in the following: "To contend successfully with a military force which now respects nothing, is armed with the most terrible weapons of destruction, and is always ready to use them to wipe out not just houses and streets but entire cities with all their inhabitants — to contend with such a wild beast one needs another beast, no less wild but more just: an organized uprising of the people, a social revolution which, like military reaction, spares nothing and stops at nothing".[24] (Bakunin's suspicions about "military science . . . with all its advanced weapons and its formidable instruments of destruction" which "work wonders" [as CNN might put it], are particularly topical.[25] They, like so much he has to say, are not and never were the stuff of an "adolescent and essentially frivolous outlook"[26], as apologists for liberal order insist.)

Bakunin later rejects any connotation of qualitative transformation here as well. The affirmative result of revolution, though it is brought about by radical negation, is still, as it were, qualitatively identical with what was negated since it is related to it as its other, and cannot be conceived in any other way. (It is difficult to imagine how different "qualities", whatever that means, might relate at all, even in a preponderantly negative way. Different qualities, properly speaking, are, from the naturalistic point of view, idealist constructions which are absolutely alien to one and other — "incommensurable", if you like.) As Bakunin puts it in *Statism and Anarchy* (a work I refer to frequently in the first part of this essay because is logically very close to *The Reaction*, despite a gap of three decades):

> Even the most rational and profound science cannot divine the form social life will take in the future. It can determine only the *negative* conditions, which follow logically from a rigorous critique of existing society. Thus, by means of such a critique [we have] rejected the very idea of State or of statism [and taken] the opposite [that is, antithetical], or negative position: anarchy.[27]

In other words, we conceive of the affirmative principle, the positive side of freedom, by reference to its concrete other, the very object of revolutionary activity, which is motivated by the negative side of freedom. Nothing qualitatively different has to be conceived outside of "existing society" in its positivity and its resulting negativity: all future affirmation is contained, implicitly, in that negative principle — as we will see.

The attempt to conceive of the future speculatively or positively, outside the scope of the dialectic *in its essential negativity*, is, in Bakunin's eyes, reactionary: an attempt to preserve order (as dreamt up by the sociological genius) at the expense of genuine (dialectical) progress. As these terms imply, this is Bakunin's criticism of Comte as the high priest of positivism. (And with Comte, all those who seek — prematurely, according to Bakunin — to "close the revolution", that is, to overcome "the predominance that the critical tendency still retains", regarding it as "the greatest obstacle to the progress of civilization".[28]) It is also his criticism of Marx as the high priest (or even the "new Moses"[29]) of State socialism. (And with Marx, all those who seek to avail of the State, one way or another, as a revolutionary means to a supposedly non-statist end [somewhere in the distant post-revolutionary, post-transitional future].)

Bakunin views this form of reaction, in its theoretical formulation, as metaphysics. Metaphysics (a term favored by Comte, though turned against him by Bakunin), modern or human idealism (Bakunin's often favored equivalent),[30] speculative philosophy (the equivalent term favored by Feuerbach), and anthropocentric philosophy (an equivalent term that I favor for reasons that will become apparent) are characterized, according to Bakunin, by the belief, explicit or implicit, that "thought precedes life", that thought precedes Being, or that the "subjective" or the human precedes the "objective" or the natural. Metaphysics thus has two aspects: *logically*, a tendency toward *speculation*; and *ontologically*, a tendency toward *anthropocentrism*. Bakunin counters both aspects: one with *dialectic* (the subject matter of the first part of this essay); and the other with *naturalism* (the subject matter of the second part of this essay). When, for example, Bakunin accuses Marx of being a metaphysician, he is therefore accusing him of an ontological prioritization of the (socialized) subject over the object, the producer over nature, and of a logical prioritization of the speculative over the dialectical. Thus his critique of Marx-the-metaphysician should not be read as throw-away vituperation, but as philosophically significant critique from an opposing point of view. Bakunin's *dialectical naturalism* (literally, *the conjunction of a negative dialectic and a positivistic naturalism, a negative logic and a positive ontology*[31]) is diametrically opposed to metaphysics in this sense. It is characterized by the belief that "life always precedes thought"[32], (ontologically) that objective or natural Being precedes human subjectivity, and (logically) that the dialectical (though it is a term Bakunin is later reluctant to use) or the negative/revolutionary precedes the speculative (which the concept of the dialectical has been widely conflated with) or the affirmative/constructive. We will comment extensively on Bakunin's critique of Marx's metaphysics later. But a word on his critique of Comte's metaphysics will orient us in this debate.

A crucial provisional observation is that Bakunin is trying to hoist Comte with his own petard. Comte, as we will see, presents metaphysics as antithetical to theology (though he contradicts himself on this by asserting at times that theology and metaphysics are substantially the same, which is precisely Bakunin's point — and Feuerbach's before him). He regards this negative theoretical and historical state with a fair amount of contempt, preferring the quasi-theological state and the "industrial" *order* of positivism. Thus Comte's dialectic, like that of Hegel and Marx, is positive, seeking a substantial preservation of the principle of order (the statist principle in the case of all three). Bakunin sees Comte himself as a metaphysician: not as a negative thinker, as Comte describes the metaphysician, but as a quasi-theological thinker who preserves the positivity of theology in a more anthropocentric form — in the form of a "religion of humanity", organized, as it were, from the top down, from the best instances of humanity and therefore the closest to God (i.e., the savants) to the lowest and least human of all (i.e., the ignorant rabble) — without submitting that anthropocentric form to the negativity of the dialectic. He sees him, and Marx, Giuseppe Mazzini, and others with him, in the terms that will emerge momentarily, as a mediating reactionary: as an advocate of, at best, whatever can be saved of order after necessary (but sufficient) progress, or, at worst, a new and more concentrated despotism — suggesting that the "government of scholars" is "the most oppressive, offensive, and contemptuous kind in the world". (Bakunin refers explicitly to Marx as a mediator in his later writings, as a revolutionary who "has manifested more strongly in recent years [a] desire to compromise with the radical bourgeoisie [the class of order, so to speak]" and "has continually pushed the proletariat [the class of progress, so to speak] into accommodations with" it.)[33]

Bakunin writes, then, again in *Statism and Anarchy*: "[Among] 'metaphysicians' we [include] positivists and in general all the present-day worshippers of the goddess science; all those who by one means or another . . . have created for themselves an ideal social organization into which, like Procrustes, they want to force the life of future generations whatever the cost . . . Metaphysicians or positivists, all these knights of science or thought, in the name of which they consider themselves ordained to prescribe the laws of life, are reactionaries, conscious or unconscious".[34] The theological terminology — worshippers, the goddess, ordination — with which Bakunin describes metaphysics is not accidental: a central philosophical thesis of his is that theology (or divine idealism) and metaphysics (or human idealism) are of a piece. The equivalence is articulated in the following way. "The difference between theologians and idealists is not great. The theologian is a sincere and consistent Idealist, and the [modern or human] Idealist is a shamefaced and hesitant theologian".[35] Idealism in its entirety (divine and human) — or what Bakunin terms theologism — is challenged only by natural science and naturalistic philosophy, from which Comte's idealist or anthropocentric positivism — his "metaphysics" — is ultimately divorced. Comte's Procrustean philosophy proceeds in the opposite direction to the dialectic. It represents the triumph of the Positive, of Order (whatever "progressive" compromise is involved — republican, social democratic, or whatever — in the order of State, whatever "the *denomination* of the State" that is brought about[36]) while the dialectic represents the triumph of the Negative, of revolutionary Progress. But let us return to Bakunin's discussion of the revolutionary-reactionary discord in *The Reaction*.

1.5 Consistent and "Mediating" Reaction

Bakunin insists that the harmonious "unification" of present discord cannot be realized through mediation (*Vermittlung*) (or reconciliation — *Versöhnung* [see 47/56]) of the Negative and the Positive because
the Negative and the Positive remain utterly incompatible (*unverträglich*).
Regarded in itself, Positives argue, the Negative would seem to have no
content. But, in itself, the Negative cannot exist at all — it can exist only
in contradiction to the Positive: "Its whole being, its content [as such]
and its vitality are simply the destruction of the Positive [*sein ganzes Sein,
sein Inhalt und seine Lebendigkeit ist nur die Zerstörung des Positiven*]" [21/41]. It is
impossible that something entirely destructive, the Negative, could ever
mediate that which it seeks to destroy, the Positive. Therefore, the notion that unity can be achieved through mediation is absurd. Thus the
logic of destruction — the negative logic — takes precedence over the
logic of mediation — the positive logic — in Bakunin's thought.

However, not all reactionaries seek such mediation. Indeed, reactionaries are, Bakunin notes, of two kinds: *Consistent Reactionaries*
(*konsequenten Reaktionäre*) and inconsistent or *Mediating Reactionaries*
(*vermittelnden Reactionäre*). Consistent Reactionaries agree that the Positive and the Negative are incompatible. However, "since they find in the
Negative only its leveling [*Verflachung*]" [26/44], since they are blind to
the affirmative side of the Negative, which includes "all that is vital, all
that is beautiful and holy" [26/43], they justifiably (on their own terms)
seek to maintain the Positive through a ruthless suppression of the
Negative. What they fail to understand, though, is that their Positive is
positive only insofar as it is opposed by the Negative; if it were to actually overcome the Negative in seeking to suppress it, it would achieve
nothing other than "the completion of the Negative" by negating itself
[22/41]. Thus it can be said that "by the very fact that they are Positive
they have the Negative within them" [27/44].

Despite the vital conflict between Negatives and Consistent Positives, Bakunin claims that both are, in some sense, honest and sincere —

both "hate everything that is half-hearted", believing that "only a whole man can be good and that half-heartedness is the putrid source of all evil" [23/42]. However, Consistent Reactionaries, in their fanaticism — in their fanatical effort to preserve themselves by excluding all other-ness — are necessarily partial and one-sided, and have no other means of expression than that of violence and hatred. Negatives, on the other hand, inspired by the "all-embracing principle of unconditional freedom [*allumfassendum Prinzipe der unbedingten Freiheit*]", can transcend the partial-ity and one-sidedness of their merely "political existence", by acting re-ligiously in their politics, "religiously in the sense of freedom of which the one true expression is justice and love". This requires that, in accor-dance with the "highest commandment of Christ", Negatives, these ap-parent "enemies of the Christian religion", love their enemy and recog-nize that it strives, in its own fashion, after the good, and that it is only due to some "incomprehensible misfortune" that it has been denied its "true destiny" [25/43].[37]

Mediating Reactionaries are studied closely by Bakunin since it is they who are viewed as the dominant party today, even among reaction-aries generally [see 30/46]. They can be distinguished from Consistent Reactionaries in two ways. Firstly, they do not reject the Negative alto-gether, but afford it a partial concession. Secondly, they lack the "energetic purity", symptomatic of an "honest nature", which is charac-teristic of the Consistent Positives. The Negatives can, then, accuse Me-diating Reactionaries of "*theoretical dishonesty*". At least it can be said of Consistent Positives that they have the "practical energy of their convic-tions" and that they express themselves clearly according to these con-victions. Mediating Positives, on the other hand, these "theorists *par ex-cellence*", "never permit the practical impulse toward truth to destroy the meticulously patchworked edifice of their theory" (later meaning socio-logical theory); after all, "it has cost [great] pains to piece such a thing together and ... it is [only by it that] one can distinguish them, the clever people, from the stupid and uneducated mob" [28-29/44-45]. (Theoretical mediation is therefore associated — long before the later critique of metaphysics — with intellectual élitism. Furthermore, since "theoretical dishonesty by its very nature almost always reverts into a practical one" [28/45], there is already the suggestion by Bakunin of practical élitism, or despotism, among Mediators — or, later, metaphysicians.) Mediators are thus distinguished both by their lack of principle and by their practical-progressive impotence.

The logic of Mediators (the logic of mediation) is based on the idea that two contradictory theses considered abstractly in themselves are one-sided, hence untrue; considered in their relation to each other, however, their truth is adjudged to arise in their mediation. Bakunin admits that the Negative is one-sided when considered in itself alongside the Positive. But since the destruction of the Positive is the sole purpose of the Negative, it would seem that any mediation between it and the Positive is impossible, as has already been stated. Only contradiction, which embraces the two one-sidednesses, the Positive as well as the Negative, can be said to be "total, absolute, [and] true". Hence, neither member can be understood in isolation; both members can only be understood in their integral union. This requires that we "grasp the contradiction in its totality in order to have truth [*den Gegensatz haben wir folglich in seiner Totalität zu ergreifen, um die Wahrheit zu haben*]" [32-33/47].

However, contradiction does not exist as such, it does not appear in its totality; it appears rather as the "conflicting cleavage of its two members". Contradiction is total truth, as it were, in the integral union of its simplicity, its unity, and its internal cleavage, its difference. Yet this nature is hidden; all that appears, again, is its cleavage, which means that contradiction itself exists one-sidedly. It exists as the Negative and the Positive in their mutual exclusivity. This presents a difficulty in understanding the *totality* of contradiction, which Mediators attempt to overcome with a "maternal" effort "to mediate the opposed members" [33-34/48]. But, according to Bakunin, this difficulty can be overcome more successfully in another way.

The Positive is positive insofar as it "rests in itself", undisturbed by anything which might negate it or, indeed, by anything which it might negate. It consists in absolute immobility, "absolute rest", since all movement involves a negation. The Positive as absolute rest is, since the notion of rest is inseparable from the notion of unrest or movement, positive only in contrast to the Negative, or "absolute unrest". That is to say, "The Positive is internally related to the Negative as its own vital determination [*das Positive ist innerhalb seiner selbst auf das Negative, als auf seine eigene lebendige Bestimmung bezogen*]" [34/48]. There are two sides to the Positive's relation to the Negative. Firstly, the Positive, resting in itself, completely self-sufficient, "contains nothing of the Negative", without which it has no meaning, without which it is inconceivable. Secondly, the Positive, as absolute rest, must actively exclude the Negative, which is, of course, an activity on its part, a negation, so that it sacrifices its positivity and becomes the Negative. Its act of exclusion must now be seen as a self-destructive act, an act of excluding itself (the Negative) from itself (the supposedly Positive). The implication of all this is the following:

> *Contradiction* is not an equilibrium but a *preponderance of the Negative*, which is its encroaching dialectical phase. *The Negative*, as determining the life of the Positive itself, alone *includes within itself the totality of the contradiction*, and so it alone also has absolute justification [35/49].[38]

It is only in the abstraction of the Negative — that is, it is only in the exclusion of the Negative from the Positive, in its abstract "self-orientation", which renders it positive — that the Negative is as one-sided as the Positive. The Positive, in the form of consistent reaction, in seeking to suppress or exclude the Negative, though, negates the Negative as such; it unwittingly "awakens the Negative from its Philistine repose" and presents it with an opportunity to realize itself [36/49].

The Positive, as a negative force, thus negates the Negative, in its positive state; in doing so, it makes it possible for the Negative to fulfill itself in the negation of all that bears the name of the Positive. The Negative, in negating the Positive, also negates itself as merely negative, and thereby establishes itself "in its affirmative abundance" — as Democracy [20/40]. This entire process of "ruthless negation" [*rücksichtslose Negieren*], then, "is the action of the practical Spirit invisibly present in contradiction", the action of the negative or revolutionary Spirit which "announces its imminent revelation in a really democratic and universally human *religion of freedom*" [36/49-50].

This process of "incessant self-combustion of the Positive in the pure fire of the Negative [*rastlosen Sichselbstverbrennen des Positiven in dem reinen Feuer des Negativen*]" is the only means of "mediating" the Negative and the Positive. It is necessitated by the very nature of contradiction. Consequently, all other means of "mediation" are "arbitrary" and contrary to "the Spirit of the times", thus indicative of either stupidity or a lack of principle [37/50].

Mediating Reactionaries admit the totality of contradiction, in this sense, but, crucially, attempt to "rob it . . . of its vitality" [37/50]. The Positive, again, is justified, not in itself but only in its negation of the Negative in its positive state. It is this negation, or act of exclusion, on the part of Consistent Reactionaries, which alone grants them vitality. It is precisely this vitality which Mediators attempt to deny. Thus Mediators retain in the Positive only that which is "worthy of destruction" while rejecting that which alone grants it vitality, i.e., "the vital fight with the Negative, the vital presence in it of contradiction [*den lebendigen Kampf mit dem Negativen, die lebendige Gegenwart des Gegensatzes in ihnen*]" [38/51].

Bakunin adds that Mediating Reactionaries relate to Consistent Reactionaries by urging them to grant Negatives, who are becoming strong, but whom they both detest, "a little space in their society". Mediation or compromise, characteristic of these "impotent half-souls", is necessary "in order not to be wholly destroyed" by Negatives. Meanwhile, Mediating Reactionaries relate to Negatives patronizingly by claiming to understand their "youthful enthusiasm for pure principles" while urging them to "yield something" (to the old world, as the object of experience); after all, "pure principles in their purity are not applicable to life; life requires a certain dose of eclecticism", that is, in Bakunin's terms, half-hearted compromise [39-40/51].

1.6 Objections

Bakunin anticipates some objections to his attack on Mediators. In the first place, people may object that Mediators, who are for the most part eminently respectable men, "honest and scientifically educated", are being presented here as "unintelligent and unprincipled". Bakunin responds that while the "inner man" is of no concern to Negatives, and while they ought never to pass ultimate judgment on this "inviolable sanctuary", men can only really be judged as they are "in the real world" — and Negatives cannot be expected to call black white [40-41/52]. (It appears to Bakunin, throughout his writings, that there is something manifestly unethical, if theoretically impressive, in the attempt to mediate rather than to fully resolve contradiction.)

People may also object (and it is a common objection) that Mediators at least seek *some* progress (through "piecemeal reform", say) and contribute more to it (if only by degrees) than Negatives do. Yet, Bakunin retorts, "the stifling of the only vital principle of our present time, otherwise so poor [*die Erstickung des einzig lebendigen Prinzips unserer sonst so armen Gegenwart*]", can hardly be called progress [41/52]. Asking that Positives cling to the old while allowing Negatives to toy with it; asking that Negatives dismantle the old, but only gradually and not entirely; none of this is seen by Bakunin to constitute meaningful *dialectical* progress.

Furthermore, people may object — from the Hegelian perspective itself — that Negatives revert to the abstraction of the Understanding (*Verstand*) in pitting two "irreconcilable extremes" against each other. Hegel *surely* refuted such abstraction by pointing out that vision, for instance, is impossible in both pure darkness and pure light, by pointing out that vision is only possible in the "concrete unity" of light and darkness [42-43/53]. It would appear, on this account, that Positive and

Negative are "concepts that are held [by Negatives] to be inert and wholly separate essences, one here and one there, each standing fixed and isolated from the other, with which it has nothing in common".[39] Hegel insists, by contrast, "that the triad (*Triplizität*) is the true form of thought", insists on the "dynamic unity of opposites", which "is the proper form of thought because it is the proper form of a reality in which every being is the synthetic unity of antagonistic conditions".[40] Bakunin's response to this objection has become evident enough in his account of the contradictory or "antagonistic" relation in which, though one element is preponderant, neither is alien. Both actively engage with the other and thereby demonstrate that they have negativity "in common", that the negative force of their contradiction "unites" them. Thus they are not in fact "wholly separate essences". But we will return to the question of the triadic form below.

It may be objected, to much the same effect, that Hegel had demonstrated that "vital existence" (that is, organic existence) requires negation from within rather than from outside (as in the case of the inorganic). Such immanent negation or vitality takes the form of "the germ of death". (As Hegel puts it, "life as such bears the germ of death *within* itself, and . . . the finite sublates itself because it contradicts itself *inwardly*".[41]) But, the Negative may respond, this "germ", immanent before the dialectical moment proper, realizes itself "as an independent principle" at that moment, that is to say, at the moment of death. Hence, "the gradual effect of the Negative [*die allmähliche Wirkung des Negativen*]" is not a true expression of the dialectic, which is revolutionary, marking natural, historical, and mental transitions "into a qualitatively new world, into the free world of Spirit [*in eine qualitativ neue Welt, — in die freie Welt des Geistes*]" [43/53-54]. We will also return to the question of the dialectic's negativity below. However, we may note here the particular importance of the historical claim. Bakunin is claiming that the gradual movement of history, bearing the revolutionary germ within it, is interrupted by moments of revolution (the agents of which will be introduced shortly), as a result of which the scope of spirit or freedom is extended. This remains his position even in his later writings.[42] (Bakunin acknowledges that Mediators, these theorizers and "dry arrangers" who exercise a certain "mastery of history", are likely to deny that very historical negativity [44/54]. This historical debate recurs between Bakunin and both Marx and Comte.)

1.7 Historical Logics: Bakunin and Kuhn

Bakunin's "historical logic", which is seen to operate in the socio-political domain, bears a striking resemblance to the historical logic of Thomas S. Kuhn, which is seen to operate in the scientific domain. Notwithstanding divisive issues of "theory-ladeness", "incommensurability" of worldviews, and so on (philosophically fashionable as they may be), Bakunin and Kuhn share the fundamental belief that history (at the very least in a particular domain) is amenable to some kind of rational inquiry and that it exhibits a certain logic, and the belief that such inquiry informs us that historical "progress" (quotation marks for Kuhn's benefit) is secured "through revolution". It is strange how many who would find Kuhn's approach perfectly acceptable and reasonable in principle would write Bakunin's off as idealist nonsense; this is why I draw the comparison at this point — as an immediate defense of Bakunin against such attacks. It seems to me that if it is a valid approach for the likes of Kuhn, it is a valid approach — in principle — for Bakunin as well. That is the level at which debates about philosophies of history ought to be conducted; accusing Bakunin and others of indulging in quasi-Hegelian idealism — especially when it is not understood — does not really get us anywhere.

At the logical level, Kuhn analyzes the structure of the scientific revolution (which he singles out as the means of scientific "progress") while Bakunin analyzes *the structure of the social revolution* (which he singles out as the means of socio-political progress). Kuhn himself admits a certain "parallelism" between scientific and political revolutions. Firstly, he notes that in both cases there is a "sense of malfunction that can lead to crisis [which in turn is] prerequisite to revolution". In the case of political revolution there is, in Kuhn's words, "a growing sense, *often restricted to a segment of the political community* [the negative party, for Bakunin], that existing institutions have ceased adequately to meet the problems posed by an environment *that they have in part created*". Secondly, political revolutions, like scientific revolutions, are created by the "*polarization*" of the community "into competing camps or parties, one seeking to defend the old institutional constellation [the positive party], the others seeking to institute some new one [implicitly, the negative party]". Furthermore, these parties represent "a choice between *incompatible* modes of community life"; hence, "once [the] polarization has occurred, *political recourse fails*" and their conflict can only be overcome by "extrapolitical or extra-institutional events", that is, revolution — the negation of one mode by the other, the creation of a new social world.[43] Bakunin shares these two convictions with Kuhn: that the revolutionary or negative impetus develops within the existing or positive order; and that no mediation is possible between the parties to a revolutionary conflict. But perhaps more can be said of the similarity between Bakunin and Kuhn.

Kuhn portrays the period of normal scientific activity as evolutionary, as gradualistic. Normal science is defined as "a *cumulative* process, one achieved by an articulation or extension of the [current] paradigm". Thus normal science is fundamentally conservative: it aims to reinforce a paradigm rather than to "produce major novelties", and its success is measured accordingly. Indeed, "novelty emerges only with difficulty, manifested by *resistance*". The eventual recognition of the anomalous and problematic, and development of novel theory which apparently explains it, opens a period of scientific crisis which can only be closed in one of three ways. Firstly, normal science may prove "able to handle the crisis-provoking problem" after all. Secondly, the problem may "resist even apparently radical new approaches" and be "set aside for a future generation with more-developed tools" to deal with it. Or, thirdly, the crisis "may end with the emergence of a new candidate for paradigm and with the *battle* over its acceptance". Should that new candidate achieve paradigm status — ultimately by "*apparent consensus*" within the scientific

community — a "paradigm shift" or scientific revolution will have occurred. Kuhn describes scientific revolutions as "non-cumulative [that is,
non-evolutionary] developmental [or "progressive"] episodes in which an
older paradigm is replaced in whole or in part by an *incompatible* new
one". This revolution, then, amounts to "a construction of the [scientific]
field from new fundamentals, a reconstruction that changes some of the
field's most elementary theoretical generalizations as well as many of its
paradigm methods and applications". Kuhn adds that such revolutions
are usually achieved by the young or those who have recently entered the
field, by those "who, being little committed by prior practice to the traditional rules of normal science, are particularly likely to see that those
rules no longer define a playable game and to conceive another set that
can replace them".[44] Such is the nature of scientific "progress" according
to Kuhn.

Bakunin, as already stated, also views (socio-political) history as a
gradual evolutionary process (bearing the revolutionary germ within it)
interrupted by progressive revolutionary "episodes" (where the germ becomes an "independent principle"). That the revolutionary germ is contained in Kuhn's period of normal science is suggested by the merely
"apparent" nature of the consensus that binds the scientific community
during the period; such consensus (idealized or absolutized by proponents of the status quo, as it is in representative democracy) conceals the
element of dissent, the negative element or revolutionary germ, that is
ever-present and continually demands that the paradigm support itself.
Without the element of dissent or the element of skepticism it is doubtful that scientific activity would be undertaken at all during periods of
comparative scientific complacency. In this sense, it is the skeptical or
negative passion that energizes science in its "normal" or positive state.

When the current paradigm cannot support itself and cannot fend
off the element of dissent, the dissenting faction (the negative party)
gains more advocates and enters into outright conflict ("battle" is Kuhn's
word) with the paradigm, such that one or other of these irreconcilable
("incompatible" is Kuhn's word) parties must prevail. Ultimately, the
only satisfactory resolution is the negation of the paradigm whose advo-

cates (the positive party) prove incapable of supporting it. This is not a merely negative resolution (consisting in the victory of the merely negative attitude toward the old paradigm); it is at once an affirmation of what has proved to be lacking in that paradigm. As Kuhn puts it: "The decision to reject one paradigm is always simultaneously the decision to accept another, and the judgment leading to that decision involves the comparison of both paradigms with nature *and* with each other". There is a ring of Bakunin's "the destructive urge is a creative urge, too" sentiment here. Kuhn adds that "To reject one paradigm without simultaneously substituting another is to reject science itself".[45] Bakunin agrees; he is no nihilist. That does not mean that Bakunin is willing to speculate on the alternative (this is hardly possible within Kuhn's scientific community either), but he is willing to conceive of it negatively or dialectically by "comparison" with what is to be negated.

Bakunin and Kuhn therefore occupy common ground at (at the very least) three points: (a) the general notion of historical "progress" through revolution; (b) the importance of resistance to the novel or change (that is, the importance of reaction — in awakening the revolutionary); and (c) the incompatibility of the old (the reactionary) and the new (the revolutionary). Fundamentally, Bakunin and Kuhn share an either-or dialectic as the basis of their historical logics. A final aspect of similarity that is worth mentioning before passing on is that (d) Bakunin too assigns a central revolutionary role to the young on the grounds that: "There is in youth a vigor, a breadth of magnanimous vision, and a natural instinct for justice which are capable of counterbalancing many pernicious influences . . . The young are disrespectful, [and] they instinctively scorn tradition and the principle of authority. This is their strength and salvation". He also notes that the young, who "do not take a direct and constructive part [as yet] in the interests of society", are more open to embracing each "new truth" than are their elders.[46] In other words, the young — by virtue of natural youthful rebellion and their relative freedom from material concerns — are more disposed toward revolutionary ideas and activity.

1.8 Popular Revolution

To return to *The Reaction*: Mediators themselves may object to the above account that, even if what the Negatives say about the nature of contradiction is theoretically sound, things are not in fact as bad as the Negatives insist they are. Negatives, though, contend that, as Bakunin puts it, "the eternal contradiction" between freedom and unfreedom, which is always the same in essence although it varies in intensity and although it develops historically, "has advanced and soared to its last and highest summit in our time". All of these illustrate this: the call of the French Revolution for Liberty, Equality, and Fraternity; the leveling activities of Napoleon; the leveling philosophies of Kant, Fichte, Schelling, and Hegel; the challenge of the philosophical principle of the autonomy of Spirit to "all current *positive* religions [or] to all present-day churches" [45-46/55]. (For the first time in the article, it becomes abundantly clear that although religion is on the side of freedom, all forms of religion to date are on the opposite (or positive) side; that although the religious principle is one with the principle of freedom, all recognized religious forms are inadequate to this principle. Again, it becomes apparent to Bakunin some years after that even the religious principle is on the side of unfreedom — that the religious principle is, with the exception of the statist principle (which is, in any case, as we have seen, inconceivable without it), the most "unfree" or enslaving of principles.)

Mediators maintain that these instances of the contradiction are in the province of past history and that the contradiction itself has now been resolved (philosophically, by Schelling himself). Negatives, on the contrary, maintain that there has been no resolution, Bakunin writes; indeed, the writings of the Left Hegelians — David Friedrich Strauss, Ludwig Feuerbach, Bruno Bauer — and even Positives themselves remain deeply imbued with the negative Spirit. Insofar as there has been a supposed resolution, the negative Spirit, the revolutionary Spirit, "has [simply] gone back into itself again, after having convulsed the whole world [at] its foundations by its first appearance" [47/56]. (To use the terminology that Bakunin would later avail himself of, this first appear-

ance was in the form of "bourgeois" political revolution; but the next appearance, as will become evident, must be in the form of "proletarian"
social revolution, the universal revolution enacted by the "greatest part
of humanity" [50/57].)

Bakunin claims that only the adoption of a universal and all-
embracing principle can satisfy humanity and resolve the great historical
contradiction — between freedom and unfreedom, between the revolutionary or negative and the reactionary or positive, between the new or
dynamic and the old or stagnant. This principle is beyond the comprehension of Positives, who pursue it in the ruins of the old world, if only
in the spirit of compromise with the new. Thus Positives might turn to
the Protestant principle. But it certainly does not qualify as the universal
and all-embracing principle since it represents "the most ghastly anarchy" and results in the most divisive sectarianism. Neither does Catholicism, which has sacrificed its "ancient splendor" as a religion aspiring to
universality and become "an obedient tool of an alien, immoral policy" [48/56-57]. That is, it has sacrificed its religiosity to the partiality of
an effectively political existence. And, as for the State, it — as an entirely
political institution — patently lacks the universality which it seeks in a
would-be universal religious ally. (That the State lacks universality is a
central argument of Bakunin against Marx, as we have seen.)

This mediation of a partial political existence and the universal religion of freedom — championed by Mediating Reactionaries, who are
thus champions of the statist principle — is not only historically lacking:
it is a logical impossibility, as Bakunin believes himself to have proved.
Mediators, who represent the perverted spirit of our times, are therefore,
Bakunin declares, "full of conflicts" and can never hope to become "whole
men", bound by a truly universal principle to all of humanity. Hence they
must "confess that our times are dismal times and that we are all its still
more dismal children" [49/57].

In spite of the claims of Mediators, the contradiction, which they
make a hopeless attempt to resolve, is not in the province of past history;
the negative spirit is coming out of itself once again and is ready to make
its "second" appearance. Importantly, Bakunin argues that the people

themselves — the poorest and most numerous class — now embody the revolutionary Spirit, that is to say, the universal, all-embracing democratic principle moving in history. Having had their rights granted to them in theory, but denied to them in fact — in fact they are condemned to poverty and ignorance, indeed to real slavery — they now endeavor to actualize these rights. Hence they are "assuming a threatening attitude". Their concrete effort to actualize their rights is therefore awaited by all with "shuddering expectation", as is the prospect of the "future which will speak out the redeeming word" [50/57-58].

The prospect of this future is sufficient reason for Positives to repent: for Consistent Reactionaries to look not in the ruins for redemption but in the creative vitality of the revolutionary Spirit; and for Mediating Reactionaries to free themselves from their "intellectual arrogance" and to accept the vital truth of the democratic principle, the principle of freedom. This principle, known immediately only in its negativity, alone offers the prospect of resolution, a prospect which in its "living fullness" has been, to Bakunin's eyes, demonstrated logically above. Thus Bakunin concludes with the truly great and greatly misunderstood exhortation:

> Let us . . . trust the eternal Spirit which destroys and annihilates only because it is the unfathomable and eternally creative source of all life. The passion for destruction is a creative passion, too [51/58].[47]

1.9 The Negative Dialectic

Some general conclusions are called for. Bakunin's concern in *The Reaction* is to examine the conflict between the reactionary principle, i.e., the Positive principle of unfreedom (the thesis), and the revolutionary principle, i.e., the Negative principle of freedom (the antithesis), and consequently also to examine the *essentially affirmative* principle of freedom or democracy which finally emerges from the "mediation" of these two antithetical principles.

This "mediation", so to speak, is distinctly non-Hegelian in that it gives primacy to the Negative, it simply expresses the Negative *fully*. The third principle, freedom, is therefore really present in, or *exists as*, the antithesis, so that in effect there are only two principles and no distinct higher mediated third. Hence Lehning writes: "There is no question here of the Hegelian trichotomy".[48] The higher third, as it were, is implicit in the Negative thesis: democracy is implicit in the negative or revolutionary principle. The revolutionary principle is, therefore, the democratic principle *as it appears*. The conflict can only be fully resolved, then, according to Bakunin, in the utter annihilation of one principle, the Positive, by the other, the Negative, by means of the Negative's self-expression, i.e., revolution.

Negation for Bakunin is also affirmation — *of the other* (the Negative itself). In this affirmation, both sides cease to exist since the Negative *qua* other obviously exists *only* in its capacity as other; with its affirmation, in the total defeat of its dialectical counterpart, it ceases to be an other, and both it and what it has negated disappear. The Negative initially then exists "only as the denial of the Positive, and therefore, it too must be destroyed along with the Positive"; but the Negative as *mere* negation, "in this evil state", engendering nothingness and to which "the whole fullness of life is necessarily external", can and must undergo a qualitative transformation, so that "from its free ground it may spring forth again in a new-born state, as its own living fullness" — as democracy [20/40].

Through revolution, in other words, freedom or democracy supersedes unfreedom, but in superseding it ceases to exist as an entirely negative principle — that is, as revolution. But democracy is not *merely* negative; it is also affirmative. It not only destroys the old, but it also, by means of a qualitative transformation, creates the new; which is to say, it also realizes its essence. The antithetical principle is, nevertheless, negative — the opposite contained within the Positive itself. Democracy, as a revolutionary force, can thus be understood only by negative reference to unfreedom, and can only concretize itself, again in "its own living fullness", by negating unfreedom.

Such a dialectical process is not characterized by sublation

(*Aufhebung*). Sublation, though it is only semi-preservative, represents, to Bakunin, a preponderance of the positive — in both its Hegelian and Marxian forms (as well as the Comtean form). It is the element of sublation in it that causes the dialectic, which is a negative moment by definition, to give way to the speculative, which is positive. But what is posited thereby is not the fullness of the negative but that which was to have been negated; in other words, the original positive is posited anew, in (as Bakunin would see it) mediated form. More importantly, though, the negative itself, the vital element, is compromised — that is, suppressed. (For that reason, to cite the most famous case, the conflict between Being and the Nothingness of such Being is resolved in Hegel's account by Becoming, which is as much the preservation of that empty Being as its negation — which, fully expressed, would, on Bakunin's account, transform such Being into what is lacking in it.) In Hegel's words, then:

> When the dialectic has the negative as its result [since it is *negatively* rational], then, precisely as a result, this negative is at the same time the positive [that required negation], for it contains what it resulted from *sublated* within itself, and cannot be [in its sublated form] without it. This, however, is the basic determination of the third form of the Logical, namely, the *speculative* or positively rational.[49]

Sublation therefore involves a negation of the Negative in its totality (or a negation of negation), and robs the dialectic of its essential negativity and vitality. It *compromises* the dialectic. To conceive of the dialectic in terms of sublation is, for Bakunin, to underestimate its force. In consequence, he undertakes to develop a "faithful" radicalization of the dialectic in *The Reaction*, and to take his place in the Left Hegelian tradition, as a thinker more Hegelian than the man himself. (Hans-Martin Sass argues that to strip dialectics of sublation is — "at least in a Hegelian understanding" — to create an "antithetics".[50] This is a useful term to bear in mind. However, Bakunin, like his fellow Left Hegelians, would have us believe that he is offering a superior, more consistent interpretation of Hegel's dialectic — a radicalization of it that is still *somehow* faithful to the original — not replacing it with something distinct. Therefore, I refer to Bakunin's "dialectic" throughout.) In this context, V.V. Zenkovsky writes that Bakunin formulated a "philosophy of negation . . . Not only did he accept Hegel's thesis concerning the dialectical value and inner inevitability of negation, but he began to give *priority* to negation as the sole bearer of Spirit's creative principle". (That is, he came around to the view that "the *creation* of the future [in all its potential, in its actuality (*Wirklichkeit*)] *demands* the *destruction* of the existing reality (*Realität*) [in its very contingency].[51]) Zenkovsky concludes that "Hegelianism was the defining element in Bakunin's turn to revolutionism; by sharpening Hegel's doctrine and interpreting it one-sidedly, he came to see creative force only in negation".[52]

In Hegelian terms, though he disputed it, Bakunin's thought might be considered one-sided or partial, thus false. He might be accused of "clinging on to one determinacy by force, an effort to obscure and to remove the consciousness of the other one that is contained in it". Or, to be precise, he might be accused of skepticism, for Hegel writes: "The dialectical, taken separately on its own by the understanding, constitutes *skepticism* . . . Skepticism contains the mere negation that results from the dialectic".[53] That is to say, Bakunin might be accused of taking a skeptical stance on all that is positive by refusing to recognize the positivity that is preserved in the positive's sublation — by refusing to recognize sublation at all, and with it, speculation.

The dialectic or the negative moment itself, however, does momentarily, as it were, affirm the other (the Negative), as a dialectical victor, which in some way contains its other (the Positive) by virtue of its original otherness — for the simple reason that one "nothingness [the negative] is specifically the nothingness [or other] of that *from which it results* [the positive]"[54] — before, that is, both the Positive and the Negative, as merely negative, cease to exist. But, for Bakunin, this momentary affirmation of the otherness of the Positive as that which determines the negation, carries with it no obligation to preserve that other in its positivity.

Hence Bakunin's negative philosophy is more complex than it may seem to be at first.

Bakunin's philosophy, as an heir to the philosophy of Hegel, is not, nor could it be, *purely* negative; it is no "crucible of total negation" in the nihilistic sense that Albert Camus has in mind.[55] Nevertheless, the negative moment defines it as, obviously, a negative philosophy, thus, in the context of history, as a revolutionary philosophy and, indeed, a philosophy of revolutionary praxis. (Bakunin himself later refers to *The Reaction* as "a *philosophically* revolutionary article".[56]) Bakunin, like August von Cieszkowski (in his *Prolegomena zur Historiosophie* (*Prolegomena to Historiosophy*) (1838)), sees this development as necessary to the project of Hegel himself. He argues that Hegel stands at the summit of theoretical understanding and, as such, "has already gone above theory", since the end of theory is at once the beginning of something else, i.e., its antithesis. Thus Hegel "has postulated a new, practical world which will bring itself to completion *by no means through a formal application and diffusion of theories already worked out* [versus Cieskowski, and later Marx and Comte], but only through an original act of the practical autonomous Spirit" — that is, the practico-revolutionary spirit [32/47].[57]

Bakunin, consistent with his dialectic (and later his naturalism), is already moving beyond the Cieskowskian synthesis in order to subjugate the theoretical to the practical, so that the theoretical becomes practical in essence: in its knowledge (from where it comes, if you like, which, if practical, can only be the positive, or reality) and its motivations (toward what it is directed, if you like, which, if practical, can only be the negative, or freedom). Conversely, Bakunin rejects the subjugation of the practical to the theoretical (implicit even in Cieskowski's synthetic compromise), which implies the rule of positive speculation, or, generally, "*the government of science*"; and to this extent he preaches "*the revolt of life against science*" (a dominant theme in his later writings).[58]

1.10 Toward Revolutionary Action

The development of a revolutionary philosophy in *The Reaction* does not represent "a decisive *turn* . . . from philosophy to action" for Bakunin, as Kelly has pointed out. Thus she refutes any notion of a dramatic "*break* with a philosophical past*" here, which, according to her, defenders of Bakunin as a political activist (including Bakunin himself) must advocate.[59] (But Bakunin does not, in fact, propose such a break here: Bakunin's reflection on *The Reaction* as "a philosophically revolutionary" article, cited above, means that he views the article as an analysis of revolution from the merely philosophical standpoint.) While Kelly is correctly dismissive of the "break" thesis — which generally suggests scholarly indolence (in the neglect of the element of continuity) — she endorses the other equally absurd extreme: the uniformity thesis. Hence, for Kelly, Bakunin "remained *all his life* the antithesis of a man of action"; that is, he remained all his life a theorist, and a poor one at that, persisting with "a *crude* dialectic to which he remained faithful *all his life*".[60] Kelly's mantra "all his life" suggests scholarly indolence too (in the inattention to or obfuscation of the element of change). (See also the Introduction, above, for a discussion of this.)

The conclusions of Kelly's work, then, are: "[(a)] As an intellectual construction [grounded on the constant "crude dialectic"], Bakunin's political ideology has little merit: [(b)] its fascination lies in what it reveals of the utopian psychology".[61] There is a basic problem with each of these conclusions, one being the conclusion to her study as (a) a study in "the *politics* of utopianism", and the other being the conclusion to her study as (b) a study in "the *psychology* of utopianism". (a) The first problem is that an assessment of the intellectual merit of a "political ideology" requires a certain understanding of that "ideology" at its most fundamental. In this case, as Kelly claims, the most fundamental aspect of Bakunin's political philosophy is his "crude dialectic". Thus an understanding of this dialectic is essential to an assessment of the ideology's intellectual merit. Kelly simply does not understand Bakunin's dialectic and therefore her assessment is worthless. This is easily demonstrated.

Kelly characterizes Bakunin's dialectic in terms of a "synthesis [sic] of . . . two [antitheses] in a dialectical *Aufhebung*" and argues that it "provides [Bakunin] with [a] classic escape from the predicament of insoluble contradictions" in overcoming opposition "by a synthesis in which each [thesis] would be both transcended and preserved". Hence "the problem of a choice between incompatible [theses is] obviated by the magic of Idealist paradox". Kelly declares that "This is, of course, a variation on the *triadic* schemes of history inspired by the myth of the *Golden Age*: the future age is seen as a reconquest, after a period of division and conflict, of an initial harmony in a new, *higher* form". Similarly, we are informed that the "goal" of this dialectic is "that eschatological vision of a unified human community which is rooted in man's sense of an inner split and his *nostalgia* for a mythical *Golden Age of primitive harmony*". Hence Kelly associates Bakunin with the "secular eschatology of Idealism, with its vision of total liberty as the outcome of a *dialectical triad* of development from unity through division to a higher unity". She adds that "man's sense of a split with nature is seen [by this tradition] as the result of a degeneration, a *falling away from a state of harmony*, when man was whole and at one with nature, a condition which he will again achieve, in *a higher and more perfect form*, in a future age when all conflicts . . . will be finally resolved".[62] If this version of Bakunin's dialectic seems unfamiliar to us, that is because it has nothing to do with his 1842 dialectic, the basis of his philosophical anarchism.

Bakunin's dialectic, to begin with, is not triadic. Yet again, there are two dialectical components, Positive and Negative, and the result of their encounter is not a "higher and more perfect" synthetic third (that is not even orthodox Hegelian, since mediation is not equivalent to synthesis), but the fullest victory, the affirmative fulfillment, of the Negative. Kelly fails to understand that Bakunin's dialectic is an either-or dialectic, not a both-and dialectic. As for the dialectic representing the three moments of primitive harmony, fall, and eventual return: unfortunately for Kelly, all three moments are lacking in Bakunin's dialectic. (i) The first moment is that of what is, the current state of affairs in its positivity. There is nothing harmonious (as the nature of its contradictions testifies) or primitive (since the present has its own past with its own contradictions, since it is historically situated) about this moment. The element of nostalgia that Kelly ties to Bakunin at this point is in fact rejected by him as reactionary. Thus, the first moment is no Golden Age to be restored but a partial state of affairs, indeed a state of enslavement, to be obliterated as such. (The pseudo-historical notion of an original Golden Age — as the moment of primitive freedom — is an idiocy that Bakunin later diagnoses in liberal theory.) (ii) The second moment is that of what is not, that which the positive is not. It is a negative moment that reveals what could or even should be in that which is, were it to be actualized. Hence it is dependent on what is while existing only to destroy both it and itself in its dependence. This moment of active contradiction of the positive is not one of falling away from the primitively harmonious for the very simple reason that, as we have shown, there is no such prior state or moment to fall away from. (iii) There is no moment of return for Bakunin because there is nothing other than the positive to return to and that is simple reaction, or the denial of the dialectic in its essential negativity. Indeed, there is no third moment of any description for Bakunin because the completion of the dialectic is the completion of the second moment. As we have asserted, his dialectic is not triadic: it concludes with the victory of the "or", not the "synthesis" of the "either" and the "or", or even their mediation. It seems fair to say, then, that Kelly utterly misreads Bakunin's dialectic and is therefore in no position to assess the political philosophy that is, as she admits, grounded on it.

(b) The second problem with Kelly's conclusions, the problem with the conclusion to her study of "the psychology of utopianism", issues from the previous problem. Utopian psychology (assuming that such a thing ever has any validity) requires a utopian personality, an appropriate subject, as evidenced by that subject's utopian vision. But Bakunin — consistent with his real (i.e., negative) dialectic — has no such vision. He rejects the speculative positing of any futuristic vision as reactionary. He disclaims all "those political and social constructs, formulas, and theories which bourgeois scholars or semi-scholars devise at their leisure, in isolation from popular life, and graciously offer to the *ignorant crowd* as the necessary form of their future organization . . . even the best of them seem [to be] Procrustean beds, too narrow to encompass the broad and powerful sweep of popular life".[63]

Indeed, as stated in the Introduction, it is Kelly who operates (in her academic sphere) in the Procrustean fashion, though she criticizes Bakunin (in spite of such passages, which are numerous) for doing so. As Morris puts it: "Kelly herself exemplifies the kind of personality that she attempts to foist upon Bakunin: the detached intellectual with a 'personal obsession' who imposes abstract categories and interpretations on the empirical reality".[64] The most relevant passage from Kelly is: "those who could claim to have known [Bakunin] best [and who is Kelly to disagree] . . . accused him of attempting to force reality into a preconceived mould founded not on observation of the external world, but on his own drives and needs, which he had universalized with the aid of the limitless subjectivism of Idealist philosophy". Those who supposedly knew Bakunin best were Herzen and Ivan Turgenev. Assuming that this is an accurate account of their views (which is debatable), it should be pointed out that Herzen offers an essentially literary account or portrait of Bakunin (what is more, from a distinct ideological standpoint), not the cold, impartial, and unquestionably truthful picture of him that Kelly, who criticizes others for taking other opinions "at face value", takes at face value.[65] Herzen, like Kelly, is some kind of liberal — though one too intelligent to deserve the embarrassing ideological admiration of Berlin and Kelly herself. It is hardly surprising, therefore, that Kelly does not question his opinion on Bakunin. Or, rather, she questions it only once, when Herzen disputes Turgenev's caricature of Bakunin in *Rudin* (1856; second edition, 1860). Thus Herzen's criticisms of Bakunin are entirely accurate, but his defense of him is misguided (heresy, surely). And this, in spite of the fact that some of Herzen's criticisms are patently unfair. For example, Herzen accuses Bakunin of being out of touch with reality since he did not *witness* those events that transpired during his imprisonment. While poor Alexander had to witness the suffering of *others* at the hands of the reaction,

Bakunin, who "had not sat by the bedside of the dying", was *himself* rotting in a cell or wasting away in Siberian exile.[66] One might ask, therefore, who — Bakunin or Herzen — has a greater understanding of the arbitrary power of State reaction. (In this context, Ulam writes: "Bakunin would have approved what another anarchist, though Christian and pacifist, Leo Tolstoy, said: 'he who has not been in jail does not know what the State is'".[67]) But aside from Herzen's criticisms, fair or otherwise, Kelly ignores the central statement by him on Bakunin, which demonstrates that for all his literary embellishment and ideological motivation Herzen is fairer to Bakunin and less fanatical than Kelly herself: "Bakunin had many defects. But his defects were slight, and his strong qualities were great".[68] It is odd that Kelly should omit this passage when she gains so much mileage from almost every other line (or at least the less flattering ones) of the few pages that Herzen devotes to Bakunin in his memoirs. Her work would have one believe that Herzen wrote tomes of detailed critical analysis on Bakunin instead of a few witty pages buried in the depths of a sprawling literary masterpiece.

In any case, all additional criticisms of Bakunin, like those of Turgenev (if they can be called "criticisms" in any meaningful sense), are most welcome. So "Turgenev was a more subtle psychologist [and therefore the most authoritative judge of a philosopher and his thought] than his critics [including Herzen, Chernyshevsky, and, in this case, Turgenev himself!] perceived him to be".[69] Two *literary characterizations of Bakunin's personality* (one of which is highly dubious as such[70]) are therefore the mainstays of Kelly's *critique of his political philosophy*. The reader of her study has been warned.

Kelly, then, partly out of ignorance of Bakunin's dialectic, partly out of ideological fanaticism (after all, another's ideology, especially when it is to the left, is always, independent of argument, "utopian"), cannot resist imposing a "utopian" vision on Bakunin. But Eric Voegelin, infinitely more attuned than Kelly to the philosophical matters at hand (though, perhaps inevitably, he has a tendency to theologize them), recognizes "the radical absence of a positive idea of order" in *The Reaction*; in fact, he recognizes this throughout Bakunin's later writings as well, noting that

Bakunin shies away "from an articulated idea of [future] society".[71] This absence, this shying-away, is no accident; it is entirely in keeping with Bakunin's logic.

So much for Kelly's general conclusions on Bakunin's "uniform" ideology with its "utopian" vision. Insofar as there is continuity in Bakunin's thought (and, as declared above, Kelly is correctly dismissive of the "break thesis"), it has nothing to do with this part-misread, part-imposed account. In any event, to dismiss the element of change in Bakunin's thought (for the sake of a neat and tidy polemic) is intellectually — even academically — reprehensible. In the present context, the emergence of a revolutionary philosophy in *The Reaction* (though it does not represent a dramatic break with the past) clearly does represent in Bakunin a transition from the speculative philosophy of his youth (the "Fichtean phase") to a *philosophy of revolutionary praxis* — which exceeds the still speculative Cieskowskian philosophy of praxis — that becomes the basis of his more active later period, or, to use Voegelin's phrase, his "revolutionary existence". Kelly, with her "uniformity thesis", cannot bear the idea that Bakunin was ever a "man of action". She is perfectly entitled to criticize Bakunin's activity (and there is much to criticize), but there is no denying that he was a committed and significant revolutionary. In any case, if this is intended as a criticism of Bakunin, it is a little rich coming from an Oxford-educated Cambridge academic. What is more, academic accusations of "superfluous existence" are frankly hard to swallow.

Again, Voegelin's scholarship in his analysis of the post-1842 Bakunin, though by no means flattering to its subject, is on a higher plane to Kelly's. (Voegelin could teach Kelly a valuable intellectual lesson: that criticism (even from another "ideological" standpoint), when sober, can be just and enlightening. Kelly's intoxicated vilification, her ideological rant, is neither. Indeed, it is too fanatical to give due credit or to be powerfully critical because it makes no effort to understand. (Here I differ from Kelly in my critique of her work: though, in my sedimented frustration with this level of scholarship, I may seem equally intoxicated, I believe I have developed a coherent argument against her analysis because *I have sought to understand it*.) Ultimately, Kelly's book seems intellectually pointless; but, unfortunately, there is more to it than that, as I suggested in the Introduction.)

Voegelin, then, who manages to place Bakunin's development of a revolutionary philosophy in its intellectual context (by comparing it with Schelling and Hegel), is worth quoting at some length:

> [A] break [perhaps better understood as a "transition" for the reasons mentioned above] occurs between the derivative Christianity of Hegel and Schelling [to which Bakunin had once more or less adhered] on the one side, and the revolutionary speculation ["philosophy" would be a better word] of [the post-1842] Bakunin [on the other]. Hegel's and Schelling's interpretations were contemplative in the sense that the understanding of history was for them the most important cathartic exercise in clarifying and solidifying their *own* existence. However far their ideas diverged from orthodox, dogmatic Christianity, however far they went in the direction of Gnosis, they still remained substantially Christian thinkers and were concerned about the order of their [own] souls. Bakunin's [distinctive] *pronunciamento* breathes an entirely different spirit. The consciousness of crisis is strongly alive in him, and he uses the historical perspective sensibly, though not impeccably [the combination of credit and criticism mentioned above], for its expression. Nevertheless, *history is now more than the cathartic means for clarifying a man's position in his world*; under the influence of Feuerbach [among others, it should be said], *it has become the legitimating basis for action*. The consciousness of crisis moved Schelling to his "inner return", toward the ground in the soul . . . The same consciousness moves Bakunin *toward revolutionary action*.[72]

Oblivious to Voegelin's insight, Kelly does not see this transition in the *direction* of activism or "*toward* revolutionary action" as significant at all but simply as an "elaboration of a new theory of the act", grounded as ever on Bakunin's, as she sees it, immutable Fichtean thought; aimed, that is, as before, indeed as ever, at Bakunin's *own* "self-realization as a real or integrated personality". Her "psychological" assessment (more suited by its very nature to the absurd egoism of Fichtean thought than to the profound universal dialectic of Hegel and the critical philosophy of the Left Hegelians — and she exhibits a poor understanding of them both) is that Bakunin continued, "generalizing from his own needs", to see "his goal as the goal of all humanity". The sole difference, that is, the sole post-Hegelian concession, is that "henceforth he would seek to realize his fantasy through the transformation of the external world", or world history. Even that is a major transition, or an expression of the transition in question, but couched in terms that aim to convey the uniformity thesis for, as Kelly notes here, "the consistency in Bakunin's thought [is] much more striking than the change". Such "Idealist fantasies" are, we are told, simply a "surrogate for action" (and would later manifest themselves, in near-identical form, as "a [utopian] *program* for revolution in the real world"). Hence, "Bakunin had rejected theory only to construct a theory of the revolutionary act wholly Idealist in its obscurity and its paradoxes".[73]

For all the evident transitions in Bakunin's thought — which might require a certain scholarly subtlety to discern — Kelly insists that it is reducible to "the limitless subjectivism of Idealist philosophy". This is a two-pronged argument. It begins with the claim that Bakunin's idealism, whether Fichtean or supposedly Hegelian, is basically egocentric. Then, when the idea that Bakunin did in fact reject Fichteanism for Hegelianism becomes too difficult to deny, Kelly turns her attention to Hegel (how he would quiver) and declares his idealism basically Fichtean anyway: "In Hegel's philosophy the objective world, for all its transitory independence, was no less the creation of thought than it was for the 'subjective' Idealists who preceded him, and it was precisely this paradox that was the secret of his irresistible charm for Bakunin".[74] Thus the first prong of Kelly's argument is the application of the uniformity thesis to Bakunin, and this is supplemented by an equally tenuous second prong: the application of the uniformity thesis to the entire tradition of German Idealism. Both prongs are from the commonsense point of view difficult to accept. After all, things rarely remain the same. Philosophically, in any case, the entire argument is just ignorant. No serious scholar of German Idealism, for example, would have the slightest sympathy for Kelly's indolent approach to a complex tradition. Furthermore, any serious scholar of Bakunin as, in some sense, a successor to this complex tradition (of which he had a sound understanding) would have to dismiss Kelly's moronic conclusions.

Even Bakunin's later naturalism is reduced to the same "limitless subjectivism", though Kelly neglects to examine it. And that is a good thing too, because it is about as untenable a claim as is imaginable. She simply comments that "From the 1860s the word 'nature' performs the function previously performed by 'Spirit' in Bakunin's vocabulary".[75] This is true: Spirit and Nature are understood by Bakunin at different stages as the dialectical overcoming of the seeming contradiction between the subjective and the objective or the social and the natural. Consistent with his dialectic yet again, Bakunin argues that this overcoming is on one side, not in mediation. In the case of Bakuninian Spirit, it is, contrary to what Kelly says, on the side of the objective. Thus Bakunin's objective idealism is already more objective and less Fichtean than Hegel's is. In the case of Nature, the overcoming is on the side of the natural, as we will see. But there is another quite coherent transition here which Kelly ignores — from objective idealism (of which she has absolutely no concept, as her statement on Hegel, just cited, demonstrates) to naturalism (which both Feuerbach and Bakunin take to be the demystified truth of objective idealism). This transition will be explored in depth in the next part of this essay.

In any event, to conclude on the transition in *The Reaction*: I have no qualms about siding with Voegelin rather than Kelly. There clearly is a transition from the speculative to the dialectical, from the "merely" philosophical to the philosophically revolutionary, in the article. (Kelly's dogged effort to obscure the transition from philosophy to philosophy of revolutionary praxis and, subsequently, to revolutionary anarchism in its essential practicality, is futile.) I see this transition as the necessary consequence of Bakunin's discovery of the Hegelian — or, to be more precise, Left Hegelian — principle of negation, the revolutionary principle. As he puts it in 1873: "merciless negation constitutes [the] essence" of Hegel's thought[76], which, for Bakunin, as we have noted, being at the summit of theoretical understanding, must necessarily give way to praxis.

The principle of negation is seen by him to be demanded for the resolution of the fundamental Hegelian contradiction, the inherent historical contradiction between the principle of unfreedom and the principle of freedom — what Bakunin sees as the principle of democracy in 1842, but what he would later see as the principle of anarchy. (There are of course transitional stages — notably of communism and Panslavism, both of which are discarded as antithetical to freedom and its revolutionary principle, which Bakunin had originally hoped to found them upon.[77]) That is to say, in Bakunin's later writings the principle of social revolution is regarded as the only possible resolution of the real contradiction between the principle of State (embodied in the "Knouto-Germanic Empire") and the principle of anarchy (the essence of the social revolutionary principle). As Bakunin puts it, again in 1873: "The [existing] State on one side, social revolution [the principle of anarchy as it appears] on the other — those are the two poles whose antagonism constitutes the very essence of contemporary public life throughout Europe". He remarks: "Between these two . . . no reconciliation is possible. It is war to the death . . . [That is,] it can end only with the decisive victory of one side and the decisive defeat of the other". It can only truly end, indeed, with the satisfaction of the most universal and all-embracing principle, the negative or revolutionary principle that alone offers the hope of "a new world for all mankind".[78]

1.11 *Preface to Hegel's Gymnasial Lectures*: Toward Naturalism

Martine Del Giudice argues convincingly that the crucial transition "toward revolutionary action" that occurs in Bakunin's thought occurs gradually, having roots in his pre-Berlin (pre-1840) period. (The "break thesis" is therefore discounted by Del Giudice too: "the abrupt dichotomy which appears in most historical commentaries dealing with Bakunin's writings and activities cannot be maintained".) The transition can be discerned earlier, even in Bakunin's supposedly conservative *Preface to Hegel's Gymnasial Lectures* (of April 1838). Del Giudice concludes that "The appeal for a 'reconciliation with actuality' [in the *Preface*], far from being a naive and uncritical endorsement of the status quo (as it has repeatedly been made out to be[79]), was rather formulated by Bakunin as a direct response to the modern crisis of alienation"; and that "through his ideal of education, Bakunin was led to take the crucial step of establishing a link between theory and practice, since, in his view, the problems of alienation *and individualism* could only be met by such a unified theoretico-practical approach". Hence, "It is in this article that, for the first time, Bakunin articulated the structured and coherent method which provided the foundation for his development of a *philosophy of action* and which formed *the basis for his subsequent revolutionary activity*".[80]

Del Giudice's reasonable conclusion could not be any more opposed to Kelly's. Instead of representing a subjectivist conservatism ("orthodox" Hegel tailored, as it were, to Fichtean needs), Bakunin in fact (a) explicitly rejects Fichte's philosophy, and (b) interprets Hegel in a non-conservative manner. The non-conservative interpretation of Hegel has been scrutinized already. What interests us here is the Fichtean component that obsesses Kelly, and overshadows any truly Hegelian component as far as she is concerned. She asserts: "[Bakunin's] temperamental affinity with Fichte was stronger than the demands of Hegelian orthodoxy".[81] However, Bakunin critiques the (Reformation) culture, even "evil", of subjectivism, which manifested itself philosophically in the person of Descartes — and thereafter, as we will see, in the persons of Kant and Fichte — in the *Preface*. Kelly acknowledges this critique of Fichte, but insists that Bakunin lapses back into Fichtean subjectivism regardless. She quotes a letter of February 1840, where Bakunin commends Fichte's "ability to abstract himself from all alien and external circumstances and from the common opinion", and expresses his desire to emulate Fichte, that is, "to rely calmly on myself and to act independently and in defiance of all that is external".[82] Of course, Bakunin is commending Fichte's personal resolve here, not his philosophical "subjectivism". This is hardly surprising since his commendation is brought on, as Kelly acknowledges, by a reading of a biography of Fichte, not by a reading of his writings. Kelly, as ever, refuses to make any distinction between personality (or the idiosyncratic elements of it, as she represents or misrepresents them) and philosophy (as she plainly misunderstands it); in fact, she simply reduces the latter (which may as well not exist, since it escapes her entirely) to an expression of the former (which is so nebulous as to escape any serious study in the first place). (This approach to Bakunin is not uncommon, as we have argued in the Introduction: the "psycho-historical" reading of Bakunin depends on it — on a simultaneous fixation with Bakunin's apparent foibles and utter ignorance of his philosophy and the tradition from which it comes. Pyziur exemplifies this approach when he writes: "it is necessary to understand the contradictions in [Bakunin's] character in order to comprehend his political deeds and their ideological rationalizations"; after all, as Pyziur declares in a flash of genius, "his character was the basis of all that Bakunin did".[83]) In accordance with this arbitrary and preposterous conflation we must assume that any commendation of a philosopher implies an endorsement of his views. No serious philosophical scholar with any feeling for the subject would accept this assumption: we all entertain feelings for philosophers whose views we reject (especially those whose views once appealed to us and who therefore inspired us in some way).

Even assuming with Kelly that this is a philosophical statement, in any case, there is nothing in it, construed as such, that compromises Bakunin's critique of subjectivism anyway. To abstract oneself from or to act in defiance of all that is "external" and constitutes mere "opinion" is not to abstract oneself from or to act in defiance of reality (properly conceived — as actuality) and the rational community which is, as such, one with it. It is not to "move back to consoling fantasy rather than forward to a critical examination of reality".[84] It is rather to divorce oneself, as a spiritual or rational subject, from a false or "alien" reality, not in order to remain within oneself but in order to seek, thereafter, as Fichte never could but as Hegel recommends, a reconciliation with actuality. If this statement is a philosophical commendation of Fichte, then it is simply a commendation of his vital contribution to the subsequent Idealist, and specifically Hegelian, tradition; but that does not make Bakunin a Fichtean or a "subjectivist", and his critique of the subjectivist or anthropocentric tradition in the *Preface* makes it abundantly clear that he is nothing of the sort.

Bakunin explains the development of the initial modern or Cartesian anthropocentrism in the following way:

> The awakened intellect, freed from the swaddling clothes of authority, was no longer willing to accept anything on faith, and, *separating itself from the actual world*, and *immersing itself in itself*, *wished to derive everything from itself*, to find the origin and basis of knowledge within itself. "I think, therefore I am". Here is how the new philosophy began in the person of Descartes.[85]

This "*new philosophy*", Cartesian *anthropocentrism*, brought about an apparent contradiction between the subject and objectivity, and resolved it unconvincingly from the subjective standpoint *with a little help from God*. That is to say, Cartesian anthropocentrism is not consistently anthropocentric, but remains part-theocentric. The theocentric dimension — and with it the Cartesian route back to the meaningfully objective — is effectively, if not explicitly, negated by Kantian anthropocentrism. Of this, Bakunin writes:

> . . . the result of the philosophy of the understanding, the result of the subjective systems of Kant and Fichte, was *the destruction of all objectivity, of all actuality*, and *the immersion of the abstract, empty I in vain, egotistical self-contemplation* . . .[86]

Bakunin's commendation of Fichte for inspiring the "defiance" of *alien* reality is well and good; but Bakunin castigates Kant and Fichte for actually destroying *all* sense of objectivity and thereby needing to determine everything on the side of the abstract, alienated subject. Kant does this implicitly, Fichte does so explicitly; Fichte is therefore the most explicit subjectivist or anthropocentric philosopher. The call for a reconciliation with actuality in its objectivity, which has been alienated by the Kantian tradition (either put aside as inaccessible or abstractly swallowed-up by the subject), is a call for the reinstatement by the subject (in its spirituality or rationality) of this objectivity, the actuality it has sought *abstractly* to make its own, an actuality with which it is *in truth* one, and apart from which it, *qua* Spirit, cannot be satisfied.

Bakunin attacks the tradition which denies this unity (noticing, in its conceptuality [in its narrowly Kantian anthropocentrism], a certain linguistic senselessness [that is, a tendency toward linguistic anthropocentrism], a predilection, shared by contemporary philosophers, for "verbal fireworks *devoid of content*, and thoughts *without sense*"). The following is the most penetrating articulation of his critique:

> [The subjectivist] necessarily bade farewell to actuality and wandered in a *state of sickly estrangement from any natural and spiritual actuality*, in some fantastic, arbitrary, imaginary world, or rose up against the actual world and *believed that with his illusory strength he could destroy its mighty existence.* He thinks that all the good of mankind is contained in the realization of the finite conditions of his finite understanding and of the finite goals of his finite, arbitrary will. He does not know, poor fool, that *the actual world is superior to his wretched and powerless individuality*, he doesn't see that sickness and evil lie, not in actuality, but within himself, in his own abstraction.[87]

This is a monumental passage in Bakunin's writings. He already sides here with Hegel over the pre-Hegelian Kantian tradition, which includes Fichte: that is, he already sides with the objective idealist over the subjective idealists by, at the most fundamental, recognizing the resistance of "mighty . . . natural and spiritual actuality" to its ingestion by the "wretched and powerless" subject. (This distinction between idealisms is, as I have pointed out above, lost on Kelly.) Indeed, Bakunin's objective idealism (which, *qua* idealism, remains an anthropocentrism, though it is socialized and, to a limited extent, naturalized) already points toward "reconciliation" on the side of objectivity (an unmediated resolution, a resolution on one side, that becomes logically possible or conceivable with the development of a negative dialectic in 1842). In 1838, Bakunin denies that the subjective can function as the ground of objectivity, asserting that the anthropocentric belief that it can do so is simply "fantastic", the stuff of metaphysics, as we will see, including that of Marx. But the possibility that the objective functions as the ground of the subjective — or that the "subjective" is simply of the "objective" — remains. This is the direction in which Bakunin moves, at any rate. Thus the transition from the subjective to the post-Hegelian objective leads quite coherently to a further transition in Bakunin's later thought, under the influence of Feuerbach in particular, to naturalism: the belief that "objective" nature precedes the "subjectively" human — which is produced within it and only conceived apart from it (by metaphysics, human idealism, or anthropocentrism) in abstraction — and is incapable of being subjugated by the subjectively human.

Bakunin therefore begins to develop what Masaryk calls his "anti-subjectivist formula" in the *Preface*. "Bakunin settles here his account with extreme subjectivism, and in particular with Fichtean solipsism. Building on a Hegelian foundation, he arrives at a position opposed to that of Kant, his former leader in philosophy, and opposed *above all* to that of Fichte".[88] This anti-subjectivism is a central tenet of Hegelian and post-Hegelian philosophy, where it is initially formulated in Feuerbach's early work *Gedanken über Tod und Unsterblichkeit* (*Thoughts on Death and Immortality*) (1830). Note the following pronouncement: "it is of the utmost necessity that the human being . . . after he has lived long enough in rapturous self-contemplation and in intoxicating enjoyment of his individuality . . . awakens in himself the need for seeking the sources of life and truth, *the determining basis of his actions,* and the abode of his tranquility, but in a place that is different from his own individuality".[89] (At this stage in Feuerbach's career, anti-subjectivism does not imply anti-anthropocentrism (any more than it does for Marx); indeed, Feuerbach is ambivalent about anthropocentrism even in his naturalist writings. Bakunin is less so, as I will argue.)

Daniel Guérin points out that Max Stirner, Feuerbach's most vociferous critic, "rehabilitated the individual at a time when the philosophical field was dominated by Hegelian anti-individualism and most reformers in the social field had been led by the misdeeds of bourgeois egotism to stress its opposite".[90] The influence of Stirner may have contributed to the libertarian aspect of Bakunin's mature socialism. Nevertheless, Stirner's egocentric philosophy represents a quasi-Kierkegaardian corruption of Left Hegelian logic — the twisting of the either-or into an absurd personalistic logic — that Bakunin would never endorse. On one of the few occasions that Bakunin mentions Stirner in his writings, he refers to the "cynical logic" of this "nihilist".[91] (The neo-Kantian or anthropocentric reaction in post-Hegelian philosophy (*post*-Hegelian, in spite of Hegel's co-option by various reactionaries, because Hegel challenges so many of the Kantian fundamentals which the neo-Kantians seek to resurrect); the reaction represented by figures like Stirner and Kierkegaard, and carried on to the present day by all manner of Nietzschean, psychoanalytic, phenomenological, structuralist and post-structuralist, pragmatist, liberal, and even Marxist philosophers; this great *philosophical reaction*, to say nothing of the socio-political reaction — for all the pretence of the economistic left, the cultural left, and left-liberals — that has accompanied it, is absolutely antithetical to the naturalist tradition to which Bakunin belongs in the final analysis. This is perhaps the central claim of the next section of this essay.) Bakunin, in any case, expresses his anti-subjectivism in the following terms in the *Preface* (drawing particular attention to the *arbitrariness* and *senselessness* of subjectivism):

> To rebel against actuality and to destroy in oneself any living source of life, is one and the same thing. Reconciliation with actuality in all its aspects and in all spheres of life is the great question of our time . . . Let us hope that our new generation will . . . come out of illusion, that it will abandon empty and senseless chatter, that it will recognize that true knowledge and anarchy of the mind, arbitrariness of opinion, are complete opposites, and that there reigns in knowledge a strict discipline, and that without this discipline there can be no knowledge.[92]

1.12 Negation: Bakunin and Bauer

I wish to supplement the first part of this essay with a brief comment on what I would suggest as a major immediate influence on Bakunin in *The Reaction*: that is, Bruno Bauer's *Die Posaune des jüngsten Gerichts über Hegel den Atheisten und Antichristen: ein Ultimatum* (*The Trumpet of the Last Judgment Against Hegel the Atheist and Antichrist: An Ultimatum*). In this seminal work of Left Hegelianism, Bauer seeks to tear "away the thin veil which briefly concealed the thought of the master", i.e., Hegel, and to reveal "the [Hegelian] system in its nakedness". Bauer's conclusion is that "the center point of this philosophy [is] its *destruction* of religion". Indeed, Bauer draws the broader conclusion that "Hegel not only is set against the State, the Church and religion, but opposes everything firm and established".[93] Bakunin, as we have shown, does not emphasize the destruction of religion as such in *The Reaction*; this side of his thought would develop in time, as we will see in the next section. (It would develop chiefly under the influence of Feuerbach, though the negation of religion *as such*, which Bakunin later champions, is a Bauerian rather than a Feuerbachian theme. Thus Bakunin supplements the genetico-historical approach of Feuerbach [which Bauer lacks] with a negative logic in the style of Bauer [which, perhaps, Feuerbach lacks].) What concerns us here is the passion for destruction expressed in Bauer's interpretation of the dialectic.

Bakunin adopts, and develops, two of Bauer's ideas on the dialectic, which result from his exposition of its "more dangerous points". First — versus "the mediating Hegelians", with their dialectic of "reconciliation" or "half-measures" — the idea that "the *negative* dialectic [is] the central principle of Hegelianism". (Bakunin, in a passage from 1873 already cited, a passage very much in the spirit of *The Reaction*, subscribes to the consistent and bold findings of the Left Hegelian interpretation. He notes that it "tore away the conservative mask from [Hegel's] doctrines and revealed in all its nakedness the merciless negation that constitutes their essence".[94] The conclusion here, including the terminology, owes much to Bauer.) And, second, the idea that this negative dialectic has practical applications. As Bauer puts it, "a theoretical principle must . . . come to the act, to *practical opposition*, to turn itself directly into praxis and action"; furthermore, "the opposition must be serious, sharp, thoroughgoing, unrestrained, and must see its highest goal in the *overthrow of the established order*".[95] (Bakunin writes in *The Reaction* that Hegel's negative philosophy "has already gone above theory . . . and postulated a new, practical world which will bring itself to completion . . . only through an original act of the practical autonomous [or revolutionary] Spirit" [32/47].) Both Bauer and Bakunin, in other words, accept that the dialectic is, as it were, theoretically negative and practically revolutionary. Thus Bauer refers to Hegelianism as "that hellish system which would blast the Christian State [note the conjunction] sky-high".[96]

Nevertheless, Bakunin and Bauer differ significantly on the question of motivation (or *what* drives the dialectic) and also on the question of agency (or *who* drives the dialectic). Bauer holds that the goal of the dialectical process is *"the freedom and self-pleasure of self-consciousness"*.[97] Bakunin, on the other hand, holds that the (theoretical) goal of the dialectical process is the *self-consciousness of freedom*. In this respect, Bakunin is closer to Arnold Ruge (when Ruge writes, for example, "Our times are political, and our politics intend the freedom of this world"[98]). On the question of agency, Bauer holds (comically, in fact) that "Philosophers are the Lords of this World, and create the destiny of mankind"; as such, they "are truly of a singular danger, for they are the most *consistent* and unrestrained revolutionaries". Put simply, philosophers are the agents of revolution. It is they who judge what contradicts self-consciousness, and who sanction the overthrow of the existing order. In Bauer's words once again, "who should it be who is to declare when a temporal institution, a regulation, is no longer to be allowed validity? To whom is it given to pass final judgment upon the 'impudence' of the established and *positive* order? Who is to give the signal for the ruin of the actual state of affairs? Now, you know that well enough yourselves! Only the philosopher!"[99] Bakunin disputes this vanguard mentality throughout his writings (later rejecting the revolutionary projects of Marx, Saint-Simon, and Comte as "metaphysical" attempts to establish the government of savants). He holds, even in 1842, that the oppressed majority is the proper agent of adequate revolution.

1.13 Bakunin and Proudhon: Toward Anarchism

At this point, considering the issue of revolutionary agency, we may note Félicité-Robert de Lamennais' influence on Bakunin, who read Lamennais' *Politique à l'usage du peuple* (*Politics for the Use of the People*) (1837) in October 1841. (Kelly's opinion on Lamennais' influence is, typically, constrained by her absurd psychological framework: "Lamennais offered the . . . breath-taking prospect of a world-historical stage on which to enact the drama of self-realization", etc.[100]) This strain of Bakunin's thought began to develop further under the influence of Weitling, whose "faith in the liberation and future of the enslaved majority" Bakunin commends in his *Confession*.[101] Under Weitling's influence, then, Bakunin writes: "The people . . . the broadest masses of the poor and oppressed . . . has always been the only creative ground from which alone have sprung all the great acts of history, all liberating revolutions. All the actions of those who are alien to the people are blighted in advance . . . [True] Communism derives not from theory, but from . . . popular instinct, and [this] is never mistaken".[102]

Weitling's influence also pushed Bakunin, more specifically, in the direction of anarchism. In *Garantien der Harmonie und der Freiheit* (*Guarantees of Harmony and Freedom*) (1842), Weitling writes: "The perfect society has no government, but only an administration, no laws, but only obligations, no punishments, but means of correction". In light of the analysis of Marx's revolutionary program above, this might be said to have more in common with the "anarchist" side of Marxian communism than with Bakunin's mature anarchism (and Bakunin, as we have seen, condemns the despotism of Weitling's communism, too). However, the suggestion of anarchism did not go unnoticed by Bakunin.[103] Konstantin Aksakov — a one-time member, along with Bakunin, of the Stankevich circle — has been suggested as the earliest influence on Bakunin in this regard. Bakunin himself reflects in 1867 that Aksakov was an "enemy of the Petersburg state and of statism in general, and in this attitude he even anticipated us".[104]

Such influences notwithstanding, Pierre-Joseph Proudhon is evidently the decisive influence on Bakunin's anarchism as such. (The notion that, for instance, Carlo Pisacane was a formative influence has been vanquished expertly by Ravindranathan, who concludes in no uncertain terms: "Carlo Pisacane had nothing to do with this development".[105]) Bakunin describes his program as "Proudhonism . . . pushed right to its final consequences".[106] There is an echo of the Left Hegelian approach here; in fact, Bakunin might be considered a Left Proudhonian, a Proudhonian faithfully (in his own eyes) drawing out the radical conclusions of the "master's"[107] thought or revealing the Proudhonian system "in its nakedness". The essence of the "master's" thought, from Bakunin's viewpoint, is twofold, as the following summary demonstrates:

> [Proudhon] armed himself with a critique as profound and penetrating as it was ruthless. Opposing liberty to authority . . . he boldly proclaimed himself an *anarchist* [in *Qu'est-ce que la propriété? (What is Property?)* (1840) and elsewhere], and in the face of [widespread] deism or pantheism he had the courage to simply call himself an *atheist* [in *Système des contradictions économiques (System of Economic Contradictions)* (1846) and elsewhere].[108]

Thus, according to Bakunin, the Proudhonian system consists, firstly, in the destruction or *negation of the political.* This negation is already formally advocated by Bakunin in *The Reaction*, but is refined, radicalized, and designated anarchist under Proudhon's influence. In Proudhon's insistence on the "absolute incompatibility" of political authority and freedom; in his contempt for those who "should undertake to reconcile them" — those mediators, those *"friends of order . . .* among revolutionaries" who, "while admitting the dangers of authority, nevertheless hold to it, as the sole means of maintaining order, [seeing] nothing beside it but empty desolation", those "in the democratic and socialistic party" who "appropriate the arguments directed against government, and upon these arguments, which [are] essentially negative, [attempt to] restore the very [positive] principle which was at stake, under a new name, and with a few modifications"; in his faith in the creativity of destruction, his faith that "negation is the preliminary requirement to affirmation", that "all progress begins by abolishing something"; in all this, we hear the Bakunin of *The Reaction*.[109] (Proudhon is not consistent here: he more frequently represents his dialectic as positive, declaring that "Reconciliation is revolution" and depicting his "whole philosophy [as] one of perpetual reconciliation".[110])

The radical edge that Proudhon contributes to Bakunin's social thought is the avowedly *anarchist*, and non-"democratic", revolutionary opposition to all state forms, including the democratic, which are, in any case, equivalent ("There are not two kinds of government . . . Government is by divine right [that is, based on the sacred or "mystical" principle of authority], or it is nothing"). As Proudhon puts his anarchist program: "Neither monarchy, nor aristocracy, nor even democracy itself, insofar as it may imply any government at all, even though acting in the name of the people, and calling itself the people. No authority, no government, not even popular, that is the Revolution".[111] Pyziur explains: "Proudhon, more than any other, was responsible for transforming Bakunin's instinctive [or general philosophical] revolt against authority into a conscious *anarchist* creed".[112]

The Proudhonian system also consists in the destruction or *negation of the religious*. Bakunin's critique of the religious — though, as we will show, shaped by the Feuerbachian and Comtean analyses in particular — is also radicalized under Proudhon's influence; thus, for example, Proudhon contributes a "Satanic" element (a preference for the "true author of human emancipation" over the "heavenly despot") to Bakunin's developing atheism: the sentiment that if after all, contrary to all reason, God really did exist, Satan — this "spiritual leader of all revolutionaries" — would be preferable.[113]

Most importantly, Proudhon stresses the intimate relation between the religious and the political — as a derivation of political authority from religious fantasy: "religion is unquestionably the oldest manifestation of government and the highway for authority".[114] Thus, the relation that Bakunin makes much of throughout his writings assumes a more pernicious character, and atheism or anti-theologism — the need to overcome the "divine phantom" — becomes a central component of his anti-political or anarchist program. It is in this sense that, as Lehning expresses it, "The atheism of Bakunin . . . is bound up with his political theory"; indeed, "anti-theologism [or] atheistic materialism [is the] key-stone of Bakunin's philosophical conceptions".[115] We must therefore study it in depth. But, before we do so, we must specify the distinction between Bakunin's outlook and Proudhon's, at least as Bakunin sees it.

Bakunin grounds his anti-theologism on a naturalism such as is lacking in Proudhon's thought; Proudhon, for all his atheism (or opposition to divine idealism), leaves the door open to (human) idealism with, for example, his psycho-centric philosophy of history, his attempt to reduce every historical element to a "psychological fact".[116] Bakunin writes: "Proudhon, in spite of all his efforts to shake off the tradition of classical idealism, remained all his life an incorrigible idealist", "unable to surmount . . . idealistic phantoms" in spite of himself.[117] It is Bakunin's purpose to rid Proudhon's libertarian thought of its metaphysicality, that is, to naturalize his anarchism — thereby overcoming its abstract, indeed reactionary, individualism and transforming it into a social anarchism. As such, Bakunin stands in relation to his "master" as, not so much Bauer, but Feuerbach stands in relation to his.

Notes to Part One

1. Bruno Bauer, *The Trumpet of the Last Judgment Against Hegel the Atheist and Antichrist: An Ultimatum* (1841), trans. Lawrence Stepelevich (Lewiston: Edwin Mellen Press, 1989), p. 62.

2. "Die Reaktion in Deutschland. Ein Fragment von einem Franzosen", *Deutsche Jahrbücher für Wissenschaft und Kunst*, ed. Arnold Ruge, Nos. 247-51 (October 17-21, 1842), pp. 986-1001. The first page number cited throughout text refers to the Nautilus/Nemo Press and Edition Moderne (Hamburg and Zürich, 1984) edition of this essay. Translated into English by Mary-Barbara Zeldin in *Russian Philosophy*, I, eds. James M. Edie, James P. Scanlan, Mary-Barbara Zeldin (Chicago: Quadrangle Books, 1965), pp. 385-406. Reprinted in *Michael Bakunin: Selected Writings*, ed. Arthur Lehning (London: Jonathan Cape, 1973), pp. 37-58. The second page number cited throughout text (for translation) refers to the latter anthology. Thus, in the case of the preceding quotes, the reference is [15 (German language edition)/37 (English translation)]. I have made only one alteration to the English translation. Since the standard philosophical translation of "*Vermittlung*" is "mediation", I felt compelled to render "*vermittelnden Reactionäre*" as "mediating reactionaries" rather than "compromising reactionaries". This sounds rather artificial, but emphasizes the Hegelianism (albeit unorthodox) of Bakunin's thought.

3. "Bakunin", *New Society*, XVI (1970), p. 451.

4. *Nausea*, trans. Robert Baldick (Harmondsworth: Penguin Books, 1963), pp. 101-02.

5. "Bakunin, Mikhail Aleksandrovich" entry in *Routledge Encyclopedia of Philosophy*, I, ed. Edward Craig (London: Routledge, 1998), p. 646.

6. *Mikhail Bakunin: A Study in the Psychology and Politics of Utopianism*, p. 297, note 55. Henceforth referred to as *Mikhail Bakunin*.

7. Encyclopedia entry, *op. cit.*, p. 647. Kelly even masquerades as the encyclopedia's "expert" on Russian philosophy in general. She may have some expertise in some area of Russian affairs, but it is evidently not philosophy. (Incidentally, the reader may be surprised to learn that the *Routledge Encyclopedia* has a disproportionately long entry for one Alexander Herzen.)

8. *Op. cit.*, p. 21.

9. *Op. cit.*, pp. 24, 114.

10. The preceding quotes are from a letter from Bakunin to his sisters [10/8/1836], *Sobranie sochinenii i pisem 1826-1876*, I, ed. Iurii M. Steklov (Moscow: Izdatel'stvo vsesoiuznogo obshchestva politkatorzhan i ssyl'no-poselentsev, 1934), pp. 325-31. Translated by Olive Stevens in *Michael Bakunin: Selected Writings*, pp. 31-36.

11. Following Bakunin, who does so for the most part, I capitalize the word "state" in all cases where the principle of State is at issue (which, in the context of this essay, is the majority of cases) rather than any particular, historical state. For the sake of consistency, I have taken the liberty of doing so even when quoting authors who do not adopt the same strategy.

12. *Philosophy of Right* (1821), trans. T.M. Knox (Oxford: Oxford University Press, 1952), p. 160 ($260); *Phenomenology of Spirit* (1807), trans. A.V. Miller (Oxford: Oxford University Press, 1977), p. 40 ($66).

13. Marx's notion of a "non-political" post-revolutionary and post-transitional State has been explored by Richard Adamiak in "The 'Withering Away' of the State: A Reconsideration", *Journal of Politics*, XXXII (1970), pp. 3-18. Adamiak's main conclusion is "although Marx and Engels anticipated the [eventual] demise of 'politics' and 'political power', the future communist society they envisioned was [for all the talk of "abolition" or "withering away" of the State] by no means anarchistic; the State was to be its one indispensable institution" [*ibid.*, p. 3]. (Bakunin says of Marx and Engels, therefore, that "They have not learned how to dismantle the religion of the State" [*L'Empire knouto-germanique et la Révolution sociale (Seconde livraison), Archives Bakounine*, VII, ed. Arthur Lehning (Leiden: E.J. Brill, 1981), p. 132]. Thus Adamiak classifies Marxism as "a statist ideology" which is, as such, antithetical to anarchism [*op. cit.*, p. 17].

    The Marxian sublation of the State represents simultaneously: (a) the abstract (post-transitional) negation of the (as Hegel describes it) "strictly political" State [*Philosophy of Right*, p. 163 ($267)]) (on the dubious basis of which Marxism identifies itself as *genuinely* anarchist); and (b) the eternal preservation of the arbitrarily designated "non-political" State (on the basis of which Adamiak rightly denies Marxism's anarchism). It represents (a) a revolutionary compromise, the compromising of the negative — in fact the compromising of anarchism in the form of a "Marxian 'Anarchism'", by the willful misrepresentation of Marxian socialism as the true anarchism. The key passage from Marx on this topic is the following (from 1872): "What all socialists understand by anarchism is this: as soon as the goal of the proletarian movement, the abolition of classes, is attained, the power of the State . . . will disappear and governmental functions will be transformed into simple administrative functions" [quoted by David McLellan in *The Thought of Karl Marx: An Introduction*, Third Edition (London: Papermac, 1995), pp. 211, 220; originally from Karl Marx and Friedrich Engels, *Die Angeblichen Spaltungen in der Internationale* (1872), *Werke*, XVIII (Berlin: Dietz Verlag, 1981), p. 50]. Engels reiterates (in the same year): "All Socialists are agreed that the political State, and with it political authority, will disappear as a result of the coming social revolution, that is, that public functions will lose their political character and be transformed into simple administrative functions of watching over the *true* interests of society [as determined by the sociological genius]" [*On Authority* (1872), *The Marx-Engels Reader*, Second Edition, ed. Robert C. Tucker (New York: Norton, 1978), p. 732; emphasis added]. Which means that "Marxian 'Anarchism'" consists in the transformation of the class-antagonistic political State, characterized by its "governmental functions", into the

classless non-political State, characterized by its "simple administrative functions".
Bakunin restates Marx's argument as follows: "the State, having lost its political, that is, ruling, character, will transform itself into a totally free organization of economic interests and communities". But even this "totally free" administration remains a State, albeit a supposedly "non-political" one. In any event, it is a State which can never properly be brought into existence given that the required transitional post-revolutionary "dictatorship [that is, the post-revolutionary State] can have [no] other objective than to perpetuate itself" as a political State, thereby "having the direct and inevitable result of consolidating the political and economic privileges of the governing minority and the political and economic slavery of the masses": the result of class division and State coercion [*Gosudarstvennost' i anarkhiia* (1873), *Archives Bakounine*, III, ed. Arthur Lehning (Leiden: E.J. Brill, 1967), pp. 148-49, 114; *Statism and Anarchy*, trans. Marshall S. Shatz (Cambridge: Cambridge University Press, 1990), pp. 179, 137 (Shatz's translation used, and referred to, in all cases below)]. (Marx comments on the transitional post-revolutionary dictatorship: "Between capitalist and communist society lies the period of the revolutionary transformation of one into the other. There corresponds to this also a political transition period in which the State can be nothing but *the revolutionary dictatorship of the proletariat*" [*Critique of the Gotha Program* (1875), *The Marx-Engels Reader*, p. 538; emphasis added]. According to Marx and Engels, "the first step in the revolution is to raise the proletariat to the position of ruling class", to bring about "the supremacy of the proletariat" [*Manifesto of the Communist Party* (1848), *The Revolutions of 1848*, ed. David Fernbach (Harmondsworth: Penguin Books, 1973), pp. 85-86]. For Bakunin, this is the first and last step of Marxian revolution; thus the "transitional period", the period in which the new ruling class gives up its power (or, in fact, does not), is decidedly post-revolutionary (or post-partial-revolution), that is, reactionary. It is a positive and not a negative stage in social development.) The point of Bakunin's critique is that: (a) Marx's State can never achieve "non-political" status — since the transition required is an impossibility; and (b) even if (hypothetically) such a transition could occur, the State's "non-political" status would be a myth, since every state — including the post-transitional merely "administrative" one — is a class-ridden and therefore necessarily political/coercive entity.

The Marxian sublation of the State represents, aside from a compromising of the negative, (b) a mystification of the preserved positive as an "ungoverned" State for all (in a classless society) — a universal State — and therefore a non-political or non-coercive State. This is a contradiction in terms for Bakunin for whom the State is political by definition, for whom "the State means *coercion*, domination by means of coercion, camouflaged if possible but unceremonious and overt if need be" [*Gosudarstvennost' i anarkhiia*, p. 20; *Statism and Anarchy*, p. 24; emphasis in original]. Bakunin denies the possibility of a "non-political" State, and believes that a mystification of the State by Hegel and Marx alone makes possible their assertion of its "non-political" side. This principle (of necessary class division and organized coercive domination of one class by another within *any* state) accords with Bakunin's principle of the partiality of the political in *The Reaction*.

The State-"administered" society is never classless for Bakunin (who, as we will see later, abhors Marxian economism, and can therefore draw non-economic elements into his analysis of *social class*, defining it fundamentally in terms of relations of domination — in order to distinguish his form of socialism — while still emphasizing the economic component which is, in any case, inseparable from it). There are at least two social classes under the hypothetical economically-classless State — the administering and the administered, those who direct affairs — ultimately by coercive means — if only in the name of learnedness, and those who are directed — by such means — in this case, on the grounds of ignorance. (Adamiak concurs, noting that "Marx and Engels appear to have remained naively oblivious to the fact that the specter of bureaucracy was haunting the specter of communism which, they boldly claimed, was haunting Europe". He adds that Bakunin "perspicaciously predicted that the implementation of the Marxian blueprint for the future society would result in a new scientific-political class, in short, that the 'classless' society of Marxian eschatology was a never-to-be-realized myth" [*op. cit.*, p. 6, note 8].)

Thus Bakunin announces that the essentially political Marxist "State [which is, as such, in a permanent condition of "transition" or, in other words, permanently despotic] will be nothing but the highly despotic government of the masses by a new and very small aristocracy of real or pretended scholars", who claim "to educate the people and raise them . . . to such a level that government of any kind will soon become unnecessary". It seems, therefore, that "for the masses to be liberated they must first be enslaved" [*Gosudarstvennost' i anarkhiia*, pp. 148-49; *Statism and Anarchy*, pp. 178-79]. Bakunin simply denies that despotic means can ever lead to free ends.

Elements of Bakunin's revolutionary practice and the "theory" which immediately serviced it certainly contradict this philosophical principle. However, to capriciously exaggerate the scope of this contradiction by absolutizing it is simple dishonesty — on the part of Pyziur and Kelly in particular. Kelly, as little qualified in psychiatry as she is in philosophy, diagnoses Bakunin's "acute schizophrenia": "while in his anarchist tracts and his polemics with the Marxists he preached absolute liberty, in his secret correspondence he was simultaneously defending a form of absolute dictatorship". (Pyziur writes in the same vein: "in spite of its vitriolic anti-State phraseology, Bakunin's doctrine does in fact reintroduce political power and does it on a scale hardly known up to his time" [*op. cit.*, p. 146].) Kelly concludes that a "strange blend of anarchism and authoritarianism . . . was Bakunin's final political philosophy" [*Mikhail Bakunin*, p. 193]. No. Anarchism is Bakunin's final political philosophy. Nowhere does he defend absolute dictatorship; that is a fabrication. To the extent that he contradicts himself in words, as opposed to deeds, it is in programmatic documents, letters, etc. that relate immediately to his contradictory deeds and simply endorse them. Nowhere does Bakunin expound an authoritarian philosophy. The contradictions are real, and I have no intention of denying them; but they have little if any bearing on the merits of the basic components of his social philosophy (our concern in this essay): it stands alone and must be assessed as such (a scholarly honor that is done, it might be said, to less radical thinkers than Bakunin [see Howard H. Harriott, "Defensible Anarchy?", *International Philosophy Quarterly*, XXXIII (1993), p. 319-20, note 2]). The attempt to jumble up supposedly weak elements of Bakunin's thought (in the case of his philosophical writings, without understanding them, and in the case of his programmatic writings, without conceding that this limits their significance and scope) and discreditable elements of his practical activity (after magnifying a highly select few), and to assess his thought on this basis is unacceptable intellectual and scholarly procedure.

For Bakunin, once again, "Liberty can only be created by liberty". The only goal of despotism is to "perpetuate itself". (This argument applies equally against the social-democratic tendencies of Marxists, or their penchant for statist — and specifically parliamentary — means in the pre-revolutionary period. Bakunin holds that "the theory of the State communists . . . enmeshes and entangles its adherents, under the pretext of political tactics, in endless accommodations with governments and the various bourgeois political parties — that is, it thrusts them directly into reaction". The final destination of the social-democratic school is clear to all by now: it is the cynical and opportunistic politics of the "Third Way" which claims to overcome the "contradiction" between socialism or equality and liberalism or freedom by reducing what are in themselves, to Bakunin, abstracted half-truths to zero, by draining all content from them. Thus, according to this account, there is no contradiction between "old" and "new" social-democracy, between (in the British context) "Old Labor" and "New Labor" — though the latter may be, in the consistency of its reaction, a little more forthright (and a great deal more efficient) than the former, for all its "socialist" and "revolutionary" bluster. Blairite politics are the logical culmination of classical social-democracy. Admittedly, however, there is a degree of integrity within the old school, for all its weaknesses, that has simply evaporated in its successor school.) [*Gosudarstvennost' i anarkhiia*, p. 149; *Statism and Anarchy*, pp. 179-80.]

In any event, Bakunin claims that the idea that the transitional form of enslavement or despotism is to be "temporary and brief" is mere consolation [*ibid.*, p. 148; p. 179]. (As such, Marx's notion of a political hereafter — that is, "non-political" hereafter — is seen to fulfill much the same function as the notion of a religious hereafter, teaching "patience, resignation, and submission" [*Fédéralisme, socialisme et antithéologisme (Federalism, Socialism, and Anti-Theologism)* (1867), *Oeuvres*, I, ed. Max Nettlau (Paris: Stock, 1972), p. 102].) Adamiak argues that the apparent convergence of Marxian and anarchist ends — at some point in the distant future — is illusory, or, rather, part of the "specious anarchistic facade ['adroitly constructed' by Marx and Engels] to ward off the successive threats from their more radical rivals, the Anarchists" [*op.cit.*, p. 17]. (Bakunin had already made this point: "Our polemics against [the Marxists] have forced them to recognize [at least formally] that freedom, or anarchy . . . is the ultimate goal of social development" [*Gosudarstvennost' i anarkhiia*, p. 149; *Statism and Anarchy*, p. 179].)

Many who acknowledge the influence of anarchism on Marxism in the formulation of *apparent* revolutionary ends (and many Marxists do not even acknowledge that) have failed to acknowledge, as Adamiak has, that the Marxist end is in fact not anarchist at all. That is, many have failed to acknowledge that Marxism and Bakuninian anarchism differ with respect to revolutionary ends as well as revolutionary means. (They also differ in philosophical fundamentals — Bakunin's negative dialectic versus Marx's positive dialectic (which gives rise to the anarchist-statist conflict in revolutionary outlook), and Bakunin's naturalism versus Marx's anthropocentrism (which gives rise to the anarchistic-economistic conflict in sociological outlook) — as I hope to show.) David Miller, then, speaks of anarchism and Marxism "Sharing the same ultimate goal" on the one hand, and of their "disagreement over revolutionary methods" on the other [*Anarchism* (London: J.M. Dent & Sons, 1984), pp. 93, 79]. George Woodcock, too, evidently misses this vital point: "The Marxists paid tribute to the anarchist ideal by agreeing that the ultimate end of socialism and communism must be the withering away of the State, but they contended that during the period of transition the State must remain in the form of the dictatorship of the proletariat" [*Anarchism: A History of*

Libertarian Ideas and Movements (Harmondsworth: Penguin Books, 1975), p. 158].

To summarize, there are two Bakuninian objections to the Marxian account. First, the transition in question is impossible (therefore the Marxian State is predicted to be highly *despotic*). Second, the hypothetical post-transitional society is State-ordered (that is "administered" by a "non-political State") anyway (therefore the Marxian State, to the extent that it embraces post-transitional elements and represents itself as the actualization of the Marxian revolutionary vision, is predicted to be highly *bureaucratic*). These predictions are "perspicacious" indeed.

Bakunin himself summarizes the entire argument — on the despotic-bureaucratic nature of the Marxian State — most succinctly in the following passage:

There will be no more class, but a government [or "administration"], and please note, an extremely complicated [or bureaucratic] government which, not content with governing and administering the masses politically, like all the governments of today [Bakunin simply rejects Marx's "non-political" rhetoric here], will *also* administer them economically . . . this will require vast knowledge [*une science immense*] and a lot of heads brimful of brains in the government. It will be the reign of *scientific intelligence* [that is, in Bakunin's terms, to be defined below, a metaphysical regime], the most aristocratic, despotic, arrogant, and contemptuous of all regimes. There will be a *new class*, a *new hierarchy* of real and fictitious savants, and the world will be divided into a minority dominating in the name of science [or "scientific socialism"] and a vast, ignorant majority. And then let the ignorant masses beware!" [*Ecrit contre Marx* (*Essay Against Marx*) (1872), *Archives Bakounine*, II, ed. Arthur Lehning (Leiden: E.J. Brill, 1965), p. 204; emphasis added except to the phrase "scientific intelligence", which is emphasized in the original].

The above statement alone seems to me to justify Bakunin's own claim for himself: "my name will remain, and to this name, which [Marxists] will have contributed so effectively to making known in the world [not least, says Bakunin, by their slander], will attach the real and legitimate glory of having been the pitiless and irreconcilable adversary, not of their own persons, which matter very little to me, but of their authoritarian theories and ridiculous and detestable pretensions to world dictatorship" [*Lettre à La Liberté* (*Letter to La Liberté*) (5/10/1872), *Archives Bakounine*, II, p. 158].

I will, I suspect, be accused of (a) giving Bakunin too much credit here. The fact that the history of Marxian-inspired despotism — and it is surely, at the very least, inspired by the (more or less) authoritarian aspects of Marxian thought (though subsequent "Marxist" thought obviously bears much of the responsibility too) — is largely congruent with Bakunin's prognosis is not the issue here, difficult as it may be to ignore. What is in question is the theoretical debate about the State, and I maintain that Marxian theory is statist, and therefore *in no way anarchist*, on the grounds that *it embraces the State as a pre-revolutionary and post-revolutionary means, and the post-revolutionary, post-transitional end*. To this extent, Bakunin's theoretical analysis seems entirely correct. This in itself need not worry the Marxist: in itself it amounts to the claim that Marxism is Marxist, that Marxian socialism is merely socialist. However, Marx claims that his theory is genuinely anarchist: that it embraces the principle of freedom as well as that of equality. The motivation for Bakunin's critique is not simply that Bakunin disagrees with Marx; his critique is also motivated by Marx purporting to agree, after a fashion, with him, or purporting to be an anarchist too, but a "better" one. The notion that a manifestly non-anarchist "anarchism" is the true anarchism — that a statist "anarchism" is liberating (from the State) — is the kind of notion that Bakunin attributes to the mediating reactionary in *The Reaction*: it is an attempt on the part of an avowed revolutionary to subvert the negative principle; an attempt which proves ultimately more reactionary — more despotic and stupefying — than consistent reaction, which at least engages "honestly" with its adversary by acknowledging it as such.

Marx's socialism, in other words, is not anarchist; his economistic egalitarianism lacks all sense of freedom. Freedom is, on this account, at best the by-product of economic equality. In this respect, Bakunin is closer to Hegel than Marx is. Freedom is no by-product for Hegel, but the very content of history, a content that becomes explicit or that is realized in the State-proper. Paul Thomas, who emphasizes what he sees as the continuity between Hegel and Marx and the discontinuity between Hegel and Bakunin, might take note of this. The discontinuity that he sees between Hegel and Bakunin is in fact illusory. Bakunin, like Hegel, regards the principle of universal freedom as the content of history. Thomas' effort to obscure the continuity through the concept of freedom by linking an individualistic concept of freedom to Bakunin — "whose *leitmotiv* is individual freedom" — is an outright falsification [*Karl Marx and the Anarchists* (London: Routledge & Kegan Paul, 1980), p. 7]. Bakunin's concept of freedom is clearly socialistic. He writes: "Liberty is . . . a feature not of isolation but of interaction, not of exclusion but rather of connection" [*Dieu et l'Etat* (*God and the State*) (1871) (the note, not the pamphlet), *Archives Bakounine*, VII, pp. 171-72]. As for the continuity between Hegel and Marx: we might simply ask what has happened to Hegel's rich concept of freedom in Marx's thought. Undoubtedly, Hegel and Marx share a statist outlook — both seek to bring about (theoretically or practically) the universal State — and are, to that extent, *political* thinkers (whereas Bakunin's anarchism is perhaps best characterized, by contrast, as *social*). But Hegel's State is the bastion of universal freedom, while Marx's is the bastion of economic equality. The difference is significant: universal freedom (though ultimately incompatible with the State as far as Bakunin is concerned) presupposes some form of equality; economic equality in itself, posited as an absolute, precludes freedom.

I suspect I will be accused of (b) ignoring Marx's response to Bakunin's critique in his *Konspekt von Bakunins Staatlichkeit und Anarchie* (*Conspectus of Bakunin's Statism and Anarchy*) (1874-75) as well. To me there appears to be little to ignore: it is a simple abusive and dogmatic restatement by Marx of his position ("when class domination ends, there will be no State in the present political sense of the word", etc. [*Conspectus, The Marx-Engels Reader*, p. 545]), without any effort to confront the issues raised by Bakunin. It adds up to a bare declaration that "I'm right, he's wrong". (Granted, the very nature of the *Conspectus* limits Marx's ability to entertain serious discussion. However, there is no suggestion that Marx is willing to do so: he simply refuses to acknowledge that Bakunin's objections pose any problems at all. And surely they do, even if ultimately they can be overcome. Bakunin, in this case as in so many others, deserves better.) Therefore, I can only agree with Adamiak's description of the *Conspectus* as "remarkably ingenuous" [*op. cit.*, p. 6, note 8]. I also share Peter Starr's view that "As a concise statement of the [theoretical] grounds for dispute in the Marxist/anarchist polemic that rocked the First International, Marx's [*Conspectus* is] quite useless". Thus I feel justified in "ignoring" it. (Starr does not ignore it at all: it may be philosophically worthless, but he finds it of "exceptional" psychological interest. According to him, it "reveals an elaborate castration drama [or "narcissistic phallodrama"] played out between polarized rivals". Starr gets stirred up by the "ejaculatory quality" of Bakunin's description of revolution, not to mention the "issues of homosexuality (the association of brothers) and anarchist cross-dressing (the brother as midwife)" that are apparent in "Bakunin's text" — which, take note, there is no evidence he has read; if he has read it, he certainly has not understood it since he defines Bakunin's anarchism as "an *unconditional* rejection of *power*" — an absurd notion given that revolution itself is a manifestation of power. Starr's indulgence in Lacanian theory (I will not dignify his analysis by classifying it as psychology) reveals more of a phallic obsession (forgive the non-technicality of my terminology) on his part than anything about Bakunin or Marx. To reduce the revolutionary notion of fraternity to an issue of "repressed homosexuality", to reduce the Socratic notion of midwifery to an issue of cross-dressing, and so forth; all of this is to compensate for evident ignorance with freewheeling, and frankly stupid, speculation based on would-be authoritative, even scientific, psycho/critico-drivel.) [*Logics of Failed Revolt: French Theory After May '68* (Stanford: Stanford University Press, 1995), pp. 17, 205-09; emphasis added.]

14.   Quoted by Herbert Marcuse in *Reason and Revolution: Hegel and the Rise of Social Theory*, Second Edition (London: Routledge & Kegan Paul, 1955), p. 12. Originally from *Dokumente zu Hegels Entwicklung*, ed. J. Hoffmeister (Stuttgart: Fr. Frommann, 1936), p. 219 f. The "mechanistic conception of the State" (Kelly's expression, intended to be derogatory [*Mikhail Bakunin*, p. 203]) is adopted by Bakunin; Bakunin draws from it the anarchistic conclusion that is implicit in Hegel's 1796 account. In 1870 he writes: "The administrative machine . . . is never [one with] the life of the people; it is, on the contrary, [the] absolute and direct negation [of popular life]. Thus the force that it produces is never a natural, organic, popular force — on the contrary, it is a completely mechanical and artificial force" [*Lettre à un français sur la crise actuelle* (*Letter to a Frenchman on the Current Crisis*) (1870), *Archives Bakounine*, VI, ed. Arthur Lehning (Leiden: E.J. Brill, 1977), p. 63]. (Note that Bakunin's depiction of the "pre-revolutionary State" — in terms of its "administrative" function — is identical with Marx's depiction of the post-revolutionary "non-political" State. As such, Bakunin is bound to reject Marx's revolutionary program as statist.) Bakunin observes that State-machinery (or "the machine of the State") necessarily requires State-machinists (or "machinists of the State") [*ibid.*, p. 53]: in the case of the Marxian State, a highly specialized élite — "*State engineers* who will form a new privileged scientific and political class" (headed, indeed, by a "*chief engineer* of world revolution" [*Lettre à la Liberté*, p. 150; emphasis added]) — to direct the dumb masses, who "require strong supervision", toward their eventual freedom in the "non-political" hereafter [*Gosudarstvennost' i anarkhiia*, p. 150; *Statism and Anarchy*, p. 181; emphasis added].

15.   *Kommunizm* (*Communism*) (1843), *Sobranie sochinenii i pisem 1826-1876*, III, ed. Iurii M. Steklov (Moscow: Izdatel'stvo vsesoiuznogo obshchestva politkatorzhan i ssyl'no-poselentsev, 1935), p. 230. Translated in Franco Venturi, *Roots of Revolution: A History of the Populist and Socialist Movements in Nineteenth Century Russia*, trans. Francis Haskell (London: Weidenfeld and Nicolson, 1960), p. 45.

16.   I use the term "actuality", rather than "reality", throughout as a translation of the German "*Wirklichkeit*" and its Russian equivalent "*deistvitel'nost'*". This is, at least when it comes to translating the German, standard procedure by now. "Reality" is a more appropriate translation of "*Realität*", which denotes the contingent existence of the essen-

tially or rationally unfulfilled, of the merely potential: in this sense, the sense critics of Bakunin's conservatism have in mind, the real (Russian reality, for all its potential, which is its sole entitlement to the claim to glory or rationality) is decidedly not the rational. "Actuality", on the contrary, denotes the concrete existence of the essentially or rationally fulfilled (that which is fulfilled in accordance with its Idea), the fulfillment of potential: the concrete existence of the rational essence (or rational content), which has no other true mode (or form) of existence. Hence Hegel's famous statement: "What is rational is actual and what is actual is rational" [Preface to *Philosophy of Right*, p. 10].

The need for a "reconciliation (*Versöhnung*) with actuality (*Wirklichkeit*)" is voiced by Hegel in this context: "it has to be seen as the supreme and ultimate purpose of science to bring about the reconciliation of the reason that is conscious of itself with the reason that *is*, or actuality, through the cognition of this accord" [*Encyclopaedia Logic* (final edition, 1830), trans. T.F. Geraets, W.A. Suchtung, H.S. Harris (Indianapolis: Hackett, 1991), p. 29 (§6)]. Bakunin, unlike his critics (who never cite it), is well aware of the significance of this passage, as his conspectus of the *Encyclopaedia* shows [see Martine Del Giudice, "Bakunin's Preface to Hegel's *Gymnasium Lectures*: The Problem of Alienation and the Reconciliation with Reality", *Canadian-American Slavic Studies*, XVI (1982), p. 181]. Bakunin understands that the reconciliation has to be actively brought about with that which is in actuality. It does not consist in the simple acceptance of contingent reality; rather it involves activity (or "actualization") on the side of both reason and the "real", or their interaction, neither side having been fulfilled (indeed, neither side can be fulfilled in abstraction from the other). His interpretation of the reconciliation is therefore "dynamic" and not "static" (though not sufficiently so, which is why he later rejects this procedure); *Kelly is wrong* [*Mikhail Bakunin*, p. 47].

Kelly completely misrepresents Bakunin's take on this issue as: "Bakunin's interpretation of 'the real is the rational' presented itself to him as a series of propositions of horrible but iron logic: all contemporary social forms [Bakunin's understanding of "actuality", according to Kelly] were sacred as manifestations of Eternal Reason; the regime of Nicholas I was thus one of the supreme manifestations of Spirit in the contemporary world. [One of . . .? In the contemporary world . . .? Sounds a little "contingent".] What might appear on the surface to be barbaric or cruel was, to all those who could see it in the light of eternal truth, rational, necessary, and harmonious. One must submit to *this* [particular] reality with its 'iron jaws and iron claws'; rebellion against it was senseless and futile" [*ibid.*, p. 51; emphasis added]. Or, Bakunin tended to emphasize "the necessity of accepting the status quo . . . as rational and just, inasmuch as it was the highest expression of Reason in history" [*ibid.*, p. 47]. This is nonsense — and the root problem is Kelly's "abysmal ignorance" [Brian Morris, *op. cit.*, p. 8] of both Hegel and Bakunin.

Kelly reveals her ignorance when she takes issue with Bakunin's "irritation at [Vissarion] Belinsky's literal-minded interpretation of 'reality'" (in other words, his irritation at the conservatism of Belinsky's reconciliation with *contingent reality*), quoting the following words of Bakunin from a letter to his sisters of March 1838 (that is, written as he was composing the *Preface*): "I do not speak here of that which is generally understood by the word reality [*deistvitel'nost*']: chair, table, dog, Varvara Dmitrievna, Aleksandra Ivanovna — all this is dead, illusory — and not living and true — reality" [*Sobranie sochinenii i pisem 1826-1876*, II, ed. Iuri M. Steklov (Moscow: Izdatel'stvo vsesoiuznogo obshchestva politkatorzhan i ssyl'no-poselentsev, 1934), p. 150; translated by Del Giudice, *op. cit.*, p. 180; see also Kelly, *Mikhail Bakunin*, p. 52]. Kelly, that is to say, simultaneously criticizes the conservatism of Bakunin's call for a reconciliation with actuality, and his very conception of actuality, which, as we have just shown, is essentially non-conservative. Del Giudice, assuming a degree of philosophical acumen which does not apply in the case of Kelly, suggests that this passage, and the letter as a whole, "has been largely [and is perhaps best] ignored or passed over in silence by historians who ascribe a conservative character to Bakunin's Hegelianism" [*op. cit.*, p. 180]. Kelly, however, cannot resist the opportunity to censure Bakunin on two counts, without recognizing that her analysis thereby collapses in self-refutation.

Incidentally, Kelly's ignorance is second-hand: her account of Hegel and Bakunin here is, to put it politely, influenced by Martin Malia's. According to Malia, Bakunin "interprets [the "real is the rational and the rational is the real" (Malia's translation, repeated by Kelly and referred to the Introduction to the *Philosophy of Right* — though it is actually in the Preface)] phrase, and indeed the whole of Hegel's philosophy, as meaning that everything which in fact existed was reasonable and hence should be accepted as necessary and just by rational men, whatever their 'subjective' feelings might be. Technically speaking [Bakunin] had misunderstood Hegel . . . [He] had made the mistake of interpreting [Hegel] statically". Again, this is just plain wrong: another instance of an historical work, devoid of philosophical merit, devoid of even bad philosophical argumentation, dismissing a philosopher who knows very well what he is talking about. Malia states: "Bakunin's . . . elaboration of this position [was] philosophically crude in a manner which would not have passed in Germany". Remarkably, Bakunin, for all his supposed philosophical deficiency, managed to get on quite well in German philosophical circles. Malia does not understand what he is talking about, and Kelly's derivative account is even worse: compare her summary of what Hegel "really" meant [*Mikhail Bakunin*, p. 47] with Malia's [*Alexander Herzen and the Birth of Russian Socialism* (Harvard: Harvard University Press, 1961), p. 204]. The phrasal similarities are surely not coincidental. It is a shame that if Kelly was going to rely on secondary sources she did not select more reliable ones; it is an even greater shame that she manages to diminish her source's account, though one might have thought that impossible in the present case.

17.   *Op. cit.*, p. 182. When quoting Del Giudice's own words or translations, I change the word "reality" to "actuality" for the reasons just given and for the sake of consistency with my text. See, *ibid.*, p. 188, note 83 for an admission of the limitations of the word "reality", and pp. 180-82 for an explication of the term "*deistvitel'nost*".

18.   Max Nettlau, *Michael Bakunin. Eine Biographie* (London: n.p., 1896-1900), p. 202. The Bakuninian "dilemma" will be commented on further below in the context of its 1867 (*Fédéralisme, socialisme et antithéologisme*) and 1871 (*L'Empire knouto-germanique et la Révolution sociale*) reformulations.

Another affirmation of atheism from this period is to be found in an article in *Il Popolo d'Italia*, 2/9/1865. [See T.R. Ravindranathan, *Bakunin and the Italians* (Kingston: McGill-Queen's University Press, 1988), pp. 41 and 251, note 21.] This article and four subsequent articles in the same publication are attributed to "*Un francese*", or "a Frenchman", the same pseudonym that Bakunin had adopted for *The Reaction*. Ravindranathan notes that the similarity to *The Reaction* does not end there, given the articles' "tirades against reactionaries, political moderates, and parliamentarians, [as well as their assignment of the leading revolutionary role to the masses,] although [they are] devoid of the Hegelian idiom and jargon of the earlier work" [*ibid.*, p. 40]. Ravindranathan also notes that two central tenets of Bakunin's mature anarchism are established in these articles. The first tenet is that of the unity of freedom and equality or "freedom in equality" [*La Commune de Paris et la Notion de l'Etat*, p. 292] (a tenet implied by the notion of the universality or non-partiality of the religion of freedom in *The Reaction*): "The liberty of each necessarily assumes the liberty of all and the liberty of all cannot become possible without the liberty of each . . . There is no real liberty without equality, not only in rights but in reality. Freedom in equality, here is justice" [*Il Popolo d'Italia*, 22/9/1865; translated by Ravindranathan, *op. cit.*, p. 41].

This tenet — "that unlimited liberty is not only compatible with unlimited equality but inconceivable without it" — is the most offensive to Berlin (and therefore Kelly, who refers to it as the principle that "'absolute liberty'" . . . is synonymous with equality" [*Mikhail Bakunin*, p. 197]), for it challenges the very basis of his liberalism. (Which is: "Everything is what it is: liberty is liberty, not equality . . . or justice"; "confounding liberty with her sisters, equality and fraternity, leads to . . . illiberal conclusions [which is true in an ideological sense, if nothing else]" ["Two Concepts of Liberty", *The Proper Study of Mankind: An Anthology of Essays*, ed. Henry Hardy and Roger Hausheer (London: Pimlico, 1998), pp. 197, 226].) Berlin accuses Bakunin of a lack of serious thought and "realism" because he "lumps together" freedom and equality by means of "glib Hegelian claptrap" ["Herzen and Bakunin on Individual Liberty", pp. 105-08]. (Kelly quotes the latter phrase approvingly, making the same vacuous accusation that Bakunin lumps together freedom and equality by "dialectical sleight of hand" [see *Mikhail Bakunin*, pp. 196-98].) However, Berlin *assumes* an antithetical and irreconcilable relationship without demonstrating it. (Berlin actually approaches here, from Bakunin's point of view, "the *metaphysics* of Kant, which loses itself . . . in those antinomies or contradictions which it claims to be irreconcilable and insoluble . . . It is clear that in studying the world with the *fixed idea* of the insolubleness of these [contradictions] . . . in approaching the existing world with this *metaphysical prejudice* in one's head, one will always be incapable of understanding anything of the nature of things" [*Appendice de l'Empire knouto-germanique: Considérations philosophiques sur le fantôme divin, sur le monde réel et sur l'homme (Appendix to The Knouto-Germanic Empire: Philosophical Considerations on the Divine Phantom, on the Real World, and on Man)* (1871), Archives Bakounine, VII, p. 267; emphasis added].)

Bakunin assumes no such conflict and therefore has no reason to lump together anything. This synthetic approach is not his style in any case; if he believed there was a conflict he would attempt to resolve it — for better or for worse — negatively, that is, in favor of the antithesis. He is quite rigorous in this respect. Berlin's understanding of Hegelian logic (and, needless to say, Kelly plays the parrot here) seems to be that any old would-be conflict (including the conflict he himself assumes) can be cast aside by means of the unifying power of the dialectic (a conception that is neither Hegelian nor Bakuninian). Berlin therefore implicitly — and mistakenly — associates a positive dialectic with Bakunin (and Kelly, it goes without saying, does likewise, as we will see). (No wonder the dialectic is seen as threatening to the partiality of Berlin's ideology.) There is a little more rigor to Hegel's approach than that: the first step is to demonstrate a contradiction, not to assume it. (That Hegel does not always manage to do this has little bearing here. What is important is that he stipulates it as a condition: that we can and should "exhibit" contradiction, which is indeed everywhere [*Encyclopaedia Logic*, p. 145 (§89)] — *except in the Absolute*, in which contradiction is overcome and therefore can no longer be demonstrated. Thus a particular contradiction can be "exhibited" in the Absolute only by abstraction from it.) It is Berlin's thought that is not to be taken seriously; he simply assumes a contradiction — and, worse still, assumes that this particular contradiction is itself absolute — because it suits him.

(The same can be said of other liberal critics of Bakunin, such as Pyziur. Pyziur expresses this dispute as one between libertarians and "equalitarians": "At one pole of political thought stands the presumption that freedom and equality contradict each other, that equality can only come from the coercion of authority, and that freedom, on the other hand, includes the freedom to be unequal. At the other pole is the equalitarian doctrine that liberty and equality are complementary and inseparable, that liberty implies equality, that the realization of the first presupposes the realization of the second, and that both are but two different facets of the same ideals". The first, especially with its "freedom to be unequal", sounds fairly nefarious; the second sounds pretty benign. However, Pyziur does not approach the dispute with any degree of objectivity. Note how inapt the term "equalitarianism" is as a description of Bakunin's position; it hints at something closer to the Marxist position that will be delineated momentarily, a position that is the corresponding one-sidedness to "libertarianism" within the assumed contradiction. But this is exactly what Pyziur has in mind — that Bakunin's principle of the indivisibility of freedom and equality leads to a prioritization of the latter over the former: "as we look more closely at Bakunin's formula of liberty and equality, we may observe that the emphasis is definitely shifted toward equality". If Bakunin lays more emphasis on equality than freedom, or socialism than libertarianism, it is for the simple reason that it is the more negative principle or revolutionary doctrine of the two in the present context. In any case, Pyziur's attempt to reduce Bakunin's anarchism to a vulgar socialism and to attack it as such — as totalitarian and so forth — from his dogmatic "libertarian" standpoint is transparent: "both common sense and historical experience tell us that liberty, in the sense of a wide choice for each individual in determining his way of life, is incompatible with a rigidly equalitarian society" [*op. cit.*, pp. 114, 121-22]. (Brian Morris treats this statement with the contempt it deserves: "Common sense and history teach us nothing of the kind" [*op. cit.*, p. 115].) Bakunin's principle completely perverted, serious argumentation goes out the window; all that remains is dogmatic libertarianism versus caricatured socialism, one-sidedness versus one-sidedness.)

Hence the "vast, polarized abstractions" that Kelly ascribes to Bakunin seem rather more characteristic of her mentor (and Pyziur) [*Mikhail Bakunin*, p. 204]. Berlin writes, for example: "The views of those who, like Herzen (or Mill), place personal liberty in the center of their social and political doctrine [and] of those [like Bakunin] for whom such liberty is only a desirable by-product of the social transformation which is the sole end of their activity . . . are opposed, and no reconciliation or compromise between them is conceivable" [*op. cit.*, p. 102]. Berlin's difficulty with Bakunin is clearly that his libertarianism (which he admits begrudgingly, but as "a by-product" of something rather sinister) is too socialist (while Marxists object to Bakunin's socialism for being too "liberal" (hence it is the "Proudhonist" side of Bakunin's socialism that Engels has difficulty with [Letter to Theodor Cuno [24/1/1872], *The Marx-Engels Reader*, p. 728]).

Herzen's libertarianism, unlike Bakunin's, is, for Berlin, only moderately and tolerably socialist (though there is little question that Berlin understates Herzen's socialism). Berlin is seemingly oblivious to his Bakuninian terminology and sentiment here: the concept of the impossibility of reconciliation or compromise is classic Bakunin. Bakunin, though, is circumspect enough in the relations he declares "contradictory", or, at the very least, more circumspect than Berlin is in this case.

Bakunin denies any polarity between freedom and equality because he regards them as the indivisible content of the negative or revolutionary principle — the "absolute" and therefore non-contradictory principle: "equality is possible only with liberty and by means of it . . . liberty is possible only in equality . . . the establishment of economic and social equality through the freedom of all: that is our present program" [*Trois Conférences faites aux Ouviers du Val de Saint-Imier*, p. 235]. The revolutionary principle has been expressed most significantly to date in the French Revolution, though not adequately even then: this revolution was merely political, a partial revolution inadequate to the content of its absolute principle. (Of this principle, Bakunin says: "Liberty, Equality, and Fraternity . . . seem to include everything that humanity could desire and achieve in the present and in the future" [*ibid.*, p. 225]; "we . . . desire noble Liberty, wholesome Equality, and blessed Fraternity. But we wish these great and beautiful things to cease being fictions [or] lies, [we wish them] to become a truth [singular] and to constitute reality. That is the meaning and the goal of what we call Social Revolution" [*ibid.*, p. 232].) Indeed, it was the very partiality of the French Revolution that bolstered the liberal one-sidedness (abstract freedom) that Berlin — ahistorically — absolutizes. Orthodox socialists have sought to counteract this one-sidedness with the principle of economic equality. But, to Bakunin, this is, in itself, an equally one-sided principle. (If it is a one-sidedness to which Bakunin feels more disposed to ally himself, that is because, again, it is the more revolutionary principle, more antipathetic to the existing order, and more given to the practico-revolutionary; it may be partial, but there is hope for at least some of those (many within the First International, for example) who are attracted to it. The other one-sidedness is a great deal less revolutionary, more sympathetic to the existing order to which it poses, practically, minimal danger — indeed, it is the partial ideology of this partial order, which emerged out of the French Revolution; there is little hope for those who are attracted to this principle (as Bakunin's flirtation with the League of Peace and Freedom in the late 1860s proved to him) since it is, practically if not according to its theory, the most reactionary of principles within the existing order.)

Nevertheless, Bakunin's anarchism or "libertarian socialism" is not a latter day "dialectical" tacking-on of one principle to the other supposedly antithetical principle (as Marxists and liberals — like Berlin — contend). (Were Bakunin simply to synthesize or even mediate these principles, his anarchism would approach the Blairite "Third Way". This mediation compromises both of the two principles that it posits as antithetical (on the grounds that we cannot have both, so we will have to make do with a little of each), sacrificing the best part of each in the process.) His anarchism is, on the contrary, based on an insistence that these principles are in fact one and have been abstractly opposed to one another by those who fear the consequences of adequate revolution, by those who have recoiled from the implications of the French Revolution, from which, historically and logically, they have abstracted themselves — by mediators of a liberal or social persuasion. (Strangely enough, advocates of one-sided ideologies spawned by partial interpretation of the revolutionary principle now criticize Bakunin for synthesizing their ideologies with those of their partial opponents. Historically, this makes no sense since Bakunin's supposedly synthetic principle (sometimes referred to by him as "justice" [see the above *Il Popolo d'Italia* quote and Pyziur, *op. cit.*, p. 117]) predates both (stretching back into the Hellenic tradition). It is they, and not Bakunin, who are guilty of abstraction — from the principle of which Bakunin speaks.) Conservatives simply deny the whole revolutionary dialectic, though, according to Bakunin, this is preferable to the attempt to manipulate it.

It is also Berlin who lacks "realism", for the history, not least in our century, of partial ideologies (those which assume a contradiction between freedom and equality and deliberately exclude one or other, or those more "moderate" versions — social democracy and left liberalism — which assume a contradiction and settle for a little of both (which they calculate in the most cynical fashion), assuming that it is the best we can hope for) demonstrates their tendency to achieve neither meaningful freedom nor meaningful equality, but a combination (in one measure or other) of despotism and exploitation. (For Bakunin, the antithesis of the revolutionary principle, the unified principle of freedom and equality, is the statist principle, the unified principle of despotism and exploitation. Hence Bakunin states that "*to exploit and to govern mean the same thing . . .* Exploitation and Government . . . are two inseparable terms of all that is called politics" [*Dieu et l'Etat* (the note, not the pamphlet), p. 191; emphasis in original]. The tension between this anarchist view and the economistic view of Marx — a partial view from Bakunin's standpoint — is evident, and will be analyzed below.) The history of these ideologies also demonstrates that Bakunin is on the right track: that the unity of freedom and equality — that this single, as Bakunin sees it, non-contradictory principle — is the sole basis of a just society. History at least appears to vindicate Bakunin's famous assertion that "*liberty without socialism is privilege and injustice, and . . . socialism without liberty is slavery and brutality*" [*Fédéralisme, socialisme et antithéologisme*, p. 96; emphasis in original].

The second tenet of Bakunin's mature anarchism that he establishes in the *Il Popolo d'Italia* articles is the federalist principle, the principle of "the organization of popular life from below upward" [*Gosudarstvennost' i anarkhiia*, p. 180; *Statism and Anarchy*, p. 219]: "Universal liberty must proceed not from the top to the bottom, nor from the center to the circumference, but from the bottom to the top and from the circumference to the center" [*Il Popolo d'Italia*, 22/9/1865; translated by Ravindranathan, "Bakunin in Naples: A Reassessment", *Journal of Modern History*, LIII (1981), pp. 194-95].

Admittedly Bakunin's federalism is rather vague, and remains so even in his lengthy programmatic documents. But this vagueness is consistent with the dialectical approach that will be explored below. The call for organization from below upward is certainly a monotonous feature of his writing and, for the most part, it does not mean a great deal — other than that an anarchist society is necessarily non-statist in form. (The notion that Proudhon's federalism (especially in his *Du Principe fédératif* (*On the Federal Principle*) (1863)) is the major influence on Bakunin's — seemingly sustained by Bakunin's comments on Proudhon in *Fédéralisme, socialisme et antithéologisme* [see p. 78] — is undercut by this dialectical "vagueness". Proudhon's federalism is (given, for example, its contractual basis) a great deal more positive or "political" in the ordinary sense than Bakunin's negative, thoroughly anarchist federalism.) What is more important than Bakunin's "below upward" phrase, therefore, is the recognition of the centralized nature of the State.

Some of Bakunin's critics (Adam B. Ulam for one) acknowledge vagueness in his "positive program" (filled as it is "with vague suggestions of purely voluntary cooperation, federalism of communes, and similar notions'): "To be sure, [Bakunin's] anarchism is excellent as a *critique* of other political systems, but hardly so as a *positive prescription*" [*Ideologies and Illusions: Revolutionary Thought from Herzen to Solzhenitsyn* (Cambridge: Harvard University Press, 1976), pp. 12-13]. This is just the point: Bakunin, as a rule, does not engage in "positive prescription", but in negation, theoretical ("critique") and practical (revolutionary activity). Camus is a more extreme case in point: he acknowledges vagueness here to the degree that it permits him, in ignorance of Bakunin's dialectic (which is portrayed as a nihilistic instrument), to criticize his thought as barren, as, at the end of the day, a wasteland — which, of course, he hopes to realize in the most indiscriminately violent way. Other critics (like Kelly) maintain, on the contrary, that Bakunin's "positive program" is exceedingly utopian. (Thus proving that radicals like Bakunin are damned if they refrain from futuristic thought — since it suggests the worst sort of skepticism or even nihilism — and damned if they engage in it — since it suggests utopianism, historicism, and all manner of evil things.) This notion also results from a misunderstanding of Bakunin's dialectic, which these critics portray as synthetically positive (though not even Hegel's dialectic is positive in that sense).

Bakunin's body of programmatic writing is extensive and includes many of what the latter critics interpret as positive statements about the shape of the future society. However, these statements, almost without exception, amount to propositions of the form "the State-ordered society is x; the anarchist society will be not-x", or propositions of the form "the anarchist society will be not-x" when the corresponding proposition, "the State-ordered society is x", is assumed on the basis of argumentation to that effect elsewhere; or this is the form they are intended to take. In any event, I am not convinced that "positive" statements of this nature are "utopian" — utopianism surely requires a speculative moment that is lacking in Bakunin's dialectic, an *imaginative* futuristic positing of something quite foreign to the present order and not simply antithetical to it. This form of speculation differs from that of, for example, Marx — who is neither a utopian (since his speculation is not imaginative but logical — grounded on a semi-preservative logic which dictates that essential elements of the present are necessarily retained in the future) nor historicist (as we will argue later). (Such is my understanding of utopianism, at least. What others mean by it is difficult to establish at times. For example, there is certainly ambiguity in the use of it by Bakunin's critics and by critics of radicalism generally. It apparently conveys to them both the notion of futuricity *and* that of unrealizability — notions which can lead to self-contradiction on their part. (Kelly, for instance, frames her study of Bakunin's "utopianism" — a term she never bothers to define — around, on the one hand, the notion of his "millenarianism" and "historicism", and, on the other, the notion of his lifelong attachment to the "Idealist fantasy" of "a unified human community", a vision which is, we are informed, unrealizable because it glosses over "contradictions [like those between freedom and equality, individual and society] which remain insoluble in history" [*Mikhail Bakunin*, pp. 292, 3, 197].) To accuse some radical simultaneously of futuristic and hence, perhaps, historicist thought, and of holding unrealizable ideals is problematic. If the future horizon is denied to others, what right does one have to it oneself: what right does one have to criticize others for "prophesizing" about society when one considers oneself the arbiter of future social possibility? Usually the way to sidestep this difficulty is to defend oneself in the name of relative scientificity (if only to the extent that one's opponent is pseudo-scientific while one depends on humble "common sense"). However, in the realm of social science *per se*, this is a weak defense indeed.) Bakunin, in any event, explicitly refers to the revolutionary program as negative in numerous places. For example: "We are called to destroy and not to build; others [in the post-revolutionary future] better, more intelligent, and fresher than we will build" [*Ispoved'* (1851), *Sobranie sochinenii i pisem 1828-1876*, IV, ed. Iurii M. Steklov (Moscow: Izdatel'stvo vsesoiuznogo obshchestva politkatorzhan i ssyl'no-poselentsev, 1935), pp. 155; *The Confession of Mikhail Bakunin, With the Marginal Comments of Tsar Nicholas I*, trans. Robert C. Howes (Ithaca: Cornell University Press, 1977), p. 93]. Elsewhere, he says of his Alliance that it "recommended to the proletariat as the only way of a real emancipation, as the policy truly beneficial for them, the exclusively *negative* policy of the demolition of political institutions, political power, government in general, [and] the State". By contrast, its "adversaries . . . pursued and [still] pursue *positive* politics, the politics of the State" [*Ecrit contre Marx*, pp. 173, 175; emphasis in original].

This interpretation of the negativity of Bakuninian anarchism or of its limits accords with Noam Chomsky's profile of the anarchist tradition generally: "Anarchism is not a doctrine about how the world is to be organized. It is a tendency in human thought and action, which seeks to enlarge the domain of freedom and justice. The anarchist typically seeks out structures of oppression, hierarchy, authority, and control, and challenges them, calling for a justification for them. Sometimes such a justification can be given, typically not. In the case of such illegitimate authority, the anarchist will seek to undermine and eliminate it. It doesn't make sense to ask whether 'anarchism is possible' [or, indeed, "utopian"], so understood" [interview response to the author, 16/8/1994].

It ought to be recorded, furthermore, that some of Bakunin's critics, exhibiting typical zealotry, even take issue with *both* his negativity *and* his utopianism. (Thus some, in the full spirit of Bakunin scholarship, wish to damn him doubly.) Pyziur is the best example of this. In the first instance, he places Bakunin among those "social reformers [who], however great their critical and destructive abilities . . . seem unable to develop a clear constructive program. Their picture of the desired future order is drawn less in terms of what it will be than what it will not be. However, this method does not allow an *exact* opposite to be deduced from the negative, and the obscurity [therefore] remains extensive". Bakunin has no desire to "deduce" an "exact opposite" because the quest for exactitude opens the door to speculation, and speculation, as he goes on to argue, opens the door to despotism. He willingly accepts "obscurity" as a price for potential liberty. Pyziur, in the second instance, noting the lack of a utopian vision, undertakes to impose one on Bakunin, and subsequently criticizes Bakunin for his utopianism (that is for the unrealizability of his non-existent futuristic speculations!). (Kelly is not without forebears.) Pyziur's justification for this is that Bakunin is not a systematic thinker so we cannot expect his assumed utopian scheme to be systematically laid out; instead, it is for us to systematize on his behalf: "Bakunin did not incorporate his ideas into a clear-cut plan. But, considering his general inability to think and write systematically, we should rather be surprised if he had. Therefore, a commentator attempting a critical exposition of Bakunin's ideas must first systematize them. In Bakunin's dispersed statements about the factors which will secure the future anarchist order, we find sufficient support for the outline given [by my good self]" [*op. cit.*, pp. 113, 125; emphasis added].

The method of systematization, modestly applied, is not entirely illegitimate. Obviously I myself am applying the method in this essay. But ordering a number of central, coherent, and frequently made philosophical arguments — in fact, basically two such arguments (for a negative dialectic and for naturalism) — because of the dispersal, varying detail, and occasional deficiency of the source material is quite different to systematizing in the absence of elements (which Pyziur all but admits) to systematize. That kind of systematization tends toward large-scale speculation. Aside from that, the elements that Pyziur pieces together are not the least utopian. The concept of federalism is the most important of these elements. Pyziur, misinterpreting Bakunin, calls it a "synthesis" of the antithetical elements in society, that is, "statism" and "destruction or amorphism" — a synthesis of the positive and the negative [*ibid.*, p. 126]. This, as we will see, is not the way Bakunin's logic operates. (Like all those who point to Bakunin's utopianism, Pyziur misrepresents his dialectic as positive.) Neither does it tally with the aforementioned vagueness of the concept of federalism, which is in fact "an absolutely negative political position". But the accusation of utopianism will arise again below; enough has been said of it for the time being.

A third tenet of Bakunin's mature anarchism that emerges in the *Il Popolo d'Italia* articles is overlooked by Ravindranathan. This tenet, anticipated even in *The Reaction*, is the supra-political (or, in more radical formulations, the anti-political) nature of social revolution, or revolution as such, which means "overthrow of the State" [*L'Empire knouto-germanique et la Révolution sociale (Première livraison)* (*The Knouto-Germanic Empire and the Social Revolution (First Part)*) (1871), *Archives Bakounine*, VII, p. 38], the negation of the political. (Contrast this with the Marxist-economistic notion of revolution: "the abolition of capital is precisely the social revolution" [Letter of Engels to Theodor Cuno [24/1/1872], p. 729]. Both notions may seem equally partial until we grasp what Bakunin means by the State or the statist principle: it includes both despotism and exploitation, and revolution is the negation of both, not merely the latter as with the Marxists.) The 1865 version — aimed at the Mazzinians — is modest enough, requiring that revolution be not merely political, but more besides (meaning that Mazzini has not gone far enough, that he has compromised the revolution, but that those "who have felt the need of a radical transformation" will go further): "radical transformation [is] not only political, but also economic and social — [otherwise] freedom for the people will always remain an empty phrase" [*Il Popolo d'Italia*, 22/10/1865; translated by Ravindranathan, *Bakunin and the Italians*, p. 42].

19. Printed in *Libertà e Giustizia*, 31/8/1867 and 7/9/1867. See T.R. Ravindranathan, *Bakunin and the Italians*, pp. 65 and 257, note 44.

20. *Predislovie perevodchika: Gimnazicheskie rechi Gegelia, Sobranie sochinenii i pisem*, II, p. 173 [translated by Del Giudice, *op. cit.*, p. 176]; *L'Empire knouto-germanique (Seconde livraison)*, p. 142.

21. *L'Instruction intégrale*, pp. 139-40. Bakunin's philosophy of education (which even his detractors admit is substantial [see Pyziur, *op. cit.*, p. 143: "In dealing with education, Bakunin showed an exactness unusual for him. He depicted it almost in detail"]) has been treated relatively extensively in the secondary literature. See Samuel Reznek, "The Political and Social Theory of Michael Bakunin", *American Political Science Review*, XXI (1927), pp. 270-96; John Anthony Bucci's PhD thesis, "Philosophical Anarchism

and Education" (Boston University, 1974); Markus Heinlein, *Klassicher Anarchismus und Erziehung: libertäre Pägogogik bei William Godwin, Michael Bakunin und Peter Kropotkin* (Würzburg: Ergon-Verl., 1998); etc.

22. *"Ihrem Wesen, ihrem Prinzipe nach ist die demokratische Partei das Allgemeine, das Allumfassende, ihrer Existenz nach aber, als Partei, ist sie nur ein Besonderes, das Negative, dem ein anderes Besondere, das Positive, gegenüber steht".*

23. A phrase from Arthur P. Mendel's frankly awful exercise in psycho-gibberish, *Michael Bakunin: Roots of Apocalypse* (New York: Praeger, 1981), p. 419. This work has much in common with the other volumes of liberal criticism of Bakunin. Firstly, it is tediously long and repetitive; that is, it repeats the same shallow arguments until one is too bored to question them. (A defense of Berlin may be that he does not share this feature with his ideological colleagues: he leaves it to others to bore us into submission.) Secondly, it is philosophically ignorant — of both those influences on Bakunin which it acknowledges and, presumably, those which it does not. Thirdly, it is couched in the most obscure — and, let's face it, ultimately meaningless — terminology, perhaps to compensate for its inability to deal with Bakunin on his own philosophical terms. And, fourthly, it is ideologically motivated; the final paragraph, where Mendel speaks fondly of the "moderate" tradition which Berlin also champions, gives the ideological element away: "there have been countless utopias — including anarchist — that adamantly rejected violence or domination as means for their realization. The apocalypse is decidedly not the only home for vision. There has always been in our culture [whose culture, may I ask?] another, older [?], and opposing heritage, that of the Pharisees and their humanist and *liberal* heirs [of course], those Bakunin so furiously despised. It is a tradition that cherishes the vision [what vision exactly?] and strives toward its fulfillment, while shunning in principle and practice the violence and authoritarianism that betray it. [Does the liberal tradition shun "violence and authoritarianism" in either theory or practice? To maintain that it does suggests an astounding ignorance of history (including the history of ideas) and our times. Bakunin — whatever his own flaws — offers a powerful argument against liberal ignorance or fantasy; small wonder, then, that he should be a figure of extreme abuse in liberal academia (that is, in Anglo-American academia in particular).] For this tradition the answer is not the maximalists' 'all or nothing', that so often disguises inaction [yes, we know: Bakunin remained all his life the antithesis of a man of action (that is, evidently, the antithesis of a reformist, parliamentarian, or dutiful academic)], but rather the realists' 'something', that accompanies serious commitment and involvement" [*ibid.*, p. 435]. The liberal form of "realism" — the effective preservation of the status quo (with all its academic and political enticements) — is indeed frequently accompanied by "serious commitment" — of the fanatical variety. It is clear where Mendel's "realistic" critique of Bakunin is coming from.

24. *Gosudarstvennost' i anarkhiia*, p. 133; *Statism and Anarchy*, p. 159.

25. *L'Instruction intégrale*, p. 120.

26. Isaiah Berlin, "Herzen and Bakunin on Individual Liberty", p. 105. "Adolescence", like "utopianism" and "voluntarism", is a constant in the characterization of Bakunin, the vacuity of which is usually veiled by psycho-gibberish (as in the aforementioned case of Mendel). Berlin, in fairness, does not pad his article with this; rather he simply arrogantly depends on his baffling reputation, the slavish endeavours of his acolytes (not least Kelly who, take note, co-edits the volume from which this quote is taken), and the

sheer ideological conformity of his claims to justify them.

27. *Gosudarstvennost' i anarkhiia*, p. 164; *Statism and Anarchy*, p. 198. Emphasis in original.

28. Auguste Comte, *Plan of the Scientific Work Necessary for the Reorganization of Society* (1824), *Early Political Writings*, trans. H.S. Jones (Cambridge: Cambridge University Press, 1998), p. 49.

29. *Ecrit contre Marx*, p. 183. Marx is accused of endeavoring to impose a prescriptive political "decalogue" on the revolutionary movement: that is to say, of seeking to impose, Procrustean-fashion, a statist order on a movement seeking genuine revolutionary progress. The revolutionary movement is best served, says Bakunin, by the "negative [i.e., non-prescriptive or dialectical, anti-political, social revolutionary] policy" of the anarchists rather than the "positive [i.e., prescriptive or speculative, statist, political revolutionary] policy" of the Marxists.

30. Bakunin distinguishes variously between "theologians and metaphysicians", "divine and transcendental [or "modern"] idealists", "religious [or "divine"] and philosophical idealism", etc. [*L'Empire knouto-germanique (Seconde livraison)*, pp. 90, 115, 139; *La Commune de Paris*, p. 300]. In general, it is evident that he is referring, on the one hand, to what I will set up as the theocentric tradition, and, on the other, to what I will set up as the anthropocentric tradition. (In the latter case, the fact that the Kantian tradition is at issue is apparent in Bakunin's use of the label "transcendental idealism".) However, this internal distinction, as it were, does not reflect a real distinction between these traditions — in fact, "one [is] nothing but a more or less free translation of the other" [*L'Empire knouto-germanique (Seconde livraison)*, p. 115]. What is being critiqued (from the perspective of materialism) here is idealism or "theologism" in general; hence Bakunin affirms a real contradiction between idealism as a whole and materialism. As elsewhere, there are two parties to this conflict, and the only meaningful resolution between them is the fullest victory of one party. This is the context in which Bakunin asks "Who are right, the idealists or the materialists?", and answers unequivocally "Without doubt, the idealists are wrong and the materialists are right" [*ibid.*, p. 87].

If Bakunin concentrates on the anthropocentric tradition (that is, one aspect of idealism in particular), it is because he consistently seeks to undermine, in his eyes, the extremely pernicious element of mediation in thought and practice. That is to say, Bakunin critiques human idealism as a mediating reaction to the revolutionary spirit of the times. (Bakunin even seems to distinguish between metaphysics and modern idealism at one point, where he suggests that contemporary idealists are not metaphysicians like Rousseau [see, *ibid.*, p. 100]; however, this is resolved later when Rousseau himself is described as a modern idealist [*ibid.*, p. 139].)

31. Kelly is confounded by this combination of quasi-Comtean ontology — to be explained in Part Two — and anti-Comtean dialectic — as explained in Part One. However, she is more than happy to write it off as contradictory and further evidence of Bakunin's arbitrary philosophical eclecticism or opportunism. (She states that "Bakunin's approach to philosophy was practical rather than scholarly [that in itself is no bad thing — but wait, here comes the punchline]: he took from it what he needed to satisfy his personal needs [something, presumably, scholars do not do]" [*Mikhail Bakunin*, pp. 32-33].) Therefore, she writes: "Thinkers who differed from [Bakunin] on fundamental issues were often pressed into service to help him score a particular point. Thus, although he was to regard Comtean positivism as irreconcilable with anarchist theory, he was taken with a brief enthusiasm for Comte at the end of the 1860s when he was

eager to discredit the religious Idealism of Mazzini and his followers" [*ibid.*, p. 175].

Bakunin does (from 1868 in the first issue of *Narodnoe Delo* (*The People's Cause*)) reject Comtean positivism as politically reactionary and, ultimately, philosophically contradictory. (As he puts it: "that positive science itself should have demonstrated [metaphysical] tendencies thus far [is a fact] we must take note of and deplore. It has done so for two reasons: in the first place, because, constituted outside of popular life, it is represented by a privileged body [of savants]; and next, because it has posited itself thus far as the absolute and final goal of all human development [whereas] it is in itself only a necessary means for the realization of a much higher goal: that of the complete humanization of the *real* situation of all the *real* individuals who are born, who live, and who die on earth" [*L'Empire knouto-germanique (Seconde livraison)*, p. 126; emphasis in original]. In other words, positivism has proven — thus far — (socio-politically) élitist and (theoretically) absurd; hence Bakunin declares it metaphysical — given to the prioritization of thought over life — in spite of itself, in spite of its avowed antimetaphysicality.) Nevertheless, Kelly does not grasp the fact that what Bakunin "was taken with" in Comte — a certain naturalistic ontology and philosophy of history (which he directs at Mazzini) — is understood by him to be quite consistent with anarchist theory — or revolutionary politics (which Mazzini, consistent with his idealism, eventually reacts against).

Bakunin credits positive science, long after his "brief enthusiasm" for it, with the following: "The immense advantage of positive science over theology, metaphysics, politics, and juridical right consists in this: that, in place of the false and detrimental abstractions [notably, God and the State] advocated by these doctrines, it posits true abstractions [i.e., natural laws] which express the general nature and logic of things". Hence positive science is, so to speak, ontologically superior to its rivals. Nevertheless, its abstractions remain abstractions, divorced — while derived — from real life. To impose such abstractions on subsequent life, Bakunin continues, is as despotic as to impose any others (notably religious and political abstractions) on life. Bakunin acknowledges the resulting contradiction: while positive science achieves theoretical access to reality — while it achieves theoretical universality — it simultaneously perverts social reality (practically) by seeking to govern it (in the name of its universal wisdom) — it renders that reality partial. "This contradiction", Bakunin states, "can be resolved only in one way: by the liquidation of science as a moral being existing outside the social life of all, and represented . . . by a body of established savants, and its diffusion among the masses". Science, that is, must become "the patrimony of all". It thereby universalizes itself in its social existence "without losing anything of its universal [theoretical] character" [*ibid.*, pp. 126, 128]. Thus positive science must transform itself into universal science, something Comte implicitly resists. Only in this way can science contribute to the "humanization", that is, liberation, of society.)

Such is the basis of Bakunin's social philosophy; furthermore, I would argue, this is central to the social anarchist tradition generally. For Kelly to miss this point — that the philosophical basis of Bakunin's socio-revolutionary anarchism is an ontological naturalism — illustrates her ignorance of Bakunin's thought amply. (The straightforward sense in which the ontological positivism and the negative logic are conjoined and the straightforward implication of dialectical naturalism is the following: what is is (is real), but is developed (or actualized) negatively according to what is not, which is implicit in (or potential to) it. This will be explained in the second part of this essay.)

32. *Gosudarstvennost' i anarkhiia*, pp. 113-14; *Statism and Anarchy*, pp. 135-36.

33. *Ibid.*, pp. 148, 151; pp. 179, 182.

34. *Ibid.*, p. 111; p. 133.

35. *L'Internationale et Mazzini (The International and Mazzini)* (1871), *Archives Bakounine*, I, Part One, ed. Arthur Lehning (Leiden: E.J. Brill, 1961), p. 33. The Feuerbachian roots of this thesis will be explored in the second part of this essay.

36. *Lettre à un français*, p. 23.
    Bakunin's central anarchist principle is *the equivalence of State forms* or "denominations": "despotism [resides] not so much in the *form* of the State or of power as in the *principle* of the State and political power itself, and . . . consequently the republican state is bound by its very essence to be as despotic as a state governed by an emperor or a king" [*L'Empire knouto-germanique et la Révolution sociale (Première livraison)*, p. 22; emphasis in original]; "the origin of [humanity's] misfortune does not reside in this or that form of government but in the very principle or fact of government [as contained in the principle or fact of State], whatever [kind] it may be" [*La Commune de Paris*, p. 293]; "the State, any state, be it vested in the most liberal and democratic forms, is necessarily based on domination, on force, that is, on despotism — covert, perhaps, but all the more dangerous" for it [*Gosudarstvennost' i anarkhiia*, p. 29; *Statism and Anarchy*, p. 34].
    Practically, of course, Bakunin recognizes the relative superiority of certain forms of government and State, or certain forms of government and State as more progressive: "Let no one think that we wish to benefit the monarchy by criticizing the democratic government. We are firmly convinced that the most imperfect republic is a thousand times better than the most enlightened monarchy". The "democratic regime", in its favor, at least "raises the masses bit by bit to [participation in] public life, something that monarchy never does". However, Bakunin reiterates his principle: "preferring the republic, we are nevertheless forced to recognize and proclaim that, whatever the form of government may be, so long . . . as human society remains divided into different classes, there will always be exclusive government and inevitable exploitation of majorities by minorities. The State is nothing else but this domination and this exploitation regulated and systematized" [*Fédéralisme, socialisme et antithéologisme*, pp. 207-08].
    A critical comment on Bakunin here might be that he draws no distinction between the State and government and implies that they are identical — while obviously they are not. Bakunin is certainly rather careless in this respect. However, the response to this objection is still evident enough.
    Bakunin's contention is that the State remains essentially the same in various forms. What distinguishes these State-forms is the form of government; thus we call a form of State republican, monarchic, or whatever, though what we are referring to is in fact the form of government. Hence, the form of government (ultimately determined by the governing class or who governs) is the variable in the equation of statehood; the constants are the other elements of the State — the military, police, and bureaucratic elements, all of which are coercive. Hence the State, whatever its form of government, is coercive.
    The variable in this equation is of minimal importance; that is to say, the form of government or the governing class (which distinguishes the form of State) has no bearing on the State as such (in other words, there are, properly speaking, no distinct forms of State); the constants are the determining elements. Thus, even under parliamentary democracy, the definition holds: "organization founded on three detestable things —

bureaucracy, police, and standing army — that is what constitutes the State today", as ever [*Dieu et l'Etat* (the note, not the pamphlet), footnote on p. 190].

The role of government, or of each particular, dispensable government, is that of "guardian" of the State [*Nauka i nasushchnoe revoliutsionnoe delo (Science and the Vital Revolutionary Question)* (1870), Archives Bakounine, V, ed. Arthur Lehning (Leiden: E.J. Brill, 1974), p. 55]. In other words, the role of the State's engineers is to oversee the State machine. Replacing one set of engineers with another has minimal bearing on the machine itself. According to Bakunin, it is the nature of the machine that determines the behavior of *its* engineers. Therefore, consistent with his naturalism, he argues from the political object to the subjects who are *of* it, from the "what" to the "who". Political revolution, at best the effort to engineer the State's destruction from within by altering the "who" and not the "what", is therefore ineffectual. (On political revolution, Bakunin writes: "What was called revolution until now — including even the great French Revolution, despite the magnificence of the principles in the name of which it was carried out — was nothing but the struggle of classes among themselves for exclusive enjoyment of the privileges granted by the State, the struggle for the domination and exploitation of the masses" [*Ecrit contre Marx*, p. 195]. Marxian revolution is political in this sense; Marxian "class war" is of this kind — an attempt on the part of the proletariat (or a limited representation of it) to achieve "supremacy" and to enjoy exclusively the privileges of State domination.) It is the program of social revolution, on the other hand, to alter the "what"; standing in direct opposition to it, it aims to negate it, necessarily from without.

Bakunin, then, is unwilling to entrust political authority to anyone because the State or political authority conditions them in a manner consistent with its coercive nature; that is, assuming that their intentions are as noble as they would have us believe, it corrupts them. (Political power should not be given to anyone, he asserts, "for anyone who is invested with [such] power by an invariable social law will inevitably become the oppressor and exploiter of society", that is, an agent *of* the State [*Gosudarstvennost' i anarkhiia*, p. 112; *Statism and Anarchy*, p. 134].) Marx, by contrast, argues from the "who" to the "what", from the class which oversees the State to the nature of the State (so, if the State is governed by the proletariat, it becomes less political, less coercive, and eventually non-political). (The formal alteration in the Marxian State is therefore dismissed by Bakunin as insignificant: "behind all the democratic and socialistic phrases and promises of Marx's program, one finds in his State all that constitutes the actual despotic and brutal nature of all states, regardless of their form of government" [*Ecrit contre Marx*, p. 205].) Again, Bakunin's naturalist/objectivist reading contrasts with Marx's anthropocentric/subjectivist reading.

37. For a discussion of Bakunin's "love for the enemy", see Eric Voegelin, *From Enlightenment to Revolution*, ed. John H. Hallowell (Durham: Duke University Press, 1975), pp. 205-06.

38. ". . . *der Gegensatz ist kein Gleichgewicht, sondern ein Übergewicht des Negativen, welches der übergreifende Moment desselben ist; — das Negative, als das bestimmende Leben das Positiven selbst, schließt in sich allein die Totalität des Gegensatzes ein und so ist es auch das absolut Berechtigte*".

39. *Phenomenology of Spirit*, p. 22 (§39).

40. Marcuse, *op. cit.*, p. 49.

41. *The Encyclopaedia Logic*, p. 129 (addition to §81). Emphasis added.

42. See James Guillaume, *L'Internationale: Documents et Souvenirs 1864-1878*, III (Paris: Cornély,

1908), p. 284.

43. *The Structure of Scientific Revolutions*, Second Edition (Chicago: Chicago University Press, 1970), pp. 92-94. Emphasis added, except to the phrase "political recourse fails".

44. *Ibid.*, pp. 84-85, 35, 64, 11, 92, 90. Emphasis added.

45. *Ibid.*, pp. 77, 79.

46. *Les Endormeurs* (*The Lullers*) (1869), *Le Socialisme libertaire*, p. 101; *Intrigi Gospadina Utina* (*The Intrigues of Mr Utin*) (1870), *Archives Bakounine*, V, p. 142.

47. "*Laßt uns also dem ewigen Geiste vertrauen, der nur deshalb zerstört und vernichtet, weil er der unergründliche und ewig schaffende Quell alles Lebens ist. — Die Lust der Zerstörung ist zugleich eine schaffende Lust!*"

48. *Op. cit.*, p. 451.

49. *The Encyclopaedia Logic*, p. 131 (addition to §81). Emphasis added to the word "sublated".

50. "The 'Transition' From Feuerbach to Marx: A Reinterpretation", *Studies in Soviet Thought*, XXVI (1983), p. 127.

51. Andrzej Walicki, *A History of Russian Thought: From the Enlightenment to Marx*, trans. Hilda Andrews-Rusiecka (Oxford: Clarendon Press, 1988), p. 120. Emphasis added.

52. *A History of Russian Philosophy*, I, trans. George L. Kline (New York: Columbia University Press, 1953), pp. 252, 257. Emphasis added.

53. *The Encyclopaedia Logic*, pp. 145, 128 (§§89, 81).

54. *Phenomenology of Spirit*, p. 51 (§79).

55. *The Rebel* (1951), trans. Anthony Bower (Harmondsworth: Penguin Books, 1971), p. 128.

56. *The Confession of Mikhail Bakunin*, p. 36. Emphasis added.

57. "... *als diese Spitze ist er schon über die Theorie, — freilich zunächst noch innerhalb der Theorie selbst —, hinausgegangen und hat eine neue praktische Welt postuliert, — eine Welt, welche keineswegs durch eine formale Anwendung und Verbreitung von fertigen Theorien, sondern nur durch eine ursprüngliche Tat des praktischen autonomischen Geistes sich erst vollbringen wird*".

58. *L'Empire knouto-germanique (Seconde livraison)*, p. 125. Emphasis in original.

59. For an example of the "break thesis", see Franco Venturi, *op. cit.*, pp. 43-44: "There is, in fact, no gradual progress from [Bakunin's] political orthodoxy to his revolutionary ideas of 1842. All the concentrated inner life of his preceding years had prepared him for a *leap*. While his Moscow friends and the young Hegelians in Germany were still discussing the need to round off classical German philosophy by practical action, and to establish within the Hegelian system the relations between politics and philosophy, Bakunin had already made the leap. He was already becoming the living example of practical action..." [emphasis added]. Venturi makes two mistakes here: he assumes that Bakunin's earlier period is one of simple "political orthodoxy"; and he assumes that Bakunin's philosophy of revolutionary activity of 1842 actually amounts to "practical action". Inevitably, then, Venturi sees a huge leap here, a leap from an imagined passive political conservatism to an imagined radical political activism. Inevitably, too, Venturi is unable to explain this "leap" satisfactorily. It will be argued below that there is — rather than a "turn" — a coherent development from a philosophical preoccupation with the problem of social alienation to a philosophical preoccupation with the need for social revolution (and subsequently to a practical preoccupation with the issues of social revolution, though I take issue with the notion that philosophical inquiry is sacrificed in the process).

60. *Mikhail Bakunin*, pp. 96, 2-3. Emphasis added. Kelly, who makes much of the antithesis

that is, according to her, Bakunin-the-man-of-action versus Bakunin-the-man-of-thought, criticizes Bakunin himself for "his uncompromising categorization of events and ideas under the opposing headings of theory and life" and his "fondness for emphasizing the gulf between theory and life" [*ibid.*, pp. 198, 204]. Thus, once again (as in the case of the aforementioned Procrustean tendencies), Kelly is guilty of the charge she levels at Bakunin.

61. *Ibid.*, p. 3. Alternatively [*ibid.*, p. 193], "[(a)] His anarchism is intellectually shallow and built on cliches: but [(b)] this does not diminish its importance as a paradigm for those who seek to understand the emotional springs of extremist ideologies".

62. *Ibid.*, pp. 205, 207, 3, 21. Emphasis added.

63. *Gosudarstvennost' i anarkhiia*, p. 164; *Statism and Anarchy*, p. 198. Emphasis in original.

64. *Op. cit.*, p. 3.

65. *Mikhail Bakunin*, pp. 2-3.

66. There is a remarkable lack of sympathy for Bakunin's plight among his critics, beginning with Herzen. This is the case especially when it comes to analysis of the period's *Confession*. Camus, for example, refers, in a tone of disgust, to Bakunin's "openly obsequious *Confession*" [*op. cit.*, p. 128]. That Camus' description may be inaccurate is secondary; the point is that it illustrates a profound lack of human feeling, not to say understanding, for the subject in question. Ditto for Kelly. She notes, again in a tone of disgust, the "servile" *Confession*'s "sugary expressions of repentance", its "preposterous flattery", etc. [*Mikhail Bakunin*, pp. 140-41]. What is most noteworthy about the case of Kelly is that her study, which is ostensibly "psychological", shows an incredible indifference to the psychological factors at play here — and they are a great deal more relevant here than elsewhere in Bakunin's biography.

Eric Voegelin, who I will contrast Kelly with further below (not as an ideological sympathizer toward Bakunin, but as a scholar with a degree of common sense and humanity), recognizes two elements which others tend to ignore. Firstly, he recognizes that "the plain, vital horror of [Bakunin's] physical and mental decay" explains, even if it does not justify, "any step that would [or could] bring relief in this respect", especially when "other persons are not endangered by" it. (A passage frequently quoted in this context (by E.H. Carr and Peter Marshall among others) is the following from a prison note of Bakunin to his sister Tatyana (February, 1854): "You will never understand what it means to feel yourself buried alive, to say to yourself every moment of the day and night: I am a slave, I am annihilated, reduced to impotence for life; to hear even in your cell the echoes of the great battle which has had to come, which will decide the most important questions of humanity — and to be forced to remain idle and silent" [*Sobranie sochinenii i pisem*, IV, p. 244-45; translated in *Mikhail Bakunin*, p. 145].) Secondly, Voegelin recognizes that the *Confession* is not quite as "obsequious" or "servile" as Camus and Kelly claim: Voegelin states that "Bakunin frequently expresses his repentance in such terms that his nonrepentance is clear" and even refuses to name names [*op. cit.*, pp. 203-04]; Carr likewise admits that the *Confession* "includes some gestures of defiance" ["Bakunin, Mikhail Aleksandrovich" entry in *Encyclopaedia Britannica*, Fifteenth Edition, I (Chicago, 1997), p. 818]; and George Woodcock remarks that it "is by no means the abject document which the Tsar doubtless expected" (indeed, Woodcock deduces from the Tsar's marginal notes that "Nicholas . . . understood, more clearly than those who have self-righteously condemned Bakunin, the defiant passages which revealed that the sinner had not repented in his heart") [*op. cit.*, p. 146]. (Thus Bakunin informs the Tsar that he is unable "in good conscience" to "confess . . . the sins of others"; he also informs the Tsar that, since "repentance in [his] situation is . . . useless", he will "simply relate the facts" of his life. In response to such provisos, Nicholas notes that a "conditional" confession "destroys all confidence" [*The Confession of Mikhail Bakunin*, pp. 33, 51].) In other words, Voegelin recognizes that the pressures on Bakunin were considerable, that his *Confession* ultimately did no harm to anybody except Bakunin himself (that is, to his revolutionary reputation), and that its tone is fairly ambivalent in any case.

The episode certainly does Bakunin no favors; however, its importance has been much exaggerated for the sake of character assassination. One wonders, if one is permitted to disclose such a fantasy, how long Kelly, for instance, might hold out in such conditions: might she sacrifice her academic reputation for her potential liberty? It is certainly a question Bakunin's critics should ask themselves. G.D.H. Cole, from this point of view, writes of his reluctance to condemn Bakunin: "I cannot be at all sure how I should behave under similar circumstances, especially if I believed the cause for which I had contended to be lost and my own chance of aiding it to be quite gone . . . I do not defend the confession; but neither do I feel disposed to hold it heavily against its author, whose subsequent conduct shows that his revolutionary faith was as sincere as it was apt to be, sometimes misguided in its forms of expression and action" [*Socialist Thought*, II (London: Macmillan, 1954), p. 215]. (Venturi goes further than Cole, dismissing any notion that the *Confession* reflects *real* revolutionary hypocrisy at this stage in Bakunin's life, quite apart from the redemption of "subsequent conduct": "Letters to his family from prison conclusively prove that Bakunin did not really believe in the ideas contained in his *Confession*, but remained faithful to his revolutionary tenets" [*op. cit.*, p. 58].) (See also Voegelin, "Bakunin's Confession", *Journal of Politics*, VIII (1946), pp. 24-43 [this article also appears in *Anamnesis: Zur Theorie de Geschichte und Politik* (Munich: Piper, 1966), but, unfortunately, is omitted from the English-language edition of the same work]; and Carr, *Michael Bakunin*, pp. 210-16; etc.)

67. *Op. cit.*, p. 12.
68. *My Past and Thoughts*, III, trans. Constance Garnet, revised by Humphrey Higgins (London: Chatto & Windus, 1968), pp. 1353, 1357.
69. *Mikhail Bakunin*, p. 75.
70. See Venturi, *op. cit.*, p. 730, note 37.
71. *Op. cit.*, pp. 200, 239. See also, *ibid.*, p. 235.
72. *Ibid.*, p. 199. Emphasis added.
73. *Mikhail Bakunin*, pp. 97-98, 111. Emphasis added,
74. *Ibid.*, pp. 2, 54.
75. *Ibid.*, p. 197.
76. *Gosudarstvennost' i anarkhiia*, p. 110; *Statism and Anarchy*, p. 131.
77. The main writing of Bakunin's "communist" period is his *Communism* article of 1843, though even this endorsement of "true communism" attacks the despotic tendencies of Wilhelm Weitling's communism in a manner that anticipates later attacks on Marxian communism, stressing its lack of liberty, as well as the economic one-sidedness of the ideology (the partiality of its interpretation of the revolutionary principle which inspired the French Revolution); stressing, that is, the Proudhonian conclusion that

"Communism is oppression and slavery" [*What is Property?* (1840), trans. Donald R. Kelly and Bonnie G. Smith (Cambridge: Cambridge University Press, 1994), p. 197]: "His is not a free society, a really live union of free people, but a herd of animals, intolerably coerced and united by force, following only material ends, utterly ignorant of the spiritual side of life" [*Kommunizm*, p. 223; translated in Venturi, *op. cit.*, p. 45].

Bakunin's notion of true communism as communism embracing liberty leads quite naturally, via Proudhon, to his mature anarchism (notwithstanding a slight economic distinction that ought to be made between communism and collectivism). However, there are diversions along the way, chiefly Panslavism. But even Bakunin's Panslavism is underpinned by the revolutionary principle that Bakunin attempts, throughout his writings, to articulate. It is the partial application of the universal principle that Bakunin eventually passes beyond, in order to develop an internationalist anarchism. In Venturi's words: "[The Panslavist] policy . . . has its Machiavellian element in the desire to use, without much belief in its value, the banner of nationalism for revolutionary ends. The expression 'Revolutionary Panslavism' can be accepted as a description of his policy, only if it is remembered that Bakunin himself put the emphasis on the adjective and not on the noun. It may be true that later in this complicated game, Bakunin was carried away and eventually overwhelmed by 'the demoniac force of Nationalism', as he once described it; and that he did not [yet] succeed in dragging it into the field of an internationalism which he conceived of as a free alliance and collaboration of democratic forces. But this only means he, too, felt weighed down by the destiny of 1848, in which the national and social elements were so entangled that neither of them could develop until everyone had realized the extent of the failure" [*op. cit.*, pp. 54-55]. (On Bakunin's Panslavism, see Benoît-P. Hepner, *Bakounine et le panslavisme révolutionnaire: cinq essais sur l'histoire de idées en Russie et en Europe* (Paris: Marcel Rivière, 1950); Lawrence Orton, "Bakunin's Plan for Slav Federation, 1848", *Canadian-American Slavic Studies*, VIII (1974), pp. 107-15; Lawrence Orton, "The Echo of Bakunin's *Appeal to the Slavs* (1848)", *Canadian-American Slavic Studies*, X (1976), pp. 489-502; etc.)

78. *Gosudarstvennost' i anarkhiia*, pp. 17, 163; *Statism and Anarchy*, pp. 20, 197. Emphasis removed from original. On the notion of reconciliation in Bakunin's later writings, see also *L'Empire knouto-germanique (Seconde livraison)*, p. 144, where Bakunin inveighs against "the doctrinaire Deists" (especially Victor Cousin), whose "openly avowed goal [was] the reconciliation of Revolution with Reaction, or, to speak in the language of the school, of the principle of liberty with that of authority — naturally to the advantage of the latter". Bakunin continues: "This reconciliation signified, in politics, the retraction of popular liberty for the benefit of bourgeois domination, represented by the monarchical and constitutional State; [and,] in philosophy, the deliberate submission of free reason to the eternal principles of faith". That is to say, compromise is still understood (in 1871) much as it was (in 1842): as a form of reaction.

79. Kelly, for instance, describes the Bakunin of this period as an "extreme conservative Hegelian who justified the despotism of Nicholas the First as a necessary manifestation of the Absolute" ["The Destruction of Idols", *Journal of the History of Ideas*, XLI (1980), p. 642]. Woodcock contends that Bakunin "advocated the Hegelian doctrine in its most conservative form" [*The Encyclopedia of Philosophy*, I & II, ed. Paul Edwards (New York: Macmillan, 1967), p. 244]. And Berlin claims that Bakunin employed Hegelianism at this stage "to justify the need to submit to a brutal government and a stupid bureaucracy in the name of eternal Reason" ["Herzen and Bakunin on Individual Liberty", p.

146]. (See also the aforementioned account of Malia, *op. cit.*, pp. 204-05; E.H. Carr, *Michael Bakunin*, pp. 66-67; P.V. Annenkov, *The Extraordinary Decade: Literary Memoirs*, trans. Irwin. R. Titunik (Ann Arbor: University of Michigan Press, 1968), pp. 21-28; etc.)

80. *Op. cit.*, pp. 162, 189. Emphasis added. I must acknowledge at this point that I am indebted in no small degree to this quite outstanding article.

81. *Mikhail Bakunin*, p. 59.

82. Quoted from a letter to Aleksandra Beyer [2/1840] in *Mikhail Bakunin*, p. 58. Originally from *Sobranie sochinenii i pisem*, II, p. 306.

83. *Op. cit.*, pp. 5, 12.

84. *Mikhail Bakunin*, p. 58.

85. *Predislovie perevodchika: Gimnazicheskie rechi Gegelia*, p. 169. Translated by Del Giudice, *op. cit.*, p. 170. Emphasis added.

86. *Ibid.*, p. 170. Translated by Del Giudice, *op. cit.*, p. 173. Emphasis added.

87. *Ibid.*, p. 167. Translated by Del Giudice, *op. cit.*, pp. 166-67. Emphasis added.

88. *Op. cit.*, p. 435-36. Emphasis added.

89. *Thoughts on Death and Immortality*, trans. James A. Massey (Berkeley: University of California Press, 1980), p. 17. Emphasis added.

90. *Anarchism: From Theory to Practice*, trans. Mary Klopper (New York: Monthly Review Press, 1970), p. 27.

91. *Gosudarstvennost' i anarkhiia*, p. 118; *Statism and Anarchy*, p. 142.

92. *Predislovie perevodchika: Gimnazicheskie rechi Gegelia*, pp. 177-78. Translated by Del Giudice, *op. cit.*, pp. 188-89.

93. *The Trumpet*, pp. 95, 129. Emphasis added. For valuable discussions of Bauer's thought, see Stepelevich's introduction to his translation of *The Trumpet* (pp. 1-56) and David McLellan's *The Young Hegelians and Karl Marx* (London: Macmillan, 1969), especially pp. 48-81 and, in the context of the interpretation of the dialectic, pp. 18-20.

94. *Gosudarstvennost' i anarkhiia*, p. 110; *Statism and Anarchy*, p. 131.

95. *The Trumpet*, pp. 68, 62-63, 96-97, 128. Emphasis added.

96. *Ibid.*, p. 66.

97. *Ibid.*, p. 97. Emphasis added.

98. *Hegel's Philosophy of Right and the Politics of our Times*, trans. James A. Massey, *The Young Hegelians: An Anthology*, ed. Lawrence Stepelevich (Cambridge: Cambridge University Press, 1983), p. 211.

99. *The Trumpet*, pp. 125-27. Emphasis added.

100. *Mikhail Bakunin*, p. 92. For Bakunin's later statements on Lamennais, see the fragment of *La Théologie politique de Mazzini: Deuxième partie* (*The Political Theology of Mazzini: Part Two*) (1871), *Archives Bakounine*, I, Part One, p. 161, third footnote; and the fragment of *L'Empire knouto-germanique, Archives Bakounine*, p. 454.

101. *The Confession of Mikhail Bakunin*, p. 38.

102. *Kommunizm*, p. 229. Translated by Kelly, *Mikhail Bakunin*, p. 115.

103. See Bakunin's letter to Ruge [19/1/1843], *Sobranie sochinenii i pisem*, III, pp. 176-77. Translation of the Weitling quote (in this letter) by Carr, *Michael Bakunin*, p. 122.

104. *Pis'ma M. A. Bakunina k A. I. Gertsenu i N. P. Ogarevu*, ed. M.P. Dragomanov (Geneva: Ukrainskaia Tipografiia, 1896), p. 201. Translation by Pyziur, *op. cit.*, p. 26. On the Stankevich

circle, see Edward J. Brown, *Stankevich and His Moscow Circle, 1830-1840* (Stanford: Stanford University Press, 1966).

105. *Bakunin and the Italians*, pp. 70-73. Ravindranathan is responding to the claims of Aldo Romano in his three volume *Storia del movimento socialista in Italia* (see, *ibid.*, p. 258, note 63). Kelly, citing Lehning, speculates on Pisacane's influence as well [*Mikhail Bakunin*, pp. 175-76]. However, Lehning observes that "The name of Pisacane does not figure in Bakunin's writings" [Editor's Introduction, *Archives Bakounine*, I, Part One, p. xviii, note 4], a sure sign with Bakunin, who is by no means above acknowledging an intellectual debt, that Pisacane's influence is negligible.

106. *La Commune de Paris*, p. 293.

107. See Woodcock, *Anarchism*, p. 141: "Proudhon is the master of us all".

108. *Fédéralisme, socialisme et antithéologisme*, pp. 77-78.

109. *General Idea of Revolution in the Nineteenth Century* (1851), trans. John Beverley Robinson (London: Pluto Press, 1989), pp. 245, 168, 103, 101. The Bakuninian tone of these lines may reflect Bakunin's influence on Proudhon, who was a great deal less familiar with Hegelian and Left Hegelian thought than Bakunin. Venturi writes: "their influences were reciprocal, for Bakunin, with Marx and [Karl] Grün, was one of those who aroused Proudhon's interest in the Hegelian dialectic" [*op. cit.*, p. 47]. This may be so; but in the present case Proudhon is clearly more influenced by the negativity of Bakunin's dialectic, Bakunin's disdain for dialectical "compromise", etc. than Marx's version of the dialectic. However, Proudhon generally presents the dialectic in a pretty confused way — simultaneously urging revolutionary compromise and revolutionary consistency (in Bakunin's sense) in the *General Idea of the Revolution*, as we will see.

110. *Ibid.*, p. 9; *Selected Writings of Pierre-Joseph Proudhon*, ed. Stewart Edwards (London: Macmillan, 1969), p. 231. See also *No Gods, No Masters*, I, ed. Daniel Guérin, trans. Paul Sharkey (Edinburgh: A.K. Press, 1998), p. 43.

111. *General Idea of the Revolution*, pp. 136-37, 126.

112. *Op. cit.*, p. 39. Emphasis added. See also, *Ibid.*, p. 32.

113. See Proudhon's *De la Justice dans la Révolution et dans l'Eglise* (*On Justice in the Revolution and the Church*) (1858), III, *Oeuvres complètes*, VIII, ed. C. Bouglé and H. Moysset (Paris: Marcel Rivière, 1932), pp. 433-34 (cited by Lehning in *Archives Bakounine*, VII, pp. 547-48, note 44); *General Idea of the Revolution*, p. 251. For Bakunin's response, see *L'Empire knouto-germanique (Seconde livraison)*, pp. 72, 88-89. Additionally, see Voegelin, *op. cit.*, pp. 195, 237.

114. *General Idea of the Revolution*, p. 248.

115. Editor's introduction, *Archives Bakounine*, VII, p. XXXVII.

116. See Alan Ritter, *The Political Thought of Pierre-Joseph Proudhon* (Princeton: Princeton University Press, 1969), p. 57.

117. Quoted in the editor's introduction to *Oeuvres*, II, ed. James Guillaume (Paris: P.V. Stock, 1907). translated in *Bakunin on Anarchism*, ed. Sam Dolgoff (Montréal: Black Rose Books, 1980), p. 26.

PART TWO

BAKUNIN'S NATURALISM AND THE CRITIQUE OF THEOLOGISM

> True freedom is present only where man is also free
> from religion; true culture is present only where man
> has become master over his religious prejudices and
> imaginations.[1]

2.1 The Totality of Nature

In his mature philosophy, Bakunin understands *nature* and reality to
be synonymous. Hence nature can be defined as the totality of reality or,
better still, *the totality of actuality*. It is not merely the totality of real things
in existence, which is "a completely lifeless concept of . . . nature" that
contradicts all experience, but the totality of possible movement, or mutual action and reaction (i.e., interaction), which embraces all real things.
Alternatively, it is *"the sum of real transformations of things that are produced and
incessantly reproduced within its womb"*. Nature, understood therefore as
"universal causality", or the totality of interactive and, as we will see, developmental causality, is both creator or cause and created or caused. Hence
it cannot properly be characterized as "absolute and first cause", since it
is the product of an infinity of particular causes. Nevertheless, embracing
all of these particular causes, conceived in abstraction, it has created all
that was, creates all that is, and will continue to create all that has yet to
be. Therefore, Bakunin writes (establishing the decisive principle of the
direct continuity of the natural and the social):

> . . . Universal Causality, *Nature, creates the worlds.* It is this
> [causality] that has determined the mechanical, physical,

chemical, geological, and geographical configuration of our earth; and which, having covered its surface with all the splendors of vegetable and animal life, still continues to *create*, in the human world, society in all its past, present, and future developments.[2]

In a sense, then, nature is the field of the possible or, we might say, the causable — which is the logical; its limit is the uncausable or the impossible — the illogical. In other words, *"All that is natural is logical, and all that is logical has already been realized or is bound to be realized in the natural world, including the social world"*.[3] Thus there seems to be a contradiction between the logical totality that is nature and the realm of actualization, or, at any rate, the realm of the actualized — that is, "the natural world". One gets the impression here that Bakunin's thought resembles (for example, and albeit only superficially) the early thought of Wittgenstein — that is, if we interpret Wittgenstein's early thought as anything other than a figurative theory of language, in other words, as having any ontological significance (which might be "unfair"), or if we interpret his thought (even in his later works) as exceeding the limits of Kantianism (which would be plain wrong in my opinion). However, that we should have to make such qualifications — and thereby appear to forgive the sheer metaphysicality of such an approach to philosophical inquiry, with its arbitrary nature-culture or natural-sociolinguistic dualisms (the products of what I refer to as the post-Kantian socio-linguistic or, more precisely, culturo-linguistic turn in philosophy, whereby philosophy became, as I will argue below, predominantly anthropocentric) — says a great deal about the not entirely healthy state of twentieth-century philosophy.

In any case, the resemblance of Bakunin's thought to that of the early Wittgenstein has three aspects. First, there is resemblance insofar as Wittgenstein portrays the world as being *directly* related to facts or states of affairs rather than isolated things or objects. "The world is the totality of facts, not of things"; "What is the case — a fact — is the existence of states of affairs"; "A state of affairs (a state of things) is a combination of objects (things)"; etc. (This is not just true of the "direct" relation for Bakunin, for whom the concept of the in any way concrete isolated object is absurd.) Second, there is resemblance insofar as Wittgenstein portrays *actuality* (*Wirklichkeit* — which is rendered as "reality" in the translation of Pears and McGuinness, but, as already explained, is better translated as "actuality") as being the existence *and* non-existence of possible states of affairs, or the totality of these possible states of affairs (alternatively, *the totality of positive and negative facts*); and *the world* as being the totality of such possible states of affairs which really exist (alternatively, *the totality of positive facts*). "The totality of existing states of affairs is the world"; "The existence and non-existence of states of affairs is actuality"; etc. And, third, there is further resemblance insofar as Wittgenstein portrays logic as being that which "deals with every possibility and [that for which] all possibilities are . . . facts".[4]

All of this results in a tension between actuality, or the possible, and the world, or that portion of the possible that has been actualized — mirroring the apparent tension in Bakunin's thought between nature and the natural world. This begs the question: How is it that something other than what really is in the universe might actually be? Wittgenstein's resolution of this in the *Tractatus Logico-Philosophicus* (1921) (by means of his highly abstract logical analysis, or reduction of everything to the completely *abstract* simple monadic object (or "substance", which is abstract in the sense that it "subsists independently of what is the case") which has the *mere* "possibility of occurring in states of affairs" [or "form"][5]) is, in its extreme abstraction, profoundly flawed. It requires the postulation of two separate realms of existence — one realm of what is and another realm where what might be is, as it were, waiting in the wings — which are grounded on some dubious metaphysical subsistent stuff that need not participate in the world at all.

Bakunin's resolution is, it seems to me, more satisfactory. Basing it on a rich concept of material causality, he can overcome the tension by showing that nature not only includes the natural world (as the possible actualized) but also that the natural world "includes" nature (as universal causality, or the totality of possibility which is actually inherent in the natural, *material* world). There is no cause that is foreign to the natural world because all causes derive from it, in its *materiality*. Nature and the natural world, while distinct in themselves, are thus identical in truth. It follows, furthermore, that matter is identical with nature (hence materialism and naturalism are synonymous); in Bakunin's words, therefore, "the *totality* of the real world [i.e., nature, is] abstractly called matter".[6] Thus matter, like nature, exists in the broader sense of the totality of its possibilities (which amounts to the totality of causality, that is, nature) and in the narrower sense of that which has been actualized (the totality of the caused, that is, the natural world). Matter, like nature, then, is not merely what "is", but is also what "can be": it exists in actuality as the totality of its potential. The principle of (immanent material) causality is the link between such potentiality and its actualization

2.2 "Dialectics" and "Materialism"

Bakunin's thought here — his materialistic naturalism — would seem to be infused with, as it were, the spirit of Hegelianism, and this will become ever more apparent in his critique of theologism. Indeed, this infusion is apparent even in contemporary anarchism. Note the dialectical naturalism of Murray Bookchin, which, it should be said, bears little relation to the pseudo-materialism or, to use Bakunin's phrase, the "economic metaphysics"[7] disguised as materialism, of Marx, or, indeed, the "crude dialectical materialism" of Engels, of whom Bookchin says: "so enamoured was [he] of matter and motion as the irreducible 'attributes' of Being that a kineticism based on mere motion invaded his dialectic of organic development". The "phenomenological strategy in the richly dialectical approach of [Hegel's] *Phenomenology of Spirit*" is fundamental to Bookchin's "nature philosophy".[8] However, Bookchin also draws from French Enlightenment thinking; specifically, he avails of Diderot's concept of *sensitivity* (*sensibilité*) — as outlined in *Le Rêve de D'Alembert* (*D'Alembert's Dream*) (1769) — for his naturalistic resolution of the philosophical tension between potentiality and actuality, as outlined above. (Bakunin was doubtless aware of the concept of *sensibilité*, given his early exposure to the Encyclopedists through his father, as well as Diderot's

influence on both Feuerbach and Comte. In any event, Bakunin's contention that matter has "action and . . . movement *of its own*", a contention
contested by idealists and mechanistic materialists alike, is redolent of
Diderot.[9]) Bookchin expresses this tension in terms of the aforementioned Hegelian distinction between *Realität* (reality) — which roughly
corresponds to Wittgenstein's notion of the world and Bakunin's notion
of the natural world — and *Wirklichkeit* (actuality) — which roughly corresponds to Wittgenstein's notion of actuality and Bakunin's notion of
nature. Hence the above (Bakuninian) description of nature as the totality of actuality.

It is worth citing Marx Wartofsky's explanation by way of a preliminary remark on Diderot's thought here: "Diderot's matter has motion
as an inherent property. It is not endowed with motion; it is not a
ground in which motion is put. Matter itself is uncreated, eternal, [and]
its motion is its essential mode of existence".[10] With *sensibilité*, with this
essentially "active concept of matter", Bookchin contends, Diderot established, albeit somewhat suggestively and tentatively, "the crucial trait of
nature that transforms mere motion into development and directiveness". Indeed, Bookchin adds, this concept of the "immanent fecundity of
'matter' — as distinguished from motion as mere change of place —
scored a marked advance over the prevalent mechanism of La Mettrie
and, by common acknowledgement, anticipated nineteenth-century
theories of evolution and, in my view, recent developments in biology".
(*Sensibilité* was, therefore, the crucial principle that enabled Diderot to
hold the following: "anyone lecturing to the Academy on the stages in
the formation of a man or animal need refer only to material factors, the
successive stages of which would be an inert body, a sentient being, a
thinking being, and then a being who can resolve the problem of the pre-
cession of the equinoxes, a sublime being, a miraculous being, one who
ages, grows infirm, dies, decomposes, and returns to humus".[11]) Bakunin's theory of self-actualizing matter, grounded on his concept of interactive and developmental or emergent material causality (that is, in
Bookchin's words, "dialectical causality", or "the differentiation of potentiality into actuality, in the course of which each new actuality [or par-

tial actualization] becomes the potentiality for further differentiation and actualization"), itself anticipated much of this aspect of Bookchin's nature philosophy. In either case, their differences notwithstanding, the result is an understanding of matter such that: "we can no longer be satisfied with the theory of an inert 'matter' that fortuitously aggregates into life. The universe bears witness to a *developing* — not merely moving — substance [that is, in Bakunin's terms, matter], whose most dynamic and creative attribute is its unceasing capacity for self-organization into increasingly complex forms [that is, in Bakunin's terms, causality]".[12]

The Aristotelian roots of the terminology here need hardly be pointed out. However, that the project to explain the related concepts of potentiality and causality is itself Aristotelian ought to be borne in mind. In other words, we owe the initial formulation of this problematic, not just the terminology, to Aristotle, whose philosophy, notwithstanding its scholastic Christian deformation, is the *locus classicus* for subsequent naturalistic philosophy and science as a whole. Hence Bakunin refers to Aristotle as "the true father of science and positive philosophy".[13] Aristotle's biological groundwork in *De Anima*, for example, and in particular his systematic distinction between the non-organic and the organic and, within the organic sphere, his notion of (unfortunately localized) biological development and differentiation (within the — in Aristotle's case — excessively metaphysical potentiality-actuality framework), is of abiding interest. However, the reason Aristotle's biology collapses, and perhaps the great flaw in his entire philosophy, is his misconception of matter as being rather empty, that is, as mere potentiality needing to be actualized (or, as it were, in-formed) from without. As a result, rejecting the Milesian emphasis on material causality rather hastily in the first book of the *Metaphysics*, Aristotle insists on four causes, and thereby provides for generations of, as Diderot puts it, "metaphysico-theological balderdash". We will return to this misconception of matter — the conception of "vile matter" — below, in the context of Bakunin's critique of the logic of idealism.

2.3 Natural Order and the "Divine Legislator"

According to Bakunin, nature "is imposed *upon* [and not *by*] our mind as a rational necessity".[14] It is manifest as a series of "inherent" laws or forms of development particular to each thing. However, it is the human mind that imposes the *form* of law on nature, since "nature itself knows no laws".[15] That is to say, there were no *natural laws* as such prior to the development of human thought; there were only natural facts and more or less regular natural processes.

Natural laws reflect the fact that, given certain conditions, certain facts or effects "invariably" follow from certain actions or causes; these laws, and the processes of which they are (true but nevertheless still abstract) reflections, are, within the context of universal causality, though, relative in character. (We should note in passing that there are two kinds of natural law. First, there are general laws [which reflect processes] which are apparently essential to all natural things, or which are, in a manner of speaking, "inherent in *matter*"; Bakunin clearly has the laws of physics, in particular, in mind, and remarks that "all the orders . . . of real existence are subject" to these [processes and their] laws. Second, there are particular and special laws, which are strictly applicable only to certain orders of things [or which reflect processes within these orders], though never entirely foreign to any other order in the unified totality that is the universe; Bakunin offers the examples of geological laws, physiological laws, and, importantly, "laws which preside over the ideal and social development . . . of man".) The (processes and their) laws which "govern" each thing determine its nature: these (processes and their) laws being relative, the nature of each thing is only relatively fixed (though, on the scale of human time, fixed to all intents and purposes). Nevertheless, it is the totality of these (processes and their) laws that accounts for the order of nature as a whole. As Bakunin puts it:

> This [to all intents and purposes] constant reproduction of *the same facts* through *the same processes* constitutes precisely *the legislation of nature*: order in the infinite diversity of phenomena and facts.[16]

This view of natural creation and natural order, of "a magnificently organized world in which every part [stands in] necessary *logical* relation to all the others"[17], rules out the existence of the personal creator, divine or otherwise. Such a creator, this "divine legislator", could only destroy the natural order by his "arbitrary personal edict"[18] or intervention in the universal causal web. To maintain that he exists, contrary to logic, is therefore plainly absurd. Bakunin reiterates: "If order is natural and possible in the universe, it is solely because this universe is not governed according to some system imagined in advance and imposed by a supreme will".[19] Or, in characteristic fashion, Bakunin offers a choice: "The existence of God can have no other meaning than the negation of natural laws, from which this inevitable dilemma results: *God is, so there are no natural laws, there is no natural order, and the world is chaotic*; or else, *the world was self-ordained* [*est ordonné en lui-même*], *so God does not exist*".[20] Bookchin argues, likewise, that the idea of a "presiding agent" or "hidden hand" that "predetermines the development of life-forms" ruptures natural order by introducing a dualism — a dualism which, as we will see, necessarily "underpins hierarchy and the view of all differentiation as degrees of domination and subordination".[21]

The ultimate source of natural order, that is, the "absolute and first cause", will seemingly always remain "unknown". Indeed, according to Bakunin, this concept of a first cause is meaningless. He asks, "how can we find the first cause if it does not exist?"[22] If nature, the totality of actuality or universal causality, consists *essentially* of the infinity of "particular" causes in their ongoing relation, it makes no sense to seek an absolute, primary, original cause among these, since, if it ever existed or meant anything (which we have no reason to believe), it has been lost and has effectively become meaningless. In fact, to seek this first cause is to arbitrarily, and artificially, render the natural order chaotic. This is the essence of Bakunin's critique of the deity of the Aristotelian-Thomist tradition, a critique largely informed by Feuerbach, who held that the concept of a first cause, and the correlative concept of "second causes", represents the "capitulation" of religious belief. If God is merely the first cause, he is evidently "an idle inactive being" of whom the natural world — "the realm of second causes" — is independent. If this is the case, God is "only a hypothetical Being [existing] not for his own sake, but for the sake of the world" — in order to explain its very existence. However, he is only required as such by the mechanistic mind, which has no understanding of the "godless self-subsistence" of the world. Feuerbach infers that "To the mechanical theorist, the creation [or the first cause] is the last thin thread which yet ties him to religion".[23] (The implication here is that Christian theology, in conjunction with Aristotelianism (which, in spite of its metaphysicality, is sufficiently naturalistic to undermine it), has lost sight of its very theocentrism; and that it contains within itself the "transitional" seed of speculative philosophy or anthropocentrism.) But, in any case, Bakunin's broader critique is aimed at the deity of the Cartesian-Kantian tradition (the transitional-anthropocentric tradition), that is, at the "phantom" of modern idealism or, in Feuerbach's words, "speculative philosophy", which, by necessity, as a *compromised* or humanized form of divine idealism, has an even more pernicious influence

2.4 The Totality of Science

The concept of *the absolute* can evidently only be attached on Bakunin's terms, therefore, to the concept of *totality*, so that the absolute cannot be conceived as a simple, abstract unity but must be conceived as a complex, concrete, many-sided unity: an *identity-in-difference*. Thus the only absolute cause, or the only sense in which one can speak of an absolute cause, is the totality of interactive and developmental causality, i.e., nature. Thus the only absolute natural law or, again, the only sense in which one can speak of an absolute natural law, is the totality of natural laws, or "the sum of all known and unknown laws".[24]

The totality of known and unknown laws is the province of *science*. Consequently, science is a unified discipline: a "unity in infinite diversity", in Bakunin's words, which can only be entirely realized — in the form of actual (or, perhaps, actualized) knowledge — when every single detail of the universe is grasped — and not merely atomistically, so to speak, but in relation to the whole. A crucial point that Bakunin is seeking to make here — one so unpalatable for contemporary metaphysicians (even when they declare themselves "philosophers of science") — is that science is historically (and methodologically), for all its diversity and all its revolutions and shifts, one, or, if you prefer, universal. This requires a naturalistic argument with respect to human nature and so on, which we will come to below, but Bakunin's case is the following:

> The world, in spite of the infinite diversity of beings that compose it, is one. The human spirit which fastens upon it . . . is also one or identical . . . This identity is demonstrated by the incontestable fact that if a man thinks at all, whatever his background, nature, race, rank, and degree of intellectual and moral development — even when he digresses and talks nonsense — his thought always develops in accordance with the same laws [that is, the laws of his nature], and this is precisely what . . . constitutes the great unity of the human race. Consequently science, which is nothing other than the human spirit's knowledge and understanding of the world, must also be one.[25]

Bakunin maintains that the project of science "evidently exceeds the capacities of one man, of one generation, or of humanity in its entirety". It is the very infinity of nature — the infinity of its "particulars" (abstractly conceived) and the relations in which they arise — that limits science or assures that it can never be exhausted. Nevertheless science alone, as distinct from theology and metaphysics, has the possibility of attaining real knowledge. Its fundamental method of attaining such knowledge, of both general and particular laws, is based on "attentive and exact observation of facts and phenomena which occur outside as well as within" man.[26] Such observation allows man to note both causal relations and the degree to which these relations are fixed, that is, the degree to which these relations are "law-governed".

Thus there are two constitutive processes in scientific inquiry, or what Bakunin calls "the realist method": the process of observation, which enables the scientist to ascertain "the certain reality of a thing, phenomenon, or fact"; and the process of, as Bakunin puts it, "comprehension", which enables the scientist "to discover, identify, and record, in [the same] empirical way . . . all its properties, that is, all its immediate or indirect relations to all other existing things".[27] Science therefore consists of both the empirical verification of (natural) objects and the understanding of these objects in relation to the whole (of nature). It is in this sense that Bakunin's "empiricism" has, yet again, a Hegelian aspect. (It ought to be noted that Bakunin uses descriptive or categorical philosophical terms more or less interchangeably (though not randomly), a habit of Feuerbach's which he has seemingly picked up. For the sake of consistency, however, I refer for the most part to his naturalism, both as a conveniently broad term and as the most adequate description of the tradition to which, as is my contention, Bakunin belongs. Empiricism, on the other hand, would seem to be the least satisfactory designation, at least if one associates it with the tradition of "British" empiricism, culminating in the Humean form of psychologism which is essentially — regardless of those issues which preoccupy scholastics — little different to Kantian idealism. Bakunin, as a naturalist, simply does not fit into this anthropocentric tradition in which pretty much everything is mediated by the human mind such that it is unknowable as it is "in itself". (Another follower of Comte, however, perhaps under the influence of his "compatriots", has properly been accused of being psychologistic: I speak, of course, of John Stuart Mill, whom indeed Bakunin calls an "apostle of idealism". He does add, however, that Mill, at the same time a "passionate admirer [and] adherent of the positive philosophy of Auguste Comte", is by no means the worst of his ilk.[28]) For Bakunin, natural things are in principle knowable as they are because they are known naturally by a natural "subject"; and to assume otherwise amounts to assuming that "subject" and "object" are qualitatively distinct, or that one or the other (usually the "subject") is somehow non-natural or super-natural, or that the process of "knowing" (even in the most limited sense) is not merely problematic but mysterious; that is, it entails unjustifiable — or certainly unjustified — assumption. Epistemology in fact survives by making such assumptions and by refusing to make them explicit. But this large issue is one to which we shall return.)

Bakunin's basic philosophy of science is not uncritical. He notes that the empirical basis of science is social, as opposed to individual (since the individual, or the individual group, is always limited in ability and experience), as well as trans-historical, as opposed to being historically — and "culturally" — imprisoned (since the method of science, the realist method, is universal). In his own words: "The basis of science . . . is the collective experience not only of all contemporaries but also of all past generations". But, importantly, he adds that science "accepts no evidence without examination [*sans critique*]". According to Bakunin, the scientist must assess evidence according: firstly, to the intellectual disposition and method of the scientist, who should display "a good realistic intellect, developed and properly trained by science [that is, by scientific practice, not academic dictate]"; secondly, to the attestable character and motivations of the scientist, who is ideally "an honest man, hostile to falsehood and seeking the truth with enthusiasm and good faith", which precludes him from being (or presumably being in the pay of) a "fantasist, poet, metaphysician, theologian, jurist, [or] politician", all of whom engage in "deception" of one sort or another; and, thirdly, to one's own scientific findings on the subject in question and those of any number of reliably scientific third parties, which are in turn open to critical examination. All science must therefore be public and subject to confirmation or refutation. Bakunin concludes that "Nothing is more inimical to science than faith, and criticism is never silenced".[29]

Theology, in contrast to science, never manages to verify — never even manages to provide criteria according to which one might try to verify — the existence of its object or objects, which are in fact always "objects of blind faith". Hence, all its peculiar speculative endeavors, which are ultimately limited to heavenly concerns, amount to nothing. (Therefore Bakunin describes theology as "the science of Nothingness".

[Indeed, Proudhon had described it in much the same manner before him — as "the science of the infinitely absurd". For Proudhon, as for Bakunin, theology deals with "terrible problems whose solution, forever attempted, forever remains unaccomplished"; that is, with "unanswerable questions", or, as Bakunin properly names them, mysteries, which pertain, by Bakunin's definition, to the absurd or nothingness.[30]]) Metaphysics, in spite of its partial awareness of nature and its doubts about the sheer nothingness of theology — that is, in spite of its critical consciousness — remains infected by the theological spirit — or the spirit of nothingness. Hence, in preoccupying itself with the "objects of transcendental speculation and more or less ingenious word-play" (an apt description of much contemporary philosophy) — the very existence of which it "has no guarantee for . . . other than the assurances [and] mandates of theology" — it never manages to ground itself, either.[31] It is hardly surprising, then, that it should eventually come to doubt *its* effectively *theological* foundations — though, unfortunately, it arbitrarily renounces all materialistic-naturalistic "foundations" as similarly "theological" (or, say, "onto-theological") in the process. (Bakunin therefore describes metaphysics as "the science . . . of the *impossible reconciliation* of Nothingness with reality" — of God with nature, of theology with naturalism, and, echoing Bruno Bauer in *The Trumpet*, of faith with reason.[32] Bakunin, here as elsewhere, reserves his vitriol for the mediators — for the metaphysicians, for the human or anthropocentric idealists who recognize the absurdity of the realm of faith, but who attempt to reconcile it with the realm of reason, which is thereby debased.)

Anticipating an immediate attack on Bakunin here, the following remark might be necessary. As far as *epistemological* gripes (or mystical forms thereof) with Bakunin's "ontological positivism" are concerned, he might justly respond that he is not compelled to enter into metaphysical discussion whereby, dare I say, a coherent approach has any number of — supposedly philosophical, but frankly quasi-religious — mysteries, absurdities, and fantasies imposed on it by crypto-theologians, old- or new-age mystics, and science fiction fanatics. In other words, the burden of justifying the non-natural, the fantastic, and the counter-scientific — be it brains in vats, visitation by extraterrestrial philosophers, the divinity of the German or French language, or whatever — rests entirely with the metaphysician. (Feuerbach argues against exactly this quasi-theological tendency in metaphysics. Ignorance of "natural, material causes", he writes, "doesn't justify you in the superstitious consequences which theology draws, on the basis of deficiencies in human knowledge, doesn't justify you going beyond the domain of natural causes . . . [That is to say, it] doesn't justify you to explain the [seemingly] inexplicable by the postulation of imaginary beings, doesn't justify you in deceiving and deluding others by an explanation which doesn't explain anything", etc.[33]) My point (one I will attempt to develop below) is this: epistemology, or the study of the (assumed) problematic, even mysterious, relation between the subject of knowledge and *its* objects (which is basically Kantian, whether in its Anglo-American or Franco-Germanic form, and which gave rise to the culturo-linguistic obsession, culminating in the philosophico-cultural commodity that is postmodernism) is a manifestation of metaphysics, of the prioritization of thought over being, or the human over the natural, which, in its various forms as they continually emerge, progressives, radicals, and other decent souls seek and have sought to overcome since the Enlightenment. Obviously, this requires elaboration.

2.5 The Logic of Materialism

Science has established, Bakunin claims, that all difference in the natural world is *quantitative*, that is, that everything real, even the "spiritual" or "ideal" in mankind, has its basis in matter and its various developments — that everything real is material, the fulfillment of some potentiality in matter. Bakunin therefore describes as "*material* everything that is, everything that occurs in the real world, within as well as outside man"; and as "*ideal* . . . the products of the cerebral activity of man". He adds, "since our brain is a completely material structure" and since, therefore, "all its functions are just as material as the interactions of all other things, it follows that what we call matter or the material world by no means excludes but, on the contrary, necessarily embraces the ideal".[34] In other words, Bakunin holds that there are no *qualitative* differences between the levels of material development.

Bookchin, by contrast, considers qualitative difference plausible from the naturalistic standpoint. Thus he opposes Bakunin's statement that "Between [the] faculties of animals and the corresponding faculties of man [including the faculties of animal and human language], there is only a quantitative difference, a difference of degree"[35]; arguing, "The dim choices that animals exercise in their own evolution should not be confused with the will and degree of intentionality that human beings exhibit in their social lives. Nor is the nascent freedom that is rendered possible by natural complexity comparable to the ability of humans to make rational decisions. *The differences between the two are qualitative,* however much they can be traced back to the evolution of all animals". Or, put simply, "we are highly intelligent by comparison with other species — *indeed, qualitatively so*". The fact that evolutionary "leaps" occur, however, does not seem to justify a belief in qualitative transformation: there may be qualitative differences *in effect,* but to acknowledge them *in fact* seems inconsistent and suggests an idealistic prejudice in Bookchin's naturalism that leaves the door open to a dualistic interpretation of it — with all the practical dangers that follow. This being the case, it seems unlikely to me that Bakunin would accept Bookchin's first nature-second nature dichotomy, and I have no doubt that he would reject some of the implications of it. It ought to be pointed out, however, that Bookchin makes the following statement of effective support for Bakunin's view: "We may reasonably claim that human will and freedom, at least as self-consciousness and self-reflection, have their own natural history in potentialities of the natural world — in contrast to the view that they are *sui generis,* the product of a rupture with the whole of development so unprecedented and unique that it contradicts the gradedness of all phenomena from the antecedent potentialities that lie behind and within every processual 'product'".[36] Is not the qualitative distinction that he himself makes a proposition of such an "unprecedented rupture" or of a, so to speak, dualization?

Another contemporary anarchist, Noam Chomsky, opposes Bakunin's view in characteristically emphatic fashion: "Any objective scientist must be struck by the qualitative differences between human beings and other organisms, as much as by the difference between insects and vertebrates. If not, he is simply irrational . . . Even the most superficial observation suffices to show that there are qualitative differences between humans and other complex organisms which must be explained".[37] Obviously, as far as Chomsky is concerned, a significant difference between humans and other animals is linguistic: "as far as we know, the language faculty is a distinctive human possession". Thus, the apparently unique and qualitatively distinct language faculty "must be explained". But how can one explain something, and distinguish it from all else, in qualitative terms? The Cartesian approach, whereby the "mental" is divorced from the "corporeal", whereby the distinctly human is abstracted from all animality, and then explained on its own terms, might seem satisfactory to some. But it transforms the problem of the relation between the human and the animal into a mystery. Thus while Chomsky acknowledges the biological status of language, in Cartesian mode he sidesteps the problem of its natural history; that is, he asserts its biological status abstractly, ahistorically, partially. This slightly controversial claim can, I believe, be demonstrated.

What, then, does Chomsky say of the biological status of language? "The evidence seems compelling, indeed overwhelming, that fundamental aspects of our mental and social life, including language, are determined as part of our biological endowment, not acquired by learning, still less by training, in the course of our experience". Bakunin would have no reason to question this statement. But Chomsky goes on: "It is sometimes argued that even if we succeed in explaining properties of human language and other human capacities in terms of an innate biological endowment, nothing has really been achieved because it remains to explain how the biological endowment developed; the problem is simply displaced, not solved". Perhaps this is a hyperbolical formulation of the quite legitimate objection that Chomsky's biological faculty lacks a natural history; that is to say, that he does achieve something, but in some degree of abstraction. Chomsky recognizes that there is a problem here, but says that "it belongs to a different domain of inquiry" and that, in any case, even in other domains of inquiry, "little is known about these matters". Nevertheless, Chomsky ventures a speculative (by his own admission) answer to "the question of the origin of human language": "It may be that at some remote period a mutation took place that gave rise to the property of discrete infinity [the distinctive characteristic of the language faculty]", etc.[38] This explanation has the air of an attempted justification for Chomsky's qualitative distinction: a quite mysterious mutation may have occurred, bringing about an evolutionary leap such that the result almost comes about *ex nihilo*. (Bookchin, for one, doubts the notion of "random mutational changes", whether conceived as dramatic, large-scale or "gradual point mutations". [Against gradualism, he remarks that "Evolution seems . . . to have been rather . . . sporadic, marked by occasional changes of considerable rapidity, then long periods of stasis". Thus Bookchin, like Bakunin, portrays (natural) history as predominantly static or "positive" (though the potential for change, the "germ of death", is ever present), and occasionally interrupted by radical changes or "negations". These changes, though not mutational, cause qualitative transformations according to Bookchin, but not Bakunin. However, the very denial of mutation and assertion of development in accordance with immanent potential leaves one wondering why Bookchin requires this qualitative element.] He maintains that "evolution includes an immanent striving" and that there is "a directiveness to genetic change itself, not simply a . . . purely fortuitous randomness". Thus, for Bookchin, evolutionary development is conditioned by the "antecedent potentialities that lie behind and within every processual "product""; these "products" never come about *ex nihilo*.[39]) But these are complex issues, and my brief treatment of Chomsky may be a little unfair (though I am convinced there is something in it). To bring this digression into contemporary anarchism to some sort of conclusion, I will say only this: while Bookchin's insistence on qualitative difference is unnecessary (and perhaps unfortunate), Chomsky's insistence (whatever the motivations — and I believe they are sound) is inevitable given his Cartesian starting point.

For Bakunin, then, the organic world is simply the direct development of the non-organic world, complemented by a new ingredient: organic matter. Organic matter itself is simply the product of new causal relations operating at the level and under the conditions of non-organic matter. It is the final determination and negation of (merely) non-organic matter and produces all that constitutes life, animal and otherwise. The human — in all its forms (religious, political, economic, intellectual, and moral) — is similarly the direct development of animality, complemented by an essential new ingredient: *reason*. Reason itself is simply the product of new causal relations operating at the level of and under the conditions of organic matter, specifically the brain. Humanity is therefore the final determination and negation of the (merely) animal in man (*qua* "spiritual" creature).

> Such is the logic of *materialism*.[40] "It is", as Bakunin puts it, "a wholly natural development from the simple to the complex, from the lower to the higher or the inferior to the superior; a development in conformity with all our daily experiences, and consequently in conformity also with our natural logic".[41] Bookchin argues, further (as if by way of explication), that "there is a 'logic' in the development of phenomena, a *general* directiveness that accounts for the fact that the inorganic did become organic, as a result of its *implicit capacity* for organicity; and for the fact that the organic did become more differentiated and metabolically self-maintaining and self-aware, as a result of potentialities that made for highly developed hormonal and nervous systems". Bookchin infers that "there is a natural *tendency* toward greater complexity and subjectivity in first nature, arising from the very interactivity of matter, indeed a *nisus* toward self-consciousness".[42] This con-

cept of directiveness, and ultimate self-consciousness, is crucial to Bookchin — and Bakunin, as we will see below.

The logic of materialism is anything but reductive: in no way does it diminish the status of humanity or vindicate the inhumane; on the contrary, it is idealism that does this. *Idealism* inverts the logic of materialism. Stripping matter of all movement, of its highest developments and manifestations — of all potentiality — and assigning these developments and manifestations — and this potentiality — to nothingness, to the phantom that is Spirit, or Mind, or God, it is forced to move from the complex to the simple, from the "higher" to the "lower", from the "superior" to the "inferior" — contrary to all logic. This move involves a mysterious, that is, an absurd, fall from the celestial to the terrestrial, from the absolute being that is Spirit, or Mind, or God to the nothingness that is nature or matter, which for some strange reason God undertook to create. Belief in this mysterious fall is, Bakunin declares, tantamount to the abdication of human reason; it represents the "triumphant stupidity of faith".[43]

The unity of "reality" (or of nature), then, can be affirmed on the grounds of its materiality: on the grounds that matter is "the true substratum of all existing things". (Of course, Bakunin does not mean to imply the subsistent existence of an abstract material substratum; matter exists only in the concrete, in more or less determined and differentiated forms, though these never exhaust its potential for further determination and differentiation.) Nevertheless, the majority of mankind through the ages has accepted, as a matter of faith, the duality of reality; has distinguished, that is, between the spiritual and the natural, the ideal and the material. In consequence, convinced materialists are compelled to pose the following question:

> *Man forms one whole with universal nature and is but the material product of an indefinite combination of material causes, [so] how did the idea of this duality ... ever come into existence, become established, and become so deeply entrenched in human consciousness?*[44]

Why and how, in other words, did *religion* and its "necessary corollary", *philosophical dualism*, ever come about in the minds of men? To ask this question is to seek the *precise* origin of religion, which, *historically*, is an impossible task since this "origin is lost in the most remote antiquity".[45] In any case, because of the diversity of mankind and because of the complexity of religious consciousness, there simply is no identifiable origin, no *particular*, original historical cause. However, religion is something essentially human: it represents a form of reason, the essential characteristic of humanity. Hence it is possible, by means of a *philosophical* analysis of reason, which is governed by principles which "always and everywhere [remain] the same", to at least speculate on some "*principal phases* observed in . . . religious development", which is what Bakunin, following the examples of Feuerbach and Comte, attempts to do.[46] Bakunin (siding with Feuerbach rather than Bruno Bauer, as we anticipated earlier) stresses the importance of this genetic component of the critique of religion: thus his critique consists not only in arriving at the "scientific [or rational] conviction" that religion is to be negated, but also, in the first place, in a genetico-historical analysis of religion, in a genetic account of the religious absurdity. (This genetico-historical component underlies his critique of the political as well since, on his account, the political absurdity is an "offshoot" of this religious absurdity.)

> As long as we [fail to] account for the manner in which the idea of a supernatural or divine world was produced and had inevitably to be produced in the historical development of human consciousness — scientifically convinced of the absurdity of this idea [as we may be] — we will never succeed in destroying it in the opinion of the majority, because we will never be able to attack it in the very depths of the human being where it had its birth . . . So long as the root of all the absurdities that torment the world — the belief in God — remains intact, it will never fail to sprout new offshoots.[47]

2.6 The Genesis of Religion

Nature, as the totality of interactive and developmental causality, is, Bakunin holds, the eternal, all-powerful creator of all that exists (though, as observed earlier, "created" as such). Among the worlds that it has created is the Earth, with its levels of material development, from the non-organic to the human. Everything, at each of these levels of development, is created, cultivated, nourished, and eventually destroyed (that is to say, transformed into some other material form) in a particular, individual way according to the natural causal relations that envelop it. Nothing that exists can overcome and control these natural relations: nature permeates everything in every way, indeed nature *constitutes* everything. Hence living creatures with any degree of consciousness cannot but be conscious of the supreme influence of nature and of their complete dependence upon it. Bakunin continues:

> Religion . . . is the direct expression of the absolute dependence which all the things and beings that exist in the world find themselves in relation to the Great All, to Nature, to the infinite Totality of real things and beings.[48]

The *consciousness of dependence* upon something supremely powerful (or "omnipotent") is the basis of *religious consciousness*. Indeed, this consciousness of dependence is originally instinctive. Every animal, every living thing, is motivated by the dual instinct for self-preservation and preservation of the species. (This dual instinct seems to be comprised of "two opposed instincts" — the "egoistic" and the "social". But, since "the individual instinct [is] a fundamental condition for the preservation of the species . . . which only lives in [these individuals] and through them", and since the preservation of the species as a whole is ultimately the sole means of preserving the individual, it is evident that these instincts are not opposed.[49]) Hence all animals are preoccupied with the danger presented to them and their species by their natural surroundings and are consequently "in a [state of] incessant, instinctive *fear*". This fear, again, is a consequence of the preservative instinct, itself the pre-conscious knowledge, as it were, of dependence. Fear is therefore the basis of religion: it "constitutes the religious relation with all-powerful nature of the individuals which belong to even the lowest species".[50]

According to Bakunin, man alone, who among all the animals is the only one capable of thought in the fullest sense (of "thought thinking itself"), raises his fear to the level of religious consciousness. With the earliest development of his reason, in his emergence from mere animality, man naturally makes his animal instincts and fears — his animal nature — the object of "nascent reflective thought". At this stage, his instinctive fear is greater than it is in any other animal. This is the case, firstly, because he is relatively poorly equipped for the struggle for self-preservation, not least because his childhood, the period of utmost vulnerability, is unusually long; and, secondly, because his infantile thought, incapable of grasping his unity with the natural world which seems so hostile to him, and thereby alienating him further from it, exaggerates the hostility of nature, representing it, "through the prism of his *imagination* . . . as a somber and mysterious power, infinitely more hostile and menacing than it is in reality".[51]

The first religion, then, is *fetishism*. Fetishism is "the *religion of fear*", grounded on the consciousness of dependence. It is the human form of nature worship, which all animals practice in varying degrees. The domestic dog, most strikingly, vies for the affection of his human master, to whom he has, in ignorance, transferred the fearful power of nature, in much the same way as man prays for the affection of his, having (also in ignorance) transferred the fearful power of nature to his *God-thing*. (The case of the domestic dog was introduced by Hegel in order to refute Friedrich Schleiermacher's equation of "pious feeling", or religious sentiment, with the "pure feeling of dependence" in the first edition of *Der christliche Glaube* (*Christian Faith*) (1821). Thus Schleiermacher's influence on Bakunin here — no doubt via Feuerbach (for reasons that will become apparent below) — is evident. Hegel's response is: "If religion [. . .] is grounded solely on [. . .] the *feeling of* [. . .] *dependence* [. . . ,] a dog would then be the best Christian, for the dog carries this feeling most strongly within itself, and its life is spent primarily in it".[52] (Hegel restates his case later as follows: "If we say that religion rests on this feeling of dependence, then animals would have religion, too, for they feel this dependence".[53]) Whatever the validity of Hegel's criticism of Schleiermacher himself, it certainly would not worry Bakunin, since his naturalistic approach does not require that he make a qualitative distinction between man and (other) animals; that a (non-human) animal might be to some extent religious, or proto-religious, is not unduly problematic for Bakunin.) The difference between these religions is that man, who alone possesses reason, is, unlike the dog, capable of abstract thought. He can conceive of his master, all-powerful nature, as an abstraction and fix that abstraction by assigning a name to it.

Language, the form of human thought, thus plays a crucial role in the development of religion. Language cannot name real objects: it can only refer by name to generalized or abstract conceptualizations of things. (In Feuerbach's words: "The particular which we mean in the context of sensuous certainty is something we cannot even express [as such]".[54] Feuerbach concludes that, in a sense, "we are hampered and misled by the nature of language and of thought itself . . . because every word is a universal, so that language in itself, with its inability to express the particular, is often taken as proof [by idealists, past and present] that the sensuous particular is nonexistent", or that it cannot be claimed to exist independently of thought.[55]) Once the God-thing, the focus of fear, has been established as *this* natural object, say, this tree, it is named, as the object of thought, and thereby becomes an abstraction, *a* natural object, say, a tree, in general. "Thus", concludes Bakunin, "with the first awakening of thought, manifested by speech", that is, manifested linguistically — in other words, with reason — "begins the exclusively human world, the world of abstractions".[56]

2.7 Reason, Freedom, and History

The *faculty of abstraction*, reason, creates for man a "second existence" alongside — or, better still, *within* — his merely natural or animal existence: a *human* existence. (The creation of a second realm of existence here bears a certain resemblance to the emergence of second nature in Bookchin's thought, yet the qualitative transformation implied by Bookchin is an idealization from the Bakuninian point of view.) As well as being what Bakunin calls a living or "natural" entity, then, man is also (in his full potential as such a natural entity) a rational or "cultural" entity. Bakunin adds, "Whatever lives . . . tends to realize itself in the fullness of its being". So, just as man was naturally compelled to develop or realize himself as a natural entity — ultimately becoming a cultural entity — so he is compelled, in accordance with his humanity or human potential, to develop or realize himself as such a cultural entity. (As Feuerbach says: "Man, the complete and true man, is . . . only he who excludes from himself nothing essentially human in man".[57]) And as a cultural or thinking entity, man must achieve self-conscious freedom in order to realize himself. The process toward self-realization is slow and ongoing, and is littered with obstacles, with "all the [theoretical] stupidities and [practical] adversities" man has had to overcome in order "to realize [even] the little [theoretical] reason and [practical] justice which now prevails in the world". Nevertheless, the end of this process remains clear: it is *freedom*. In Bakunin's own words:

> The last phase and the supreme goal of all *human* development is *liberty*.[58]

Man's past is in *animality*, in "slavish" (or un-self-conscious) obedience to nature ([including society] the potential of which is as yet unfulfilled). His future — negatively or antithetically conceived — is in *humanity*, in self-conscious freedom (in the fulfillment of natural potential — nature being understood as, in Bookchin's words, "a nascent domain of freedom, selfhood, and consciousness"[59]). Man's present existence exhibits the tension between this past, and what he has retained from it, and the future, and what he (actively) projects into it. Thus the antagonism between the past, which is characterized by "slavery" (real slavery in terms of social history), and the future, which promises freedom — in other words, this dialectic — is the basis of the drama that constitutes human existence or *history* — in all its forms: religious, political, economic, intellectual, and moral. (Bookchin concurs with this broad characterization: "History is the painful movement of human beings in extricating themselves from animal existence, of the emergence of tensions from a combination of non-human and human attributes, and of progressively advancing toward a more universally human state of affairs, however irregular and unsteady this advance may be".[60] Which is to say that Bookchin, like Bakunin, acknowledges that this process is arduous, periodically regressive (though, as we have seen, regression or "reaction" may, objectively, have its "revolutionary" role to play), and not *strictly* or *narrowly* teleological or predetermined in any speculative sense.) It is upon this conception of historical progress, and of freedom as the *end* of history, that Bakunin bases his critique of, for example, Rousseauean liberalism, "according [to which] natural or wild man [that is, "primitive" or "animal" man] alone is completely free".[61] This seminal act by Jean-Jacques Rousseau of locating the historical end at the beginning of human history — in some primitive "Golden Age" — is quite literally reactionary. Hence Bakunin describes Rousseau as "the true creator of modern reaction".[62]

The dynamic principle within this historical process, the concrete mode of practico-historical transformation, is, according to Bakunin, the *principle of revolt*, which together with the *principle of human animality* and the *principle of reason* constitutes the (distinctive) human essence — at least in its abstract expression. (It has been said, therefore, that Bakunin "expounded . . . revolt as an anthropological principle".[63] An anthropological principle it may be, but not in an anthropocentric sense since it is a principle that, as we will see, is not qualitatively distinct from the principle of animal will. In other words, it is an anthropological principle with a natural history [thus a naturalistic principle], not an anthropocentric principle [such as the metaphysico-liberal principle of free will, which is basically how Marx saw it, thus accusing Bakunin

of voluntarism. Bakunin, however, rejects this very principle in no uncertain terms: *"we absolutely deny free will*, in the sense attached to the
term by theology, metaphysics, and jurisprudence; that is to say, in the
sense of the spontaneous self-determination of the individual will of
man (for instance, when he enters into some imaginary past social con-
tract), independent of all influence, natural or social"[64]].) The principle
of reason, in its theoretical form, is concretely embodied or realized in
science (or what Bakunin calls "universal science"). The principle of rebellion, the practical fulfillment of reason, is concretely embodied or
realized in (actual) *freedom*. And the principle of human animality,
which is the fundamental principle underlying all others (as naturalism
requires), is said by Bakunin to be concretely embodied or realized in
"*social and private economy*".[65] This I regard as a quasi-Marxian lapse on
Bakunin's part; that is, an isolated (though not unique) statement contradicting his naturalistic critique of Marxianism (and, to put it controversially, as I will formulate this issue below, other Kantian or anthropocentric philosophies).

In any case, man himself secures the development of human existence, again in all its forms, as he overcomes all impediments to self-
conscious freedom. He is compelled to overcome these impediments
and to realize himself. Like all animals, he is driven by the instinct to
act in accordance with his natural needs. This instinct is manifest in all
animals as *will*. It is purely instinctive in "lesser" species. Man, though,
possessing reason, by means of which he can consider and order his
own real needs, can be said to possess a "*free will*". Of course, his will is
only relatively free; man cannot arbitrarily determine nature or the totality of interactive and developmental causality. Nevertheless, only
man can "regulate and modify [his natural urges] by making them conform . . . to what at different epochs of intellectual and moral development he calls just and beautiful".[66]

Reason, then, is the means or, if you like, the faculty by which
man achieves the consciousness of freedom. "Free will", the practical
dimension of reason, is (within the natural limits that are imposed on

it) the means by which he secures actual freedom. (We may say therefore that man's will is the basis of the principle of revolt, which is
therefore ultimately grounded on the natural faculty of reason.) Hence,
reason is the emancipatory force in history. Since man alone possesses
reason, it can be concluded that freedom is the concern and goal of man
alone — indeed, that freedom is the "destiny" of mankind, the fulfillment of human potential. (Hegel had expressed this idea in the following terms: "Just as it is only the human being that thinks, and not the
animal, so it is only the human being that has freedom; and then only
because he is capable of thinking".) History emerges, then, as the rational progress of mankind toward freedom. (Hegel had abstractly expressed this idea in the following terms: "it is Spirit, and the process of
its development, that is the substance of history . . . freedom is the only
truth of Spirit . . . [therefore] history is the progress in the consciousness of freedom".) This process is gradual and distinguished by ever-
increasing degrees of freedom. Bakunin's attempt to trace this process
from the philosophical or rational perspective, and to make explicit its
implicit direction and potential, that is, to determine its direction and
to outline the stages in the movement toward its goal and the fulfillment of its potential, might be referred to as a *phenomenology of freedom*. It
is not a phenomenology of Spirit since Bakunin rejects the Hegelian
attempt to spiritualize or idealize the material and the natural, seeking
instead (with Feuerbach and Comte as we will see below) to material-
ize or naturalize Spirit or Freedom. Thus Bakunin (like Feuerbach) rejects, or inverts, the Hegelian claim that "While matter has its
'substance' outside itself, Spirit is autonomous and self-sufficient, a Be-
ing-by-itself [*Bei-sich-selbst-sein*]".[67]

Religious consciousness is, for Bakunin, merely the first concrete
step in the direction of self-conscious freedom: it is the dawning of self-
conscious freedom, the primordial negation of animality — of natural
"slavery" — and affirmation of humanity — of freedom. However,
though religion is in this sense a form of reason, it is in fact "*reason...in
the form of unreason*". It is *not reason "in the form of reasoned reflection which*

recognizes and is conscious of its own activity"; rather, *it is reason in the form of "imaginative reflection"*, as has already been suggested. As a result, religious emancipation from natural "slavery" is at the same time enslaving; thus Bakunin speaks of "the [new] slavery . . . of religion".[68] As an inadequate expression of the rational, then, man must necessarily negate religion if he is to attain a greater degree of rationality and move toward freedom. Bakunin takes up his analysis of this process once again.

2.8 Fetishism, Polytheism, and Monotheism

As we have already ascertained, for Bakunin, the first religion is fetishism, the religion of fear. Primitive man, conscious of all-powerful nature and of his complete dependence upon it, makes this all-powerful force — which he attaches to a particular natural object, the God-thing, by means of his imagination, and generalizes, that is, names, by means of language — the object of his infantile thought. The natural object, fetishized, then becomes a supernatural object. It is in this way that reason, in the form of imaginary reflection or unreason, creates religion in its purest, most unrefined form. Consequently, fetishism is to be understood as "the most religious, that is to say the most absurd, of religions".[69] However, primitive though this religion is, Bakunin contends that (unspecified, though conceivable) traces of it remain in the practice of Catholicism.

With fetishism, the first major step in the development of religion is taken. As always, this first developmental step is the most difficult but also the most important since, once taken, "the rest unfolds naturally as a necessary consequence" of it. The first step is thus irreversible and conclusive. In the case of religion, this vital first step "was to posit a divine [or supernatural] world as such, outside the real [or natural] world".[70] Man, lacking the consciousness of natural unity, thereby severed the imaginary, that is, the primitively rational, and the real, or the ideal and the material, not realizing that in each case the former is simply the "highest manifestation" of the latter, and not qualitatively distinct from it.

The second religion — or rather a religion related to the first and generally coexistent with it — is, according to Bakunin, *sorcery*. Sorcery is scarcely any more adequate as an expression of the rational than is fetishism, but it seems more natural to us because it is still common. We are accustomed to sorcerers, to all manner of spiritualists from clairvoyants to priests, who declare themselves "*subducers [forceurs]* of Divinity, which submits to their enchantments" and responds to their "mysterious formulas". The only difference between modern sorcery — for example, the sorcery of the Catholic priest — and that of the primitive sorcerer is that the God of the former has achieved — through theological speculation — a greater degree of complexity. The god of the primitive sorcerer, by contrast, exists only as an essentially indeterminate "All-powerful", totally lacking moral and intellectual content. Nevertheless, the practice of primitive sorcery reveals much about the character of its god: "it is egotistical and vain; it loves flattery, genuflection, the humiliation and immolation of men, their worship and their sacrifices, and it cruelly persecutes and punishes those who do not want to submit: the rebels, the proud, the impious".[71] This, according to Bakunin, is the nature of all deities, chiefly, as we will see, Jehovah, God of the Jews and Father of the Christians.

The god of primitive sorcery is present only as mediated by the sorcerer. That is to say, there is a certain identity of god and sorcerer: the sorcerer *is* God; he is effectively the *man-God*. But with the development of the believer's mental or critical faculties, and the inability of the primitive sorcerer to cope with this development, the contradiction between the sorcerer's roles as limited man and all-powerful god becomes apparent. He cannot, therefore, be regarded as integrated man-God, as identical to or one with God. He "remains . . . a supernatural being, but only for an instant, when he is possessed".[72]

Neither the fetish (the God-thing) nor the sorcerer (the man-God) is capable of containing the divine: both are formally inadequate to their content. Therefore, both fetishism and sorcery must be overcome in the development of religious consciousness. That is, the divine must be sought outside both the supernatural object and the supernatural man. Therefore, "Man . . . seeks Divinity far away from him *but still among things that have real existence:* in the forest, on a mountain, in a river, and later still in the sun, in the moon, in the sky. [Thus] Religious thought begins to embrace the universe".[73]

This brings us to the second religion proper: *polytheism.* Bakunin offers little by way of an introductory remark on polytheism. However, in Comtean terms (and, as we will see, it is largely in these terms that Bakunin presents his argument), polytheism is distinguished from fetishism in the following way: whereas fetishism conceives particular natural objects as being alive or supernatural, and divine in that sense, polytheism conceives natural objects as being inert, but subject to the will of divine agents, which govern objects of particular kinds. (This recognition of *kinds* of objects demonstrates the relative rationality of polytheism — relative, that is, to fetishism.) Thus, while fetishism divinizes the natural object, polytheism externalizes the divinity, actually conceives it as being separate from the natural object and related to it only insofar as it governs it. Nevertheless, because of this relation, which is essential to the divinity, Bakunin contends that "The pagan gods were not yet *strictly* the negation of real things; they were only a fantastic exaggeration of them".[74] But religion, having posited the divine outside the real, that is, having posited the material outside itself, inevitably went on to negate the material, to reduce it to nothingness by denying its essential motion and energy and attributing its manifestations and potentialities to the (necessarily singular) absolute creator of all things — God — from whom all things *emanate.* Therefore, the second major step in the development of religion encompasses its historic development from polytheism through to Christianity: it is the transition from the materialistic polytheism of the pagans to the spiritualistic monotheism of the Christians.

The third religion, which is, more accurately, only the culmination of the second, is, according to Bakunin, *pantheism.* With pantheism, man finally begins to transcend religious consciousness in its immediacy. Pantheism represents man's emerging consciousness of the *totality* of real things — of real things in their interaction, of universal causality, of nature as such. Such consciousness represents in itself a development of reason, the faculty of abstraction, such that it becomes capable of grasping, albeit in a limited way, the identity of the universe in its difference and the difference of the universe in its identity; such that it becomes capable of conceiving of nature as such. Bakunin adds, "it is . . . man's thought which creates [the *idea* of this] unity and transfers it to the diversity of the external world". The identity or unity is thus (in the pre-scientific epoch) abstract; the abstracting faculty is thus unifying. In the act of unification, consequently, something is abstracted, something is lost: diversity, the essence of life. The greater the degree of abstraction, therefore, the more that is lost of life, of the diversity of concrete reality. As we will see, abstraction pushed to its limit, divested of all real content, unifies everything in indeterminate being — that is, nothingness — that is, God. In Bakunin's words:

> *God is then the absolute abstraction*, the product of human thought itself, which, as the power of abstraction, has passed beyond all known beings, all the existing worlds, and, thus having divested itself from all real content . . . poses before itself — without, however, recognizing itself in this sublime nudity — as the *One and Only Supreme Being*.[75]

The development of reason, by virtue of which the pantheist conceives of nature, enables man, by making himself the object of his own thought, to abstract his "inner" or spiritual life, as a thinking entity, from his "outer" or corporeal life, as a living entity — enables him, that is, to distinguish between body and "soul". Ignorant as yet of the nature and limitations of his thought and will, as well as of the fecundity of matter, he necessarily conceives of the soul as master of the body. Transferring this abstract duality into the natural world as a whole, man "begins to seek the invisible soul of this universe of appearance".

Nature, as Bakunin understands it, is thereby split in two, so that it consists now of two empty abstractions: *vile matter* and *pure spirit*. This is the critical moment in the transition from materialistic polytheism, or primitive religion, to spiritualistic monotheism, or what Bakunin calls "true Religion", and, with it, true theology.[76]

Primitive religion, grounded on the consciousness of dependence upon some almighty power, and guided by the imaginative reflection of man, located this power, the divine, within the domain of nature, in a particular natural object or in a particular man or even in abstractly conceived nature as a whole. In the aftermath of pantheism, however, the divine has been spiritualized in the manner outlined above; it has become "an invisible and extra-mundane spiritual God". Furthermore, the divinity has been universalized. The limited divinities of primitive religion, condemned to share the natural order with their non-divine counterparts, have taken to the heavens, have merged to constitute the (necessarily) singular, all-powerful, all-creating "Being of Beings . . . the great All".[77] This is the basis of the third religion proper: *monotheism*.

The *universal* and *spiritual* God of monotheism is a product of naive reason, of human thought which lacks the consciousness of its own abstracting activity. Unaware of the "subjective origin" of God, then, man inevitably considers Him an "objective being". Unaware of the unity of all-powerful, all-embracing nature, man posits all-powerful, all-creating God in opposition to intrinsically worthless material nature. Consequently, natural laws, properly understood as laws relating to processes inherent in nature, come to be understood as "manifestations of the Divine Will, God's commandments imposed from above upon nature as well as upon man". (As Feuerbach expresses this process, "Radically distinguished from nature, God becomes a despot, ruling over the world, over nature" (though, remarkably, he "governs entirely in accordance with natural laws", relative as they are).[78]) Monotheistic man therefore accepts God as his creator and master. Bakunin claims, and will later demonstrate, that he has thus "laid the foundation for his own political and social slavery".[79]

With monotheism, God, the creation of human thought, is transformed into the creator of all things — the Supreme Being — and man duly worships Him. All the qualities that man discovers both in himself and in everything around him must therefore be attributed to this Supreme Being, of whom, by definition, there is nothing (or no positive quality) which cannot be predicated. Yet, as we have said, God, the so-called Supreme Being, is in fact the product of man's thought, its ultimate abstraction — or more precisely, the "power of abstraction [i.e. reason] positing itself as its own object". In other words, God is, in himself, indeterminate being, nothingness. It is only by assuming all determinations, by appropriating all perceived natural powers and human virtues (including those that created him), that he can be represented as Supreme Being. Hence, as Feuerbach himself might have put it, "anthropomorphism [is] the very essence of all religion" — or, at least, the consummate religion.[80] Maintaining the Feuerbachian tone, Bakunin writes elsewhere:

> [T]he religious heaven is nothing but a mirage in which man, exalted by ignorance and faith, discovers his own image, but magnified and inverted — that is, *divinized*. The history of religions, of the birth, rise, and fall of the gods who have succeeded one another in human belief, is therefore nothing but the development of the collective intelligence and [self-] consciousness of mankind.[81]

Bakunin insists, however, that God does not just appropriate the human: he also defiles it, and thereby sets it against itself. Reason, then, the essence of humanity, its means "of recognizing the truth", is transformed by religion into divine reason, the means of consecrating the absurd. Similarly, love, the basis of human solidarity, is transformed by religion into divine love and religious charity, historically "the bane of humanity". And justice, the basis of human equality, is transformed by

religion into divine justice or, in theological terms, divine grace, the basis of human conquest and privilege, as will become apparent. Nevertheless, it is only through religion that truth, equality, justice, and liberty emerge in the first instance — but submerged in falsehood, ine-
quality, injustice, and slavery. Thus, while religion is historically necessary (to rational development) and is by no means "an absolute evil", as
an obstacle to man's ultimate freedom and humanity, it must be overcome.

> Through religion, the human animal, in emerging from [mere]
> bestiality, takes the first step toward humanity; but so long as
> it remains religious it will never attain its aim, for all religion
> condemns it to absurdity . . .[82]

Religion in fact condemns man to slavery — to a new slavery at
the hands of the absolute being. This absolute being, this divine authority, sanctions all supposedly legitimate human authority and is therefore the true founder of the State. God, having appropriated human morality, leaves man himself without morality — that is, renders him incapable of distinguishing between good and evil. For that reason, God
himself must impose a morality upon man and must impose order upon
human society. It is the task of the elect, God's (self-appointed) chosen
legislators, to preach this morality and to maintain this order which,
issuing from God himself, must of course be adhered to unquestion-
ingly. Or, as St. Paul warns, "Every person must submit to the authori-
ties in power, for *all authority comes from God*".[83] (It is at the level of revolutionary consciousness that this principle of authority — religious,
political, and scientific — is finally challenged.)

Bakunin insists that this *pernicious relation of religion and human authority*, all too convenient for those who govern and all too inconvenient
for those who are governed, must be examined closely. Since God is
merely the product of human thought pushed to its extreme, that is,
since he is in himself the emptiest of abstractions, nothingness, "He
can . . . establish nothing", impose no morality, dictate no social order,

or, indeed, appoint any legislators or rulers and ground their authority. The sole basis of human morality and social order is humanity itself, which, as ever at the level of religious consciousness, "gave, while it believed itself to be the recipient".[84] The legitimation of human authority by divine authority is therefore merely a fantastic self-legitimation or mystification of human authority. Bakunin's conclusion on the mystifying role of religion is the following:

> . . . divinity, once established on its celestial throne, has become the bane of humanity and the ally of every tyrant, every charlatan, and every tormentor and exploiter of the popular masses.[85]

2.9 The Development of Christianity

Christianity, together with the "doctrinaire and deistic metaphysics" that is founded upon it ("at bottom a disguised theology [*une théologie masquée*, to be "unmasked" as such]", Bakunin remarks in Left Hegelian fashion), is — historically — the greatest obstacle to man's self-conscious freedom. This explains why all modern statesmen, who are seemingly neither theologians nor metaphysicians, and most likely are non-believers, "passionately and fiercely" defend Christianity: the so-called "religion of love and forgiveness" which is actually "founded upon blood and historically baptized in it". Thus Bakunin describes Christianity as "the religion *par excellence*": the most impoverishing and enslaving religion of all.[86] For this reason, it is necessary for him to trace its development in some detail — in line with his genetico-critical method.

He identifies four key factors in the development of Christianity. (We ought to bear in mind that the first three factors are three important elements in the transition from nature religion to spiritual religion proper, and determinate religion to the consummate religion, in Hegel's lectures on the philosophy of religion.[87]) The first of these is the *Judaic* factor. Bakunin characterizes Jehovah, sole God of the Jews (and Father of the Christians), in two ways. Firstly, this god is "an excessively national God", the god of a chosen people alone. And, secondly, he is, like all primitive deities, a primarily material god — one still rooted in nature — who undertook to convince his followers with crude "material arguments". Indeed, as Bakunin points out, such an existence does not seem to rule out the existence of other deities, though Jehovah jealously demands absolute allegiance in the First Commandment, where he says: "I am the Lord thy God [and] Thou shalt have no other god *before* me" (or, as Bakunin's French version has it: "*Je suis ton Dieu et tu n'adoreras pas d'autres Dieux que moi*"). In fact, Jehovah admits to this jealousy in the Second Commandment. Jehovah, as a national and material God, then, is merely the "first draft" of the Supreme Being of spiritualistic monotheism. This God must, by definition, be the complete negation of matter. It must also be universal; it must be the sole God, a God for all humanity. Hence it is necessary for the development of the Supreme Being of Christianity, firstly, that metaphysics arise in order "to spiritualize the gross Jehovah of the Jews", and, secondly, that humanity be realized in place of multiple nationalities.[88]

The second key factor in the development of Christianity is the *Hellenic* factor. It was the ancient Greeks who created metaphysics and who thereby facilitated the spiritualization of Jehovah. As Bakunin puts it: "In relation to spiritualism, the Greek metaphysicians were, much more than the Jews, the creators of the Christian God. The Jews added only the brutal personality of their Jehovah". The Greek philosophers, then, took the religion of the Greek poets as their starting point; however, to their credit, they did not generate a theology from it, that is, they did not attempt to reconcile its gods with reason. Rather, they "addressed themselves directly to the *divine idea*", the idea of divinity or the divine order as such, which confronted them "as a tradition, as a sentiment, [and] as a habit of thought". Their project, the metaphysical project, consisted therefore in the development and perfection — the complete spiritualization — of this divine idea. Thus the intuitive Socratic quest for self-knowledge "in fact amounted to nothing", since the

Greek philosophers (Socrates himself excepted, it might be argued) remained unaware of the subjective origin of the divine idea that preoccupied them.[89] Greek metaphysics, then, produced a conception of divinity as spiritualistic but impersonal. It was in conjunction with the imaginary god Jehovah that this divine idea was personalized.

The third key factor in the development of Christianity is the *Roman* factor. The brutal conquests of the Romans, their destruction of national institutions and negation of cultural differences (including "national forms of worship [*cultes nationaux*]"[90]), "created . . . the first — doubtless entirely gross and negative — draft of humanity".[91] This negative realization of humanity as a homogeneous conquered mass was the basis of the universal religion of Christianity. (Thus Theodosius I eventually prescribed Christianity as the official religion of the Empire in 392.) Jehovah, personal God of the Jews, was therefore spiritualized by the Greek metaphysicians and universalized by the Romans.

The fourth key factor in the development of Christianity is the specifically *Christian* factor: Jesus Christ. The three previous factors Bakunin regards as "historical elements", that is, "*general* conditions of an actual [historical] development". Such elements must be supplemented or, as Bakunin puts it, impregnated by "a living, spontaneous fact" if they are to result in concrete "historical transformations". In the case of Christianity, this fact was "the propaganda, martyrdom, and death of Jesus Christ". (There is a suggestion here of David Friedrich Strauss' influence on Bakunin. Elsewhere, at any rate, Bakunin credits Strauss with the interpretation of the historical Christ as an "actual historical figure . . . endowed with great genius" who "left after [him] a profound impression on history" by the force of his character — together, of course, with the needs and expectations of his contemporaries (as produced by "general historical conditions" of the kind that Bakunin mentions) and the efforts of his disciples to perpetuate his teachings orally and, later, in the writing of the Gospels.[92]) The Christ of the Gospels, insofar as it is possible to say anything about him, was undoubtedly a friend of the oppressed, to whom he promised eternal life, and an enemy of oppressors, by whom he was eventually crucified. It was in this sense that Christ inspired "the first awakening, the first elementary revolt of the [proto-]proletariat"; and it is in this inspiration that the "great honor [and] incontestable merit" of Christianity lies.[93]

Nevertheless, the initial success of Christianity, its appeal as a *form* of revolt, is attributed by Bakunin to the severe intellectual and political oppression of the ancient world. He adds that there must have been "an almost absolute impoverishment of mind" in this epoch for it to have embraced Christianity, which, again, as a *form* of revolt, represented "not just the negation of all the political, social, and religious institutions of antiquity", but also "the absolute inversion of common sense [and] all human reason" — as spiritualistic monotheism necessarily does. In other words, *Christianity expresses the rational principle of revolt in merely intuitive form*; or, Christianity is an inadequate form of revolt since, as Bakunin will argue, it contradicts both reason and freedom. Bakunin concludes that Christianity spoke to the ancient proletariat's "heart, not to its mind", which had not yet developed to the point where it could recognize the absurdity of its faith. While the initial success of Christianity, then, is attributable to the slavery of the ancient world, its continued success was assured by "the invasion of the Barbarians", who, for all their admirable "natural force", were as blind as the ancient "proletariat" to the absurdity of Christianity, and were therefore ever susceptible to conversion.[94]

Christianity, thus established, and upheld by the might of the Church, flourished for a millennium. The Church being the arena of discourse and the sole educator, Christian dogma remained unopposed. Hence the "double belief" in the existence of God and the duality of reality was entirely dominant in this period and became "the ideal basis" of European civilization — of the public and private existence of every class.[95] This double belief, yet to be shaken off once and for all, was challenged for the first time by the heroes of the *Renaissance*, such as Lucilio Vanini, Giordano Bruno, and Galileo. The movement of the free mind initiated by the Renaissance, and incorporating the Reformation, the Enlightenment, and the Great French Revolution, has, Bakunin says, continued to the present day and culminated in the proclamation of atheism and materialism. Nevertheless, the Christian absurdity has persisted in the form of what Bakunin calls *modern idealism*, represented by notable reactionaries, as he sees them, like Rousseau, Jules Michelet, and Mazzini, and it therefore requires further examination.

2.10 Christianity, Reason, and Freedom

Bakunin makes two fundamental claims with regard to Christianity. Firstly, he claims that, theoretically, it implies *the abdication of human reason* (that is, that Christianity is a form of theoretical or intellectual slavery). And secondly, he claims that, practically, it is *the negation of human liberty* (that is, that Christianity is a form of practical or real slavery). Of course, this is really one and the same claim: that the Christian religion implies the abdication of humanity (that is, that Christianity is the negation of theoretical and practical freedom). We have already partially examined the theoretical dimension of this claim in the context of Bakunin's analysis of monotheism. Briefly, we concluded that the universal and spiritual God of monotheism is the ultimate product of the faculty of abstraction positing itself as its own object; that is, that this God is, in itself, nothingness, and that it only determines itself by appropriating the human, principally human reason (the essence of the human), which thereby becomes divine reason, the antithesis of human reason — meaning that human reason, at the level of religious consciousness, negates itself. However, it is the practical dimension of this claim that Bakunin emphasizes, declaring his intention "to treat this question . . . solely from the point of view of its social and moral utility".[96]

In what sense, then, is Christianity the negation of human liberty? The Christian God, having appropriated the human, indeed the natural as a whole as Bakunin understands it, establishes himself as All and thereby reduces his true creator, man, and his ultimate basis, nature, to nothingness — that is, to indeterminate beings in themselves. With this miraculous transformation of the created into the creator, nature and man become dependent upon God, who alone has the power to determine them, to lend them a little of *his* beauty, to grant them a little of *his* justice, and so on. Hence God becomes their master and they become his slaves. The ramifications of this relation are, of course, highly significant. In Bakunin's words: "Slaves of God, men must also be slaves of the Church and the State, *insofar as the latter is consecrated by the Church.* [The Church naturally consecrates itself on God's behalf.] Christianity has understood this better than all the other religions that exist or have existed".[97] Religion therefore underpins the political so that human authority (at least *insofar as it attempts to legitimate itself* and thereby uphold and extend its dominion indefinitely) *originally* springs from divine authority.

Bakunin's first proposition here, then, is that the existence of God implies the slavery of man. However, as we have seen earlier, Bakunin also maintains that man, as a rational being, *needs* to be free, that freedom is his peculiar object. Hence Bakunin's famous anti-Voltairean slogan: "*if God really existed, it would be necessary to eliminate him*". Incorporating the second proposition, that man needs to be free, then, Bakunin — typically — expresses his argument in the form of a dilemma: "If God exists, man is a slave; man can [and] must be free, so God does not exist. I defy anyone to escape this circle; and now let all choose". In response to the mysterious claim by modern idealists that God is in fact "animated by the most tender love for human liberty", Bakunin argues that a master, liberal or otherwise, remains precisely that: a master, an enslaver of all beneath him. In any case, Bakunin continues, if this liberty-loving God of modern idealism really existed, the "single means [by which he could] serve human liberty [would be] by ceasing to exist".[98]

Christianity, as the abdication of human reason, represents the disavowal of the logic of materialism (that is, as we have seen, the logic of natural development from "simple" matter to its complex manifestations) and the affirmation of the illogic of idealism (that is, as we have seen, the supposed logic of causal degeneration from the Absolute Being that is God to the nothingness that is matter). And yet, as the negation of human liberty, Christianity also represents "the triumph of the most crass and brutal materialism" over human idealism.[99] That is to say, the illogic of Christian idealism produces the crudest materialism. (Bakunin will argue, by extension, that the illogic of Marxian idealism produces the crudest despotism.)

Bakunin renders this conclusion more generally in the following manner: "*theoretical idealism incessantly and inevitably transforms into practical materialism*" (while "theoretical materialism necessarily leads to practical idealism"[100]). He proposes four examples. First, that of ancient *Roman* civilization, which, in contrast to ancient Greek civilization (which was "more materialistic . . . in its [religious and philosophical] point of departure" yet "more humanly ideal in its results"), was "more abstractly ideal in its point of departure" yet "more brutal in its consequences". Roman civilization assigned man the ideal status of citizen while subjecting him to the brutal materialism of Caesarism, the forerunner of modern statism. The second example is that of modern *German* civilization, which, in contrast to modern Italian civilization, for example (which initiated the movement of the free mind), represents, for all its philosophical idealism, rampant statism. The third example is that of the *Catholic Church*.

> What is there more sublime, in the ideal sense, more disinterested, more detached from all the interests of this earth, than the doctrine of Christ preached by that Church? And [yet] what is there more brutally materialistic than the constant practice of that same Church . . .?[101]

The Catholic Church was, according to Bakunin, the first to fully recognize and take advantage of the material relation between power, wealth, and spiritual faith, between political oppression, economic exploitation, and spiritual propaganda. It recognized fully that power generates wealth, that wealth yields power, and that together power and wealth (which are properly inseparable, "the two inseparable terms of the reign of the divine ideality on earth",[102] that is, of divine authority in human form [again, for Bakunin, unlike Marx, despotism and exploitation tend to be as one]) assure the success of "Christian propaganda". Hence the Catholic Church dedicated itself to assuming a corporate structure, wherein wealth flows from the broadest possible bottom to the narrowest possible top, and absolute authority is imposed from above — all in the name of God's will, needless to say.

This brings us to the fourth example, that of *Protestantism*. Protestantism understood the relation between power, wealth, and spiritual faith as well as Catholicism did. But Protestantism expressed an aversion to centralized authority, or at least that of the Catholic power or spiritual power as such, which formerly had a tendency to conflict with temporal power. The Protestant Reformation, this merely religious, this partial revolution (for all its idealism), stood for the material-coercive interests of this temporal power — for its separation or independence from the spiritual power which formerly dominated it (though never entirely), and for the domination by this power of the Church (such that the temporal power ultimately absorbs [for its own purposes], though never negates, the spiritual power altogether, such that statism achieves what Catholicism never quite did — it becomes absolute or absolutely despotic). Bakunin writes: "The Reformation put an end to this struggle [between Church and pre-modern "State"] by proclaiming the independence of states. The sovereign's right was recognized as proceeding immediately from God, without the intervention of the Pope or any other priest, and, thanks to this wholly heavenly origin, it was naturally declared absolute. In this manner the edifice of monarchical despotism was erected on the ruins of Church despotism. The Church, having been the master, became the servant of the State [became, in effect, a political or temporal institution]".[103] The Reformation represented, then, a mere shift in the locus of power, the conquest of power by a different — a non-sacerdotal — class. This class set about instituting a State structure identical to that of the Church: a corporate structure, wherein wealth flows from the broadest possible bottom to the narrowest possible top, and absolute authority is imposed from above — in the name of the absolute right of the State. As a challenge to authority, Protestantism had some merit as far as Bakunin is concerned; however, its historical consequence was an absolute State despotism.

In any case, Bakunin deduces from the latter examples that the idealism of Christianity produces the crude materialism of the Church, in the case of Catholicism, and (subsequent to the French Revolution) the bourgeoisie, in the case of Protestantism. In both cases, this practical materialism is the privilege of the few, be it the papacy and the clergy or the wealthy and the propertied. The grand ideals of Christianity, on the other hand, are for the politically oppressed and economically exploited majority, which is promised due compensation in the hereafter for its consequent material sufferings. As Bakunin explains, Christianity functions as "the eternal mirage which leads the masses off in search of divine treasures, while, much more restrained, the dominant class contents itself with sharing among all its members — most unequally . . . and always to the advantage of the [already] advantaged — the paltry goods of the earth and the spoils of the people, naturally including their political and social liberty".[104]

Christianity is therefore associated by Bakunin, as a form of "theoretical or divine idealism", with the abdication of human reason, and, as a form of practical materialism, with the negation of human liberty. As a form of theoretical idealism, there are a number of implicit contradictions within it which Bakunin, having merely suggested, seeks to make explicit. He begins by accepting the logic of materialism, which — as the logic of natural, progressive development from "simple" matter to its complex manifestations, including humanity, from which emerges the rational and the ideal — alone is coherent. The logic of idealism is the absurd inversion of this logic: it is the supposed logic of causal, qualitative degeneration, of counter-intuitive — indeed counter-scientific — regression, from the complex to the simple, from the ideal to the material, from Absolute Being to nothingness. Accordingly, history is, for the idealist, "nothing but a *continuous fall*" within which the Absolute Being "is flattened out, loses consciousness of itself and never recovers it".[105] This disoriented divinity is, nevertheless, given to the miraculous.

Quite how and why this singular, universal Absolute Being, as pure spirit, managed to spin matter out of itself, to act upon it as something qualitatively distinct, and to combine it with the spiritual in man, remains unknown — as does quite how matter contains and thereby limits spirit in man. As does quite how the spiritual becomes individualized and therefore divisible in man. As does quite how and why the Absolute Being would itself "become flesh", and yet remain one with itself. These are simply examples of "those questions which faith alone, that passionate and stupid affirmation of the absurd, can resolve". More fundamental, anyway, is the following question: given that "man has neither seen nor can see pure spirit, detached from all material form, existing separately from any animal body", why should anybody believe in the spiritual (so conceived) at all — let alone accept it as the basis of "legitimate" authority?[106]

Thus the Christian faith, in conclusion, denotes the following: firstly, theoretically or intellectually, "the sacrifice of logic, of human reason, [and] the renunciation of science"; and, secondly, practically, collusion with the "oppressors and exploiters of the popular masses". (These two themes further demonstrate the influence of Feuerbach, who had already argued that religion implies both the abdication of reason ("To place anything in God, or to derive anything from God [such as political authority], is nothing more than to withdraw it from the test of reason, to institute it as indubitable, unassailable, sacred, without rendering an account *why*") and the negation of liberty ("wherever right [say, the absolute right of the State] is made dependent on divine authority, the most immoral, unjust, infamous things can be justified and established").[107] This side of Feuerbach's thought reveals a radicalism with which he is rarely credited.) Bakunin imagines that these two reasons "should be sufficient to drive every great mind

[and] every great heart from [divine] idealism".[108] How is it then that the Christian absurdity retains its appeal, not only for the weak-minded, but also for so many intellectual giants? To answer this question, Bakunin must pose the *why* of Christian faith.

2.11 Forms of Christian Faith

Bakunin identifies three forms of Christian faith and characterizes each form in terms of its particular cause or motivation. The first form is the faith of *the masses*, which has two causes. The first cause is the *ignorance* of the masses. This ignorance is inevitable given their traditional upbringing, their poverty, and the best efforts of Church and State (both of which recognize the faith of the masses as essential to their own survival) to promote and reinforce it. In general, the conditions of the masses are detrimental to critical thought and turn the Christian faith into little more than a "mental and moral habit". As Bakunin puts it:

> Crushed by their daily labor, deprived of leisure, of intellectual intercourse, of reading, in short of almost all the means and the better part of the stimulants that develop reflective thought in men, the people generally accept religious traditions, in their entirety, without criticism [*sans critique*] ...[109]

The second cause — obviously closely related to the first — is the actual *economic condition* of the masses. (Which is not to say that the economic factor determines religion as such; it simply accounts for the persistence of certain forms of religious faith at a certain stage of historical development. But this debate must be deferred.) More specifically, it is the masses' natural or instinctive urge to escape their economic condition, their "instinctive and passionate protest ... against ... a wretched existence", which reduces them, "intellectually and morally as well as materially, to the minimum of human existence ... without horizon, without outlet, without even a future if one is to believe the [bourgeois] economists". (Thus Bakunin, echoing Feuerbach, states that religion, though it may be "an aberration of the mind", is actually, in this class at least, the product of "a profound discontentment at heart".)[110]

Three means of escaping their "wretched existence" are available to the masses. The first two, between which there is little difference, are the tavern, a terrestrial church, and the Church, a celestial tavern. The relation between these means of escape is defined by Bakunin as follows: "In church and tavern alike [the people] forget, at least momentarily, their hunger, their oppression, and their humiliation, and they try to dull the memory of their daily afflictions, in the one with mindless faith and in the other with wine. One form of intoxication is as good as the other".[111] (Marx's famous "opium of the people" line comes to mind.) The third means of escape is Social Revolution, the only adequate means, since it consists not in intoxicated oblivion but in the complete negation of present conditions and — representing nothing more or less than the direct antithesis of these conditions — the creation of a "harmonious" new world.

The second form of Christian faith is that of the *oppressors and exploiters of the masses*. This reactionary class includes, Bakunin tells us in classical Proudhonian style, "priests, monarchs, statesmen, soldiers, public and private financiers, functionaries of all sorts, policemen, gendarmes, jailers and executioners, monopolists, capitalists, extortionists [*pressureurs*], entrepreneurs and proprietors, lawyers, economists, politicians of all shades, [. . .] the smallest vendor of sweetmeats", and, dare I say, so on.[112] Whether this class really does believe or not is of little consequence; the point is they need to be seen to believe, to share the faith of the masses, without which their position is untenable. Hence, they share the sentiment of Voltaire: "If God did not exist, it would be necessary to invent him". Elsewhere Bakunin speculates further on the question of their belief. He suggests that this class simultaneously believes ("Man always believes easily . . . in what does not contradict his interests", or, as Feuerbach put it, "That to which the heart is open is also accessible to the mind"[113]) and disbelieves ("One cannot . . . admit that they have believed in *every* absurdity that constitutes faith"). While this resolution seems contradictory, Bakunin simply comments that "In the great majority of cases people live in contradiction with themselves" — not least at the level of religious consciousness, at any rate.[114]

The third form of "Christian" faith is that of the middle or "mediating" party, the modern idealists. This "quite numerous class" Bakunin characterizes as intelligent but cowardly. Recognizing the "particular absurdities" of Christianity — the particular matters of faith, such as "all the miracles" — which they abandon, they insist on the "principal absurdity", that is, the existence of God, which is in fact responsible for all the particular absurdities. Rejecting the "brutally positive God of theology", therefore, they espouse a "nebulous" God — a God without content, a stubborn absurdity.[115] (This form of belief in "a merely negative existence, an existence without existence" (perhaps the dominant form today) had been challenged by Feuerbach before Bakunin, when he wrote: "The denial of determinate, positive predicates concerning the divine nature is nothing else than a denial of religion, with, however, an appearance of religion in its favor, so that it is not recognized as a denial; it is simply a subtle, disguised atheism" — atheism without the strength of its convictions. Nevertheless, this form of belief reveals much about the development of religious consciousness, and is perhaps, in spite of itself, a crucial stage in its negation, for, as Feuerbach adds, "Only where man loses his taste for religion . . . does the existence of God become an insipid existence — an existence without qualities".[116])

Such is the nature of the *Mediating Positive* at the level of religious consciousness, who recognizes the dialectical vitality here in its negativity, but who seeks to subvert it by attempting to reconcile faith in God's existence, or, in broad terms, *theologism*, with the rational recognition of its absurdity, or, in broad terms, *atheism*. This pseudo-dialectical attempt is, again, considered impossible by Bakunin (after Bruno Bauer, for one, as shown above); thus he berates the modern idealists for "endeavoring to reconcile the irreconcilable". (At the level of political consciousness, this class insists (and its insistence is not accidental), despite its apparent revolutionary or libertarian fervor, on a different absurdity — the State — and therefore represents an equally absurd mode of thought — *statism*.) Bakunin concludes: "[These idealists] are uncertain, sickly souls, disoriented in the present civilization, belonging to neither the present nor the future, pale phantoms eternally suspended between heaven and earth".[117]

The three forms of Christian faith depicted above, then, represent the dialectic at the level of religious consciousness. Present are the Positive or Consistently Reactionary element (as the faith of the reactionary class), the Negative or Revolutionary element (at least *potentially* as the faith of the masses), and the Mediating element (as the faith of the modern idealists). The contradictions implicit in Christianity are therefore revealing themselves, or, as it were, making themselves explicit, and, in consequence, Christianity is becoming ruptured. However, it persists, albeit it in somewhat negative form (as the *mere* belief in the existence of God), as we have pointed out. We must therefore ask on what grounds it is posited as such.

According to Bakunin, the existence of God is treated by modern idealists "as a fact universally accepted", across the ages, "and, as such, [it is] no longer an object of doubt". Thus "the *antiquity* and *universality* of a belief" is regarded by them, "contrary to all science and all logic, as sufficient and incontestable proof of its truth".[118] We must therefore see whether these criteria hold. The standard example of Ptolemaic geocentrism, an ancient and near-universal belief called into question by Aristarchus of Samos and Nicholas of Oresme, and overcome by Copernicus, Kepler, Galileo, and company, would suggest that in fact they do not. But Bakunin offers a more thorough analysis, firstly of the criterion of antiquity.

It is, he says, quite logical that older beliefs and theories are more flawed and that ancient peoples are more ignorant, given man's animality. Emerging from natural animal "slavery" and ignorance, human history "consists precisely in the progressive negation of the primitive animality of man by the development of his humanity", that is, the development of his reason. In other words, man becomes, in general, progressively more knowledgeable (at least of the limits of his reason). Hence, the antiquity of a belief ought to lead us to doubt it rather than to accept it. Of the criterion of universality, on the other hand, Bakunin says that it simply demonstrates "the similarity, if not the perfect identity, of human nature in all ages"; that is, that the universality of a *particular* belief, rather than proving it, shows only that it reflects a *particular* development of human reason. This, in the case of religion, has been Bakunin's contention all along. Therefore, Bakunin's conclusion regarding the ancient and universal belief in the existence of God is the following:

> Nothing, in fact, is as universal or as ancient as the iniquitous and absurd; truth and justice, on the contrary, are the least universal and youngest features in the development of human society.[119]

2.12 Bakunin and Kant

This is the extent of Bakunin's analysis of religious consciousness and his critique of theologism. What remains to be established here is the lineage of his thought and his place in the philosophical tradition. Bakunin acknowledges four very definite influences on him in this context. The first of these is Immanuel Kant, who he claims, despite the imperfection and metaphysicality of his criticism, in effect "demolished the objectivity or reality of the divine ideas".[120]

Charles Taylor has said of Kant's moral philosophy that it is "radically anthropocentric" (since it situates all components of morality within the rational human agent).[121] This might be said — perhaps controversially, but defensibly — of his philosophy as a whole, and Bakunin evidently holds this to be the case. The implication here is that the epistemoligization of philosophy, the reduction of philosophy to a series of metaphysically conceived Kantian problems, transforms pre-

Kantian philosophy into explicitly anthropocentric philosophy (though philosophy had made an implicitly anthropocentric turn — away from theocentric philosophy — with Descartes). Thus Kant proclaims (by dubious analogy) his Copernican Revolution, according to which the object is henceforth taken to conform to or to be determined by the subject in some fundamental sense.

The epistemology of the *Kritik der reinen Vernunft* (*Critique of Pure Reason*) (first edition, 1781; second edition, 1787), effectively renders that which is beyond the grasp of human consciousness (which is to say, the thing-in-itself (*das Ding an sich*) — as opposed to the synthesized thing as it appears) meaningless. The relation between *the thing-in-itself* and the *noumenon* is difficult to conceive; it seems, however, that the onto-logically assumed thing-in-itself is somehow epistemologized in terms of the noumenon. As Henry Allison puts it, "The concept of a noumenon . . . is the epistemological concept *par excellence*, characteriz-ing an object, of whatever ontological status, considered *qua* correlate of a non-sensible manner of cognition".[122]

Kant's definition of the noumenon as "a thing which is not to be thought as object of the senses but as a thing in itself, solely through a pure understanding", and as "a merely *limiting concept*, the function of which is to curb the pretensions of sensibility", shows that, unlike the thing-in-itself, it has no ontological standing, but is accorded epistemo-logical status only.[123] The gulf between the real (ontological) object and the ideal (epistemological) subject — the very mystified essence of Kant's metaphysics — is bridged even more mysteriously in the first edition of the first *Critique* by means of the *transcendental object*, which is the thing-in-itself divested of its immediacy or rendered "non-empirical" [A109]; or, it would be more truthful to say, the onto-epistemological transcendental object mediates between the ontologi-cal thing-in-itself and the strictly epistemological noumenon. (This me-diating principle disappears from view in the second edition, or disap-pears in name, since, as Allison writes (though the relative evaluation might be disputed), "The distinction between the positive and negative senses of the noumenon, which is the essential feature of the Second Edition account, is really only a more explicit and somewhat clearer reworking of the contrast between the noumenon and the transcendental object drawn in the First Edition".[124]) To summarize this issue:

> [Kant] mainly uses the term "Transcendental Object" when he conceives of . . . objects . . . as being what *we* have to conceive as being the underlying, unknown ground of appearance and experience; while the term "Thing-in-itself" is mainly employed when he conceives of them as existing *independently* of whatever we may conceive or believe. And in very many contexts the two concepts are interchangeable, the former merely stressing a relation to our own subjectivity which the latter prefers to ignore. The term "Noumenon", or object of pure thought, is also applied in both contexts, though, at times, with the additional feature that it is the appropriate object of awareness not called into action by sensuous affections, but in some manner directly constitutive of its object, or at least directly apprehending it, in the very act of conceiving it. The Thing-in-itself, the Noumenon, and the Transcendental Object therefore all point to the same sort of unapparent source of all that is apparent, in which Kant profoundly believes . . .[125]

The thing-in-itself is an ontological assumption on Kant's part; its elusiveness may be accounted for by the fact that the consciousness that posits it is a mere epistemological assumption, a groundless epistemological agency; the ontological status of the subject itself remains a mystery. (Bookchin's forceful critique of the abstraction of Kantian epistemology merits citation here (not least because it will be reintroduced as a critique of Marx below):

> [Kantian epistemology] lacks all sense of historicity. If it looks back at all to the history of mind, it does so within a context so overwhelmingly social and from historical levels so far-removed from the *biological genesis of mind* that it can never make contact with nature. Its very claim to "modernity" has been a systematic unraveling of the interface between nature and mind that Hellenic thought tried to establish. This interface has been replaced by an unbridgeable dualism between . . . mind and external reality. Thus, the problem of nature's

knowingness [is] seen from the knowing end of a long social history rather than from its beginnings. When this history is instead viewed from its origins, *mentality and its continuity with nature* acquires a decisively different aspect. An authentic epistemology is the physical anthropology of mind, of the human brain, not the cultural clutter of history that obstructs our view of the brain's genesis in nature and its evolution in *society conceived as a unique elaboration of natural phenomena.*[126])

Thus arises Kant's contrived dualism of epistemological or ideal subject and ontological or real object (willfully obscured to this day — by essentially Kantian scholastics of one sort or another, as Feuerbach diagnoses them — by the metaphysically supposed contradiction between the nebulous epistemological subject and its fallen epistemological object). Hence David-Hillel Ruben sketches the subsequent development in German philosophy (which I will elaborate below) as follows:

> Essentially, the dilemma in Kant arises by trying to wed an idealist theory of knowledge to a realist ontology . . . Hegel's response to that problem was the adoption of an idealist ontology, in order to suit the theory of knowledge . . . Conversely, Feuerbach's reply was in favor of the retention of the realist ontology. [That is,] For Feuerbach the essential independence of nature is retained.[127]

Bakunin's understanding of Kant is that the thrust of his philosophy is in keeping with his own anti-theologism, that is, that (in irreparably damaging the concept of the divine) it is *implicitly* atheistic (a covert or compromised atheism). Nevertheless, Bakunin challenges the metaphysicality of Kant's criticism — its compromise — which retains, in the concept of the thing-in-itself, a "false" and "dangerous" concept of the unknowable or "inaccessible ground" of all things; so that while it has "the air of excluding the absolute from the domain of science [or knowledge], it [in fact] reconstitutes it [and] confirms it as a real being", which amounts to affirming "that all of this phenomenal world — the apparent, sensible, known world — is only a sort of outer envelope, a husk . . . inside of which is hiding, like a kernel, the being not determined by external relations, the non-dependent and non-relative being, [in other words,] the absolute".[128] (Kant's division of the inner and outer worlds therefore reintroduces the theological division of the realm of the Absolute and the determined realm, of heaven and earth.) As the naturalist sees it, by contrast, the Absolute (the non-determined, the non-relative, and the non-dependent) is Nothing. Kantian metaphysics or anthropocentric philosophy therefore stands opposed to naturalistic philosophy; but the ultimate expression and negation (though, as contemporary philosophy illustrates, by no means the final form) of the anthropocentric philosophy, that is to say, the philosophy of Hegel, was to usher in the naturalistic philosophy.

This apparent contradiction in Kantian anthropocentrism — between the "atheistic" exclusion and "theologistic" reconstitution of the Absolute — is articulated with utmost clarity by Feuerbach, who demonstrates that divine idealism and modern idealism, as Bakunin denotes the theocentric and anthropocentric philosophies in the account outlined above, are essentially identical and non-contradictory. Feuerbach states: "Kantian idealism, in which the objects conform to the understanding and not the understanding to the objects, is therefore nothing other than the realization of the theological conception of the divine mind, which is not determined by the objects but rather determines them . . . [Therefore,] Kant's idealism is idealism still bound by theism".[129] The blurred distinction — or, in fact, the identity — of the theocentric philosophy and the anthropocentric philosophy — between divine idealism and modern idealism (Bakunin), or between theologized religion and speculative philosophy (Feuerbach), or between the theological philosophy and the metaphysical philosophy (Comte) — is a theme which will reemerge below.

2.13 Bakunin and Hegel

The second major influence on Bakunin here is Hegel. According to Bakunin, Hegel, after Kant, consciously "tried to replace [the divine ideas] upon their celestial throne". However, he did not restore God, he restored the Absolute (as is evidenced by the very fact that, as Bakunin says, "Hegel never speaks of God [as such], he speaks only of the Absolute"[130] — in the interests of "expediency" as we have seen). For Hegel, the Absolute is the divine idea humanized, so to speak; it is the "divine" idea that is available to human consciousness as its own implicit content and its own ultimate product. Thus Bakunin says of Hegel that he "took away from these ideas their divine halo by showing . . . that they were never anything other than a pure creation of the human mind running through the whole of history in search of itself". This was Hegel's achievement in the *Phänomenologie des Geistes* (*Phenomenology of Spirit*) (1807), an achievement which amounted to killing "the good God for once and for all".[131]

It is in the introduction to the *Phenomenology* that Hegel attempts to overcome the Kantian bifurcation. He shows that there is in fact no contradiction between cognition and the Absolute, between consciousness and what it is conscious of, between knower and known, between subject and object — or, at least, none that cannot be resolved. In other words, there is nothing that consciousness cannot become conscious of. As he puts it elsewhere, "Two things must be distinguished in consciousness: first, the fact *that* I know; and second, *what* I know. In self-consciousness, the two — subject and object — coincide".[132] How does Hegel arrive at this conclusion? He argues that the object of consciousness exists both *for it*, as the object *of* consciousness, and *in itself*, as the *true*. But since truth is affirmed by consciousness itself and since it is the criterion by which consciousness itself judges what it knows, it can been seen that both the object as a being-for-another (or *Concept* (*Begriff*)) *and* the object as a being-in-itself (or the true) lie within consciousness. As Hegel puts it, "Concept and object, the criterion and what is to be tested, are present in consciousness itself". The movement or development of consciousness therefore embodies the ongoing tension *within* consciousness between the Concept and the object, between the being-for-consciousness and the being-in-itself. This tension is not overcome by the Concept adapting itself to the object, as would seem to be the case. Rather, it is overcome by the object adapting itself to the Concept, as *must* be the case since, as Hegel says in the Preface, "truth has only the Concept as the element of its existence", meaning that it is "the criterion for testing [i.e., the being-in-itself or the true] [that] is altered when that for which it was to have been the criterion [i.e., the Concept] fails to pass the test".[133] The complexities of this argument need not concern us here; suffice it to say that the ultimate reconciliation *herein* is accomplished when Concept and object correspond to each other.

The dialectical interplay of Concept and object constitutes the *experience* (*Erfahrung*) of consciousness — phenomenological experience, so to speak. However, the precise direction of this dialectic, the logic of this experience, is apparent only to the phenomenologist, not to consciousness itself: as Hegel famously puts it, the dialectic goes on "behind the back of consciousness".[134] (At the level of World History, this somehow concealed dialectic represents the equally famous "Cunning of Reason".) The task of the *Phenomenology* as a whole, then, is to trace the development of consciousness, not merely to reveal it to the oblivious consciousness, as it were, but as a necessary stage, in itself, in the development of the Absolute.

Thus the *Phenomenology* expresses the development of consciousness from its beginnings in the supposed immediacy of sense-certainty to the fullness of its being as Absolute Spirit — which is a philosophical enterprise, since only philosophy can express the rationality of this process — the rationality that is the end of this process — in explicitly rational form. Religion, on the other hand, can only express this rationality, its implicit content, in imaginative form: it is merely representative. It is in religion that Spirit (through natural-symbolic religion and Greek-aesthetic religion) arises for consciousness (in the revealed Christian religion), but the subject of religion and its object are not conscious of their identity as yet. In other words, in religion Spirit, though conscious of itself as such, remains unfulfilled, since it is conscious of itself as other. As Walter Jaeschke puts it, "The consummation of the history and the actuality of spirit are attained when . . . the self 'beholds the determination of the object as its *own*, [and] consequently beholds *itself* in the object'. But even [in] the Christian religion . . . the self does not behold itself as itself, and reconciliation remains something represented . . . It is only when [Spirit] frees itself from its representational objects that it can, as self-conscious, become an object to itself — and this happens in philosophy". Thus the *Phenomenology* declares the form of religion to be inadequate to its content. But, more than that, it also achieves an identification of the human and the divine that becomes so crucial in the Left Hegelian tradition. As Jaeschke puts it, once again:

> More clearly than the later lectures [on the philosophy of religion], the religiohistorical conception of the *Phenomenology* is that of an incarnation of God in human form. Hegel accordingly links the unfolding of the content of the revelatory religion to the shape of the incarnate God, the very shape in which spirit recognizes the absolute being to be a self-consciousness . . . [Therefore,] the history of religion leads up to the christological idea that . . . "the divine nature is the same as the human, and it is this unity that is beheld".[135]

Of course, as far as the philosophy of religion is concerned, the *Phenomenology* is not Hegel's sole contribution; indeed, it is a relatively early work in Hegel's *oeuvre*. However, the *Phenomenology* is important because — apart from the specific reason just mentioned — it situates Hegel's philosophy of religion within the context of the broad scope of his thought. As such it served as the *locus classicus* for Left Hegelian interpretation of Hegel, as a touchstone for the Left Hegelian movement. This is not to deny the influence of Hegel's *Vorlesungen über die Philosophie der Religion* (*Lectures on the Philosophy of Religion*) (first edition, 1832) on individual members of the Left Hegelian movement, who were clearly familiar with them in some form or other. For example, Strauss' lecture notes from the 1831 series have recently been discovered; Bruno Bauer edited the 1840 edition of the lectures; and Feuerbach attended Hegel's 1824 lecture series. Since we are especially concerned with Feuerbach (for reasons that will become apparent presently), it is necessary to say a little about the 1824 lectures.

The two ideas that we have extracted from the *Phenomenology* — the idea of the formal inadequacy of religion and the idea of the identity of the human and the divine — are also present in the 1824 lectures. Hence Hegel speaks, in the first case, of the unity of "the infinite *form* of knowledge [and] the absolute *content*" which "can only be apprehended *speculatively*". In the second case, he says: "it is to be noted that there cannot be two kinds of reason and two kinds of spirit, a divine and a human reason or a divine and a human spirit that would be strictly distinct from one another, as if their essence were strictly opposed. *Human reason, human spiritual consciousness or consciousness of its own essence, is reason generally, is the divine within humanity*".[136] This passage can be taken to serve as a prelude to our discussion of Feuerbach below.

There is another aspect of the 1824 lectures which is distinct from both the *Phenomenology* and the 1821 lecture manuscript; that is, Hegel's dispute with Schleiermacher (or the Schleiermacher of the 1821 edition of *Christian Faith*). This aspect foreshadows Feuerbach's later (post-1844) writing, where Schleiermacher's influence is obvious, indicating continuity in his thought (from 1824 to at least 1851) — a point which proponents of the "break" myth ought to concede. (We will address this question in greater detail later.) Hegel, in his attempted refutation of Schleiermacher, distinguishes between the subjective and objective elements of religious experience. Of the subjective element — in Schleiermacher's account, feeling — Hegel writes: "If in regard to God we could appeal only to feeling, then we have to wonder how any kind of objectivity is still attributed to this content, i.e., to God". He notes that at least those who advance "materialistic . . . (empiricist, historicist, and naturalistic views) have been . . . consistent in this respect. They have regarded spirit and thought as something merely material, a combination of material forces; they have reduced spirit and thought to feeling and sensation, and accordingly taken God and all representations [of God] as products of feeling, and denied objectivity to God. The result is then atheism".[137]

This is precisely what Feuerbach does in his later work, where, as we will see, he takes materialistic naturalism and atheism to be synonymous. Nevertheless, Feuerbach does not accept that the "reduction" of the subjective element of religious experience to feeling implies the "reduction" of the objective element to something which *"is only for me"*, which "is not independent in and for itself". The *supposed* object of religion — God — may be for me, though more accurately it is, in itself, simple nothingness. But the real object of religious experience does subsist "in and for itself", independent of subjective feelings about it. Indeed, Hegel anticipates Feuerbach's analysis of the early 1840s when he states that "in the philosophy of religion it is . . . God, or reason in principle, that is the object".[138] Feuerbach later developed this anthropocentric view of religion (which thereby stands as a naturalistic view of Christianity) into his naturalistic view of religion in which the subsistent object is nature. But the basic point to be made here is that the 1824 lectures seem to have contributed to Feuerbach's critique of religion, and, indeed (in keeping with Feuerbach's profound influence on Bakunin), are consistent with Bakunin's critique as well.

Bakunin shares two of the implicit Hegelian convictions. First, he accepts that the idea of the absolute, the divine idea, is the product of human consciousness. Second, he accepts the inadequacy of religion as a form of reason — that is, the need of human consciousness to develop beyond religion in order to realize itself. Thus the influence of Hegel on Bakunin in this context is, unlike that of Kant, (at least somewhat) positive — insofar as Hegel offers Bakunin a phenomenological method of analysis (in addition to the logic that we discussed in the first part of this essay) and an elaborate example of such analysis — a profound analysis of human consciousness in all its forms — in the *Phenomenology*. However, the influence of Hegel on Bakunin in this context is also negative — insofar as what Bakunin, like his fellow Left Hegelians, ultimately takes from Hegel is a critical approach to religion as a form of human consciousness — an approach which was to lead to the conclusion that, in Marx's words, "the critique of religion is the prerequisite of every critique".[139] Marx's words these may well be, but, dare I say, the sentiment itself is closer to the heart of Bakunin.

2.14 Bakunin and Feuerbach: On Religion

This brings us to the third major influence on Bakunin here: that of his "beloved philosopher", arguably the greatest Left Hegelian thinker, Ludwig Feuerbach.[140] According to Bakunin, it remained for Feuerbach, after Hegel, to finally "put an end to all the religious insanities and the divine mirage" by showing "how the divine ideas . . . were successively created by the abstractive faculty of man".[141] Hence it was Feuerbach who developed Hegel's insight into the inextricable relation between human consciousness and the divine idea — between man and God, between religious subject and religious object — most satisfactorily, demonstrating that the divine idea — God, the Absolute, the Supreme Being — is in fact limited by human consciousness and that religious developments consequently reflect developments of human consciousness itself. The focus of Feuerbach's analysis of religion (or the consummate religion at any rate) is therefore man, the supposed subject of religious experience, rather than the divine idea as such, the supposed object of religious experience — *whatever this object may be called*. As Feuerbach himself expresses this in the Preface to the second edition of *Das Wesen des Christentums* (*The Essence of Christianity*) (first edition, 1841; second edition, 1843):

> This philosophy has for its principle not the Substance of Spinoza, not the *ego* of Kant and Fichte, not the Absolute Identity of Schelling, not the Absolute Mind of Hegel, in short, no abstract, merely conceptual being, but a *real* being, the true *Ens realissimum* — man.[142]

Feuerbach's critical analysis of religion, then, is an attempt, as he sees it, to translate the propositions of religion — predications of the religious object — into "plain speech" — into predications of the religious subject. In other words, what he calls his "historico-philosophical analysis of religion" aspires to be "the revelation of religion to itself [i.e., the religious subject], [or] the *awakening of religion to self-consciousness*". The negative conclusion of this analysis is that "the object of religion in general, the Divine essence, in distinction from the essence of Nature and Humanity . . . is only something in the imagination, but in truth and reality nothing".[143] Feuerbach must therefore ask the central question: how this nothingness came to be represented as Absolute Being.

Religion has its origin, according to Feuerbach, in the unique and defining "inner" existence of man, that is, in man's unique capacity to converse with himself — so that he is at once both I (or subject or individual) *and* Thou (or object — to himself — or species-member). Thus, religion has its origin in man's unique capacity to relate to his own nature as a member of a distinct species, through the faculty of understanding (which simply designates "the thinking power" in general here). Feuerbach continues: "Religion being identical with the distinctive characteristic of man [once again, his inner existence, governed by thought], is then identical with self-consciousness — with the consciousness which man has of his own nature". But since religion is, by definition, consciousness of the infinite, it follows that man's nature is itself infinite. As Feuerbach puts it, "in the consciousness of the infinite, the conscious subject has for its object the infinity of its own nature", or, more accurately, the theoretical "infinitude of his species", which transcends the limits of his individuality. Feuerbach concludes:

> *Man has his highest being, his God, in himself;* not in himself as an individual, but in his essential nature, his species.[144]

Religion, the consciousness of the infinite or God, is therefore nothing but the self-consciousness of man. Nevertheless, religious consciousness is characterized by ignorance of this identity: to it the divine and the human are antithetical. (This contradiction mirrors that which Hegel had already exposed in religious consciousness.) The development of religious consciousness, however, consists in the emergence of such an identification, so that "what was formerly contemplated and worshipped as God is now perceived to be something *human*". (This is a philosophical achievement according to Hegel's *Phenomenology* account — or an achievement of *speculative* philosophy, as Feuerbach himself will argue.) Religion, then, culminates (and transforms into speculative philosophy) in the recognition that "the antithesis of divine and human is *altogether* illusory, that it is nothing else than the antithesis between the human nature in general and the human individual". So, once again, the divine arises within human consciousness — it is the product of the dialectic between man as subject and man as his own object, that is, the I-Thou dialectic. Specifically, it is the product of man's subjective objectivity — his nature or his species being as a rational creature — being projected outside of him, into the realm of nothingness, and subsequently opposed to him. Feuerbach expresses this in the following manner:

> The divine being is nothing else than the human being, or, rather, the human nature purified, freed from the limits of the individual man, [and] made objective — i.e., contemplated and revered as another, a distinct being. All the attributes of the divine nature are, therefore, attributes of the human nature.[145]

Since all divine attributes are in fact human attributes, all religious predicates are anthropomorphisms. Feuerbach maintains, furthermore, that "If thy predicates are anthropomorphisms, the subject of them is an anthropomorphism too". This means that all religious statements, all religious propositions, can be transformed into human statements, so to speak, or anthropological propositions, by means of the method of inversion — by simply inverting the subject and predicate of every religious proposition. Feuerbach describes this method in the following way:

> . . . that which in religion is the predicate we must make the subject, and that which in religion is a subject we must make a predicate, thus inverting the oracles of religion; and by this means we arrive at the truth.[146]

The truth of religion, then, is that "God is the nature of man regarded as absolute truth". However, since the nature of man is regarded differently in different ages, as man attains greater degrees of self-consciousness, different religions emerge and the very nature of God changes, from "mere nature-god" (as portrayed in Feuerbach's later writings) to the "God-man" of Christianity, reflecting man's emergence from the "state of savagery" to the state of "culture". Man is therefore the measure of God — the Absolute Being; or, in Feuerbach's words, "Man, especially the religious man, is to himself the measure of all things, of all reality". In consequence, Feuerbach declares that "Religion has no material exclusively its own" — which implies that, as we have said, the Absolute Being of religion literally amounts to nothing. Everything in the province of religion has merely been lent to it by man, who has transferred all that he values in his nature, in the species as a whole — these "divine" qualities — to the Absolute Being that is God. (Feuerbach's influence on Bakunin here is evident when he writes: "To enrich God, man must become poor; that God may be all, man must be nothing".)[147] However, man, at the level of religious consciousness, that is, in ignorance, has forgotten the debt. Impoverished, then, he has no choice but to bow down before his master. The gradual development of self-consciousness, on the other hand, represents the reclamation of these qualities, the reclamation of the human from the divine.

Feuerbach does not draw the obvious atheistic conclusion from his argument here that others, including Bakunin, do. In the antithesis of the human and the divine, the divine is not negated as such. Rather, it is tied to the human and the human is itself established as the divine. (As we observed earlier, Feuerbach does not endorse the Bauerian dialectic.) To negate the divine in this relation, Feuerbach claims, would be to negate the human. "Hence he alone is the true atheist to whom the predicates of the Divine Being [in other words, human qualities] . . . are nothing; not he to whom merely the subject of these predicates is nothing". In fact, to the true atheist *mystified* human qualities *are* nothing — *in themselves*. Nevertheless, this dubious claim is the basis of Feuerbach's conception of a new religion, a religion of man — that is, of his vain effort, in the face of his criticism, "to vindicate *to life a religious import*". However, Feuerbach acknowledges the inevitability of this conclusion at the outset:

> My work . . . being evolved from the nature of religion . . . has in itself the true essence of religion — is, in its very quality as a philosophy, a religion also.[148]

2.15 Interlude: Bakunin and Marx

In this context, it is worth considering Marx's fourth and sixth theses on Feuerbach. Marx states in his fourth thesis, quite correctly in light of the above, that Feuerbach's "work [at this point] consists in resolving the religious world into its secular basis", but points out that "the secular basis detaches itself from itself and establishes itself in the clouds as an independent realm". Thus Marx recognizes, and disputes (only to reestablish in his own work, as I will argue), the *mystification of the human* that is the result of Feuerbach's *demystification of the divine*. Bakunin would not disagree in principle with Marx on this issue; however, I believe that there is an important distinction to be made between the grounds for their dispute with Feuerbach. In the sixth thesis Marx states, again quite correctly, that "Feuerbach resolves the religious [though it would be more accurate to say the Christian] essence into the human essence". But Marx impugns Feuerbach's conception of the human essence as an "abstraction inherent in each single individual", since "In its reality it is [merely] the ensemble of . . . *social* relations". Feuerbach's ahistorical conception, as Marx sees it, "can with him be comprehended only as 'genus', as an internal, dumb generality which *merely naturally* unites the many individuals".[149]

Bakunin does reject Feuerbach's (as yet) abstract conception of the human essence or human nature and his mystification of the human. However, influenced by Comte and Darwin, as we will see, he also believes in a *relatively* ahistorical human nature, that is, human nature subject to evolution and therefore biologically determined, and does believe that this nature alone makes possible the initial development of religion and its ultimate negation. Religion proper only arises in the mind of man because it reflects something peculiar in the nature of man — and its development is always constrained by the development of his evolving mental faculties, which ultimately allow him to overcome it or emancipate himself from it. (Versus Marx's claim that the "religious sentiment" is itself a social product".[150]) This does not mean that Bakunin rejects the social factor — or, what is the same thing, the economic factor — which Marx stresses; but he never fully embraces the doctrine of historical materialism. He speaks of it, rather, as:

> a principal which is *profoundly true* when one considers it in its true light, that is to say, from the *relative* point of view, but which, [when] envisaged and posited in an *absolute* manner, as the only foundation and first source of all other principles, . . . becomes *completely false.*[151]

This distinction between Bakunin and Marx is crucial. It accounts for Bakunin's accusation that Marx "cannot free [himself] from the sway of abstract, metaphysical thought" — or at least lends philosophical weight to this aspect of the invective between them.[152] Indeed, this rejection of "absolute" historical materialism, or of historical materialism as such (the theory — understood either as all-explaining, or in Popper's terms, unfalsifiable or irrefutable economic determinism [whatever the precise mechanisms at work], or as grand metaphysical construct — is absolutist by its very nature) unites anarchists from Bakunin and Kropotkin to Bookchin and Chomsky. David Miller concurs, and states that "The most fundamental difference [between anarchists and Marxists] concerns the materialist conception of history", which, as he puts it, is "often regarded by Marxists as the crowning glory of their system, but looked on with less favor by anarchists". Hence, Miller contends, "It would be quite wrong to suppose that the [famous] disagreement over revolutionary methods was all that divided them. This disagreement was an inevitable outcome of differences at a more fundamental [philosophical] level".[153]

A note on the "absolutism" and "metaphysicality" of historical materialism must be appended here to clarify the above, to place what follows in context, and, indeed, to pre-empt an inevitable and premature attack. First we must elucidate our understanding of the materialist conception of history. There are well documented difficulties here, not least among them the apparently conflicting statements made, for example, in the 1848 manifesto (where the determining relations of production within the economic base are seemingly prioritized) and the 1859 preface (where the determining forces of production within the base are seemingly prioritized)[154]; the relation between the (economic) base and the (politico-juridico-religio-philosophico-artistic) superstructure itself is also problematic. Thus the exact nature of the base-superstructure framework and the connection between the forces of production and the relations of production within the base, to say nothing of the consequent problems of class, revolution, ideology, and so on, have occupied scholars for decades.

Regardless of such debates, the basic point of historical materialism is that, as Engels puts it, "the *ultimately* determining element in history is the production and reproduction of real life"; he adds, "if anyone twists this into saying that the economic element is the *only* determining one, he transforms that proposition into a meaningless, abstract, [and] senseless phrase".[155] A dubious distinction indeed: the economic factor is the one that counts, the one that alone or at the end of the day — take your pick — determines history. Hence Engels says of Marx: "Just as Darwin discovered the law of development of organic nature, so Marx discovered the law of development of human history"[156] — no less, and in complete isolation from natural science (and, as I will argue, naturalistic philosophy). (Isaiah Berlin, with his talent for getting things the wrong way round, duly claims that historical materialism "is not guilty of Hegel's reckless and contemptuous attitude towards the results of the scientific research of his time; on the contrary, it attempts to follow the direction indicated by the empirical sciences and to incorporate their general results".[157] It seems to me that this is historically or biographically untrue. In any case, we will see what Marx has to say about the natural sciences below, passing comment here only on his view's influence on postmodernism, which, to quote from one of the significant works of our time, in large part "regards science as nothing more than a 'narration', a 'myth', or *a social construction* among many others".[158])

In fact, the implicit diremption here — of "organic nature" and "human history" — is essential to Marx's thought. He lacks all sense of the direct continuity between the natural and the social (hence, as we have seen, he lacks all sense of a biologically-determined human nature), between what he portrays as the "realm of necessity" and the "realm of freedom", which is why he conceives of human liberation in terms of the domination of nature, and social fulfillment in terms of equality of exploitation (of natural resources). As he puts it: "Just as the savage must wrestle with nature to satisfy his wants, to maintain and reproduce life, so must civilized man, and he must do so in all social formations and under all possible modes of production . . . Freedom . . . can only consist in socialized man, the associated producers, rationally regulating their interchange with Nature, bringing it under their common control, instead of being ruled by it as by the blind forces of Nature".[159]

This may, on reflection, be laughable in theory (the image of "wrestling" with the natural opponent (wrestling with a blind opponent at that), as if originally independent of it to some extent and potentially free of it to a great extent); but it has been catastrophic in practice — leading (directly or indirectly, but leading all the same) not only to ecological devastation, but also to very real social enslavement in the name of a myopic anthropocentric ideology. Thus I accept, in the case of the latter result, Bookchin's logical and historical argument that Marx "placed considerable emphasis on *human domination* as an unavoidable feature of *humanity's domination of the natural world*".[160] In the fanatical quest to subjugate nature by means of highly organized forms of production, it becomes necessary to maintain structures of authority within society (the function of which is said to be merely "administrative" rather than "governmental", though it is questionable which function sounds more sinister). Hence the realm of freedom collapses into, at best, a realm of partial freedom, or, more likely, as history confirms, into a realm of all-pervasive authority. Bookchin concludes that "To structure a revolutionary project around . . . a harsh opposition between 'man' and nature", and to make "domination . . . a precondition for freedom, debase[s] the concept of freedom and assimilate[s] it to its opposite".[161] Of course, this authoritarian rationale is not uniquely Marxist. Bookchin writes:

> It [is] one of the most widely accepted notions, from classical times to the present, that human freedom from the "*domination of man by nature*" entails the *domination of human by human* as the earliest *means of production* and the use of human beings as instruments for harnessing the natural world. Hence, in order to harness the natural world, it has been argued for ages, it is necessary to harness human beings as well, in the form of slaves, serfs, and workers.[162]

Despite Marx's diremption of the natural and the social, some scholars portray Marx as a materialistic naturalist, if an unorthodox one. Alfred Schmidt, for instance, writes that "The dialectic of Subject and Object is for Marx a dialectic of the constituent elements of nature", a dialectic of "external nature" and "human practice", both of which are "natural" in some sense. But Schmidt acknowledges that "It is the socio-historical character of Marx's concept of nature which distinguishes it from the outset". In other words, for Marx, "external nature", though it is supposedly the "natural basis" of the historical subject, is always mediated by "human practice" or productive activity; as we have seen, the objective (nature) is always mediated by the subjective (the practico-historical agent). (Though, again, "in all this the priority of external nature remains unassailed".[163] Quite how Marx can assert that nature is prior to that by which it is essentially mediated is beyond me. But this problem reveals his Kantianism: while insisting on the principle of mediation, he assumes an in-itself. Schmidt maintains, however, that Marx, as "an exponent of a theory of mediation", is close to Hegel — who, in fact, attempted to overcome mediation in the figure of absolute Spirit. This misrepresentation (of Marx as Hegelian rather than Kantian) is familiar enough.) Marx-the-would-be-materialist, therefore, as Schmidt puts it, "accepted the idealist view that the world is mediated through the Subject". As such, his materialism, indeed his materialist conception of history, is distinct from "philosophical materialism" or what Marx himself calls "naturalistic materialism" — insofar as it is not materialism at all.

Schmidt thinks otherwise; he thinks Marx is a materialist and that his materialism is continuous from, and an improvement on, "naturalistic materialism". After all, "naturalistic materialism", and the very concepts of matter and material nature, are bourgeois and must be overcome! In Schmidt's words: "Matter in its physical or physiological determinateness [that is, dare I say, the subject matter of natural science] is the central preoccupation of the materialism of the bourgeois Enlightenment of the seventeenth and eighteenth centuries". But Marx — influenced by (anti-bourgeois?) German idealism — "placed [these] traditional objects of materialist thought in the background insofar as he conceived them in their social function and genesis". The social genesis of matter is a fascinating topic without doubt. Schmidt, of course, realizes that this kind of materialism, which is clearly more akin to Kantian idealism than genuine materialism, is difficult to square with the materialist tradition: "The kernel of philosophical materialism contained in [Marx's] theory of history and society and implicitly presupposed by it does not come so plainly into view and is difficult to establish". But he makes the following lame effort to establish it: "It would be quite wrong to see in materialism a uniform idea in whose history there has been only an immanent intellectual development. If one disregards certain formal characteristics of materialist philosophy in general, it can be shown that materialism is subject to socio-historical change in its method, its specific interests, and, finally, in its substantial features". Certainly, materialism can change in many respects; but for it to change in "its substantial features" — in the process of idealization, for example — simply means that it ceases to be materialism.[164]

Others have called Marx's materialism into question. Anthony Giles-Peters, in a penetrating article on Marx's theses on Feuerbach of 1845, observes that it is the very materialism of Feuerbach, framed in terms of his "respect for the independence of nature from man" (or the priority of nature over man), that "drew Marx's critical fire". Marx, in distinguishing himself from Feuerbach, distinguishes himself from the materialist wing. (This is evident in the first thesis where Marx, to all intents and purposes, rebukes "all hitherto existing materialism, that of Feuerbach included", for its lack of idealism, or for not conceding enough ground to or compromising with idealism; that is, for not conceiving "reality . . . subjectively", as mediated by *"human sensuous activity"*.[165] Nature must therefore be conceived as socially mediated.) More generally, Giles-Peters states that the theses "are incompatible with any non-social (non-human) nature; hence with the ontological independence of nature from man; hence with *any* materialism, historical or otherwise". So, if they "are taken — as they are, say, by Engels — as the 'germ' of Marx's later world view", one may fairly doubt all Marx's claims to materialism, including those claims made for the "materialist conception of history".[166]

Even Sebastiano Timpanaro, a Marxist himself, concedes that there is "a lack of clarity [on the subject of materialism] that goes right back to the origin of Marxist theory and was perhaps never completely overcome even in Marx's mature thought". Timpanaro formulates the issue much as I have done above (bearing in mind, again, that materialism and naturalism are understood to be synonymous in this context). He defines materialism, ontologically, as the "acknowledgement of the priority of nature over 'mind' [or] the socio-economic and cultural level", and, "cognitively" or epistemologically, as the belief that "experience cannot be reduced . . . to a production of reality by a subject (however such production is conceived [whether mental (in the solipsistic sense), speculative (in sense explained above), economic (as in Marx's case), or whatever])". As regards Marx, then: "If a *critique of anthropocentrism* [bravo!] and an emphasis on the conditioning of man by nature are considered essential to materialism, it must be said that Marxism, especially in its first phase . . . is not materialism proper". Rather charitably, Timpanaro continues: "the gigantic labor to which [Marx] had dedicated himself in the field of political economy did not permit him to develop [in his "later phase"] a new conception of the relation between man and nature which would fully replace that outlined in his youthful writings". In other words, Marx's fixation with his elaborate anthropocentric-economistic system made him incapable of improving upon it, even though he became (instinctively?) "much more materialist" in later years.[167] (Timpanaro's position seems essentially correct; my major contention is that I view the effort to reconcile Marxism and materialism as hopeless.)

Mainstream critics of historical materialism — notably Karl Popper — have focused on the question of the legitimacy, or, more precisely, illegitimacy, of Marx's approach or method, categorizing it as historicism, that is, supposedly, the Promethean attempt to get a handle on history, which is deemed impossible, or dangerous, or passé. Popper in fact distinguishes two elements in historical materialism. The first element is *economism* (the would-be materialistic element), that is, "the claim that the economic organization of society, the organization of our exchange of matter with nature [whatever that means], is fundamental for all social institutions and especially for their historical development". This claim Popper broadly supports — though no more than Bakunin does. In any case, the economistic element of Marx's thought, the economistic basis of his metaphysics of history, is, from the naturalistic standpoint, its real weakness. This is a view Popper does not share.

The second element in historical materialism is, on Popper's account, then, *historicism*, the "belief in *scientific fortune-telling*" or "the age-old dream of revealing what the future has in store for us". This element Sir Karl (like Sir Isaiah) rejects outright, on the basis, dare I say, of a certain fanaticism for the so-called "open society" and paranoia about anything which threatens it (such as the belief in the possibility of socio-political progress). He accuses Marx, therefore, of having "misled scores of intelligent [though presumably not intelligent enough] people into believing that *historical prophecy* is the scientific way of approaching social problems", and of being "responsible for the devastating influence of the historicist method of thought within the ranks of those who wish to advance the cause of the open society".[168] Frankly, it seems to me that Marx's "predictions" and "prophecies", as Popper has it, are few and far between and generally pretty limited in scope. That is to say, if, as Popper holds, Marx is possessed of a will to historicize (which is doubtful in the extreme), he fails to provide any significant historicizations: his "futuristic utterances" are speculative only in the logical (see Part One), and not in the prophetic, sense. In other words, that is not the main point of Marx's thought; the question of his economism or, as Bakunin labels it, "economic metaphysics", however, would seem to be of far greater consequence — unless, of course, something more, something more balanced, remains to be said of historicism.

Eric Hobsbawm offers what is perhaps a more enlightening definition of historicism as "the more or less sophisticated extrapolation of past tendencies into the future". But even this definition is ambiguous: does Hobsbawm mean the extrapolation of past tendencies into the future of the past, in other words, the present and perhaps beyond; or does he simply mean the extrapolation of past tendencies into the future of the present, with little or no concern for the present itself? (With Hobsbawm, I maintain, though not uncritically, that historical facts are precisely that, and that they are accessible, contrary to the "fashionable" postmodernist belief that "what we call [historical] 'facts' exist only as a function of prior concepts and problems formulated in terms of these . . . [and that] The past we study is only a construct of our minds" — a belief shaken when we question historical events like the Nazi holocaust accordingly.)[169] The latter approach, though conceivable, is hardly credible; it could only result in an extremely abstract and practically irrelevant *meditation on history*. The former approach, on the other hand, which consists in drawing at least limited conclusions about the world as it stands, on the basis of past events or historical facts broadly speaking, seems reasonable. However, it does assume (as history, though not as philosophy) a certain historic unity, a certain fixedness of the historical subject: in its more legitimate and fruitful forms, a biologically determined and defined human nature. (This [non-psychologistic] link between the natural and the social [that is, the naturalization of the social, in contrast to the prevalent post-Kantian metaphysical — or, as Feuerbach explains it, quasi-theological — socialization of the natural] may be regarded as its defense against the accusation of relativism, since it operates within a given and, more controversially, accessible framework. That is to say, the naturalistic overcoming of anthropocentrism represents some kind of threat to relativism, with all its political trappings.) Hegel expressed this conviction, albeit in inverted fashion or spiritualistic terms, as follows:

> The only thought which philosophy brings with it, in regard to history, is the simple thought of Reason — the thought that Reason rules the world, and that world history has therefore been rational in its course. This conviction and insight is a *presupposition* in regard to history as such, although it is not a presupposition in philosophy itself.[170]

So which approach does Marx, the supposed historicist, adopt? Once again, as I see it, he is not the *scientific fortune-teller* that Popper depicts. But might he be the aforementioned *meditator on history*? Surely not; it would surely be unfair to accuse him of merely extrapolating past tendencies into the future of the present; his thought is neither that abstract nor that irrelevant; indeed, he is anything but indifferent to present circumstances and needs. (Thus Bakunin writes: "one might say without flattery that [Marx's] entire life . . . has been exclusively devoted to the greatest cause of the present day, that of the emancipation of labor and the worker".[171]) Of course, this defense does not imply that his historical understanding of those circumstances and needs, that is, his understanding of the relation of the present to the past and the future, is adequate. Bakunin clearly thinks that it is inadequate — restrictive, partial, one-sided, abstract — and therefore, "set down in an absolute manner", or metaphysically formulated, *qua metaphysics of history*, false. In other words, Marx is not a historicist in the third sense either, since his conclusions about the future of the past, so to speak, lack the cohesion or historical unity that an account — either naturalistic or *objectively* idealistic — of the historical subject generates.

The account of the historical subject, if idealistic, cannot be that of the subjective idealist, who makes no attempt to explicate the concrete relation of thought to being, of cultural subject to natural object; for him everything is on the side of thought or culture, whether nature is granted independence (*merely conceptual* in any case) or not. Hence, on the one hand, the subjective idealist sends nature into investigative exile; and, on the other hand, as a result, he — to all intents and purposes — denies the biological status of the historical subject, that is, its derivation from and intimate, unbreakable union with nature. Consequently, the subjective idealist's account of the historical subject is partial. The objective idealist, in his favor, confronts nature, relates to it, at some stage at least, as *resistant other*. Hence, on the one hand, the objective idealist rescues nature from its place of exile; and, on the other hand, as a result, he achieves a recognition, admittedly perverse, of the intimate union of nature with the historical subject. The crucial difference, then, is this: while the object is *for* the idealist of the subjective and objective varieties, the objective idealist, unlike his subjective counterpart, acknowledges the resistance of the object to its ingestion by the all-devouring subject. Feuerbach argues, as we will see below, that the idealistic account of this dialectical confrontation with objective otherness, or the object conceived as other, necessarily leads to naturalism: essentially, the view that the object is not merely resistant to but also independent of, prior to, and constitutive of the subject. In spite of this, Marx, I contend, perhaps influenced in this fundamental regard by Max Stirner, never progresses beyond a "materialization" of subjective idealism; to this extent I regard him as Kantian, or of the Kantian tradition. I contend that Bakunin, by contrast, achieves a naturalization of objective idealism; to this extent I regard him as Hegelian, or of the Hegelian tradition.

The basic objection to Marx's metaphysics of history, however we characterize it with regard to historicism, is that it is partial; that is, relatively, though not absolutely, false — or, indeed, as Bakunin has already stated, relatively, though not absolutely, true. In other words, it is a partial interpretation of the present, conceived economistically or in terms of the capitalist mode of production. This interpretation is supposedly supported by a wealth of historical material. However, it might be argued that this material has the partial interpretation foisted upon it; that is, that the present (or "determining" elements of it) is telescoped out into the past. (And, likewise, into the future. This telescoping of the present into the future is, however, hardly prophetic, since the "foretold" changes are non-substantial. Hence it is essentially conservative, anticipating a mere shift in economic and political power, while insisting on the productive imperative or the human quest to subjugate nature for the sake of one interest group or other. [Bookchin regards the Marxian notion of "class interest" as another form of self-interest, as a socialized egoism, and therefore characterizes Marxism as "the alter ego of traditional capitalism".[172] Given the formative influence of the classical British economists, not to mention Stirner, on Marx, there is a certain coherence to this line of argument.] Such conservatism is represented by Marx as the scientific approach; anything that insists on the possibility of substantial change is represented as utopian or voluntaristic.) Thus it may be that Marx progresses from a conception of capitalism to an appropriate conception of *its* past; that is, from a specific conception of a dominant element of the present to a universal economistic conception of the past which supports it.

Eric Voegelin — perceptive, for all his flaws — shares this view of the partiality of Marx's analysis. But what he objects to in particular is the absolutization of this partial analysis. He asks why thinkers like Marx "expressly prohibit anybody to ask questions concerning the sectors of reality [for example, nature, the whole of reality on the naturalistic account] they have excluded from their personal horizon? [Why] do they want to imprison themselves in their restricted horizon and to dogmatize their prison reality as the universal truth? [And] why do they want to lock up all mankind in the prison of their making [all too literally, in the case of Marx's disciples]?" Furthermore, Voegelin notes that such thinkers have a tendency to employ "the dignified tactic of not taking cognizance of fatal criticism [*Statism and Anarchy*, though imperfect, is about the most fatal critique of Marx], and the less dignified procedure of personally defaming the critic".[173] Engels tried to defend Marx and himself against the first charge: "Marx and I are ourselves partly to blame for the fact that the younger people sometimes lay more stress on the economic side than is due to it. We had to emphasize the main principle *vis-à-vis* our adversaries, who denied it [Bakunin does nothing of the sort], and we had not always the time, the place or the opportunity to allow the other elements involved in the interaction to come into their rights".[174] But for all Engels' protestations to the contrary, Marx clearly did hold the materialist conception of history to be as good as absolute. As a result (and in line with Voegelin's second charge), he censures all those who dare to oppose his views — notably the anarchists — for their utter ignorance. For example, Marx patronizes the "petty bourgeois" Proudhon by suggesting that, as such, "he is *incapable* of understanding economic development".[175] He also calls Bakunin an "ass" for claiming that economic factors in and of themselves do not bring about social revolution. Typically, Marx writes: "He understands *absolutely* nothing about social revolution; all he knows are its political phrases. For him its economic requisites do not exist ... *Will power* and not economic conditions is the basis of his so-cial revolution".[176]

That Marx's allegation (that Bakunin is his partial ideological counterpart, that he absolutizes the other (and "wrong") principle, while, like Marx himself, he should absolutize the ("correct") economic one — an accusation based on a false antithesis from Bakunin's stand-point, as we have demonstrated) is false is obvious to anyone of inde-pendent mind who cares to read *Statism and Anarchy*, to which Marx is referring. Paul Thomas, for example, is clearly not of independent mind. Sheepishly following Marx, he speaks of Bakunin's "extreme volunta-rism", of his "emphasis on the primacy of revolutionary will", and, worse still, adds that "To Stirner and Bakunin *alike* the source of revolu-tionary liberation was the will of the revolutionary ... [This] will, once extended, is capable of destroying the state and its 'hierarchy' [I dread to think what Thomas might mean by those quotation marks]".[177] As I will show below, this is nonsense, unbelievably churned out more than one hundred years after the original "debate", repetition of a simple falsehood without, apart from any degree of insight, the slightest im-pact of hindsight. (Thomas is not unique in this respect: Kelly, for dif-ferent ideological reasons, writes of "the genuinely Bakuninist faith [after Fichte, needless to say] that it is possible by [a simple] effort of will to transform reality into what one would wish it to be".[178]) It should be made simple for Thomas and his ilk, before we restate the argument in a less patronizing manner. The question of "will" arises because Bakunin is skeptical about the notion of historico-economic "necessity", of economic determinism. Bakunin's *Essay Against Marx*[179] of 1872, that is, just one year before *Statism and Anarchy*, makes this quite clear, if Thomas cared to read it (Marx, in his defense, could not have done so). Bakunin's point is merely that revolution requires a "subjective" element, that it cannot simply be "determined" in a void, in the absence of any *natural* agency (a class in Marx's sense hardly consti-tutes an agency, never mind a natural agency, but the instrument of mysterious and supposedly objective — though in fact socio-subjective — forces). For Bakunin the subjective element is a human agency (in the case of social revolution, a "class" which need not be confined to the glorified urban proletariat), with its capacity to "will", or to initiate change, within naturally determined bounds, certain social circumstances permitting. There is no reason to suppose Bakunin thinks this is tremendously perceptive or original; he thinks it is obvious enough; he thinks that to deny this dimension of revolution, with Marx, is to conceive of it metaphysically. (Some years after Bakunin, Peter Kropotkin, who contends that "It was Bakunin who initiated . . . the critique of Marxism", restates this fundamental criticism of "Marx's belief in the fatalism of capitalism's self-negation":

> "Economic materialism" [is] passed off as a rigorously scientific theory according to which revolution will come *of itself* through the development of productive forces, and all efforts to bring it about are therefore useless.[180])

Therefore, while Bakunin is, like his contemporary compatriot Dostoyevsky for example, critical of deterministic "scientism" (as much as of theologism and statism), he is neither an arationalist nor a voluntarist, which Dostoyevsky may (or may not) be.[181] In fact, Bakunin continually declares himself a determinist; but, unlike Marx, he is a naturalistic determinist (that is, he believes that the objective, nature, ultimately determines the subjective, the human, for the simple reason that the subjective is of it and in no way distinct from it), not a metaphysical or anthropocentric determinist (who believes, conversely, that the subjective, the human, determines the objective, nature, in some supernatural way or other — thereby presupposing some qualitative distinction). It is Marx, not Bakunin, who exaggerates the subjective side (or socio-historical side) of revolution and history in general; hence one might refer, as much as to his socialized egoism, to Marx's socialized subjectivism. He is close in this respect to his Kantian colleagues, the socio-linguistic subjectivists (who coincidentally or otherwise are opposed by contemporary anarchists such as Chomsky and Bookchin).

Bakunin writes in *Statism and Anarchy*, then, of the revolutionary will (which, as we have seen, he views as a naturalistic principle) being incited by "an extreme degree of poverty", that is, by the economic factor generally speaking. He maintains that both this will and the economic factor are necessary conditions for social revolution, but that *neither is a sufficient condition*. As he puts it: "The most terrible poverty . . . even when it strikes a proletariat numbering in the many millions, is not a sufficient guarantee of revolution" because, quite simply, "Nature [including any number of social factors] has given man an astonishing, and, indeed, sometimes despairing, patience". Bakunin holds that man must be "driven to desperation" before "revolt becomes . . . a possibility". It is this desperation, this "sharp, passionate feeling", which "draws him out of his dull, somnolent suffering", and eventually awakens the negative or destructive passion (a constant theme in Bakunin's work), that is, the revolutionary will. As if to respond to Marx's allegation directly, then, Bakunin writes: "This negative passion is *far from sufficient* for achieving the ultimate aims of the revolutionary cause. Without it, however, that cause would be inconceivable, impossible".[182] Bakunin, here as always, therefore, counters the crude socio-subjective (masquerading as objective) determinism of Marx (as Bakunin represents it in his *Essay Against Marx*, for example) with the simple Hegelian point (contrary to the conventional caricature) that historical transformation is the result of the real interaction of "objective" and "subjective" factors, of, say, the state of social nature and the potentially determining natural human agent. In Hegel's spiritualistic terms, "There are two elements that enter into [the] topic [of history]: the first is the Idea, the other is human passion; the first is the warp, the other the woof in the great tapestry of world history that is spread out before us". Hegel says of the latter element, we may note, that "*nothing great* has been accomplished in the world *without passion*" — passion for that which is lacking, which, ultimately, for Hegel and Bakunin, is freedom.[183]

In spite of *all* this, scholars of anarchism have often mistaken Bakunin for an historical materialist. Arthur Lehning, no less, says that

"Bakunin adopted [Marx's] historical materialism".[184] Daniel Guérin takes it as given that Bakunin "*fully* accepted the materialist conception of history".[185] Brian Morris, likewise, asserts that "Bakunin was a dialectical or historical materialist, not a mechanical one", which, literally, is true, but in the Marxian sense is false. Morris makes this assertion on the strength of his argument that "Bakunin's conception of reality, like that of Marx, is dialectical, materialist, and deterministic", which is valid for the most part, but the "like that of Marx" clause is troublesome, since Marx's materialism — beyond the metaphysical web of historical "materialism" — is, once again, difficult to establish.[186] This mistake is understandable. On occasion Bakunin voices what is seemingly the staunchest support for Marx's position, not least in the following cases:

> [Marx] advanced and proved the incontrovertible truth, confirmed by the entire past and present history of human society, nations, and states, that economic fact has always preceded legal and political right. The exposition and demonstration of that truth constitutes one of Marx's principal contributions to science.[187]

> . . . the entire history of humanity, intellectual and moral, political and social, is a reflection of its economic history.[188]

As regards the second passage, the relativity of economic causality is brought into view by the more consistently naturalistic claim, a matter of pages later, that history "consists precisely in the progressive negation of the primitive animality of man by the development of his humanity [that is, of his reason, theoretical and practical]".[189] Thus human history consists in the emergence, and continuous fulfillment, of a specific natural, neural development. Any historical account that obscures this fundamental dimension of human history (in its continuity with the rest of natural history), and proclaims a more immediate, local cause within history absolute, is highly dubious. The very absolutization of a local human cause, i.e., the economic cause (or the economistic prioritization of the human over the natural), is exactly what has been characterized here as anthropocentrism.

As for the previous passage, Pyziur acknowledges it, but concludes — properly, in light of the foregoing considerations — that "As a rule, Bakunin dilutes Marx's historical materialism to a point where it becomes little more than an insistence that the economic factor is *one* of the important [or relative] causes of *social* change" (in other words, one of the local factors in social history).[190] Bakunin may overstate the importance of this factor on occasion, but then he is also prone to overstating other factors that are relative too (and, as social factors, relatively minor in comparison with general natural laws or episodic natural events, such as so-called "catastrophes"). As an instance of the overstatement of a non-economic factor, note the following:

> Whoever is in the least concerned with history cannot fail to see that at the basis of the most abstract, sublime, and ideal religious and theological struggles there is always some great material interest. No war between races, nations, States, and classes has ever had any purpose other than *domination*, the necessary condition and guarantee of possession and enjoyment [of wealth].[191]

Bakunin, in more consistent mode, therefore criticizes Marx for paying "no heed to [non-economic] elements in history, such as the effect — though obvious — of political, juridical, and religious institutions on the economic situation".[192] Which is to say that Bakunin simply does not accept a base-superstructure framework wherein the political, the juridical, and the religious are merely elements of an economically-determined superstructure. This framework, which is accorded relative merit by Bakunin, is, in any case, profoundly ahistorical in itself since it does not take account of man's development from the pre-human condition to the human condition by physiological (chiefly neural) and, by extension, rational (including religious) development. It simply assumes the presence of a metaphysically modeled economic creature.

Curiously, such reservations indicate to Kelly — a liberal scholar demonstrating a cowardly intellectual reverence for Marx (as she does throughout her malicious and philosophically naive book) — that "Bakunin never gave serious attention to economic materialism". (Kelly obviously misunderstands Bakunin's relation to historical materialism. She claims that it "provided Bakunin with an impressive intellectual foundation for his atheism", which, from the above account, is clearly untrue; historical materialism is in fact one of the targets of Bakunin's anti-theologistic critique, the foundations of which have been demonstrated to lie elsewhere. She also claims that it "came to represent for him the final stage in [the] process of emancipation from the thrall of metaphysics", which, again, from the above account, is obviously untrue; Bakunin's major reservation about Marxian thought is precisely due to its perceived metaphysicality and non-naturalism.)[193] It would be more truthful to say Kelly never gives serious attention to Bakunin's thought. (Though, for example, she seems fixated upon the far more important subject of his financial affairs — a subject that is, we must infer, close to her heart — so that her book might as well be subtitled "A Study in the Psychology and Politics of the [sin of "bourgeois" sins] Bad Debt".) However, others share my view of a fundamental philosophical distinction. K.J. Kenafick, for example, writes: "As far as Marx's works are concerned, Man might have had no pre-human and little or no pre-political history. Marx, that is to say, never treats Man as a biological phenomenon, but . . . as an economic subject" (an argument which — modified such that the "economic subject" becomes a "culturo-linguistic subject" in general — might be directed at all Kantians). Bakunin, though, influenced by Feuerbach, especially Comte, and also Darwin, "clearly recognized Man's biological character and wrote and acted on that assumption".[194]

Marxists have responded by attacking this "assumption" (in spite of the fact that, in principle, its validity has been firmly established in various fields of science from genetics to linguistics). István Mészáros, for example, accuses Bakunin of sharing with liberals "an arbitrarily assumed [notion of] 'human nature'".[195] To the extent that Bakunin makes any *specific* (or contentious) "assumptions" in this regard, he has little in common with the liberal tradition, which he considers (in its conception of liberty) resolutely metaphysical. But, for the most part, all Bakunin "assumes" is the biological meaningfulness of "human nature", and this "assumption" can hardly be discounted as "arbitrary"; indeed, its validity has never been in less doubt. This belief, which I take to be fundamentally sound, is, in fact, a constant in social-anarchist philosophy, from Proudhon ("Man has but one nature, constant and unalterable"[196]) to Chomsky ("Human nature exists, immutable except for biological changes in the species"[197]). I acknowledge here that Proudhon's account of human nature, which is overly psychological or "idealistic" and insufficiently naturalistic, is not satisfactory. Marx recognizes this, and Bakunin agrees, in part at any rate, with his analysis: "Undoubtedly there is a good deal of truth in the merciless critique [Marx] directed against Proudhon. For all his efforts to ground himself in reality, Proudhon remained an idealist and a metaphysician".[198] But, as we will see momentarily, Marx adopts an even less satisfactory position — by abandoning human nature, or at least making it contingent upon economic history. That is to say, he replaces Proudhon's psychocentric attempt at naturalism with an outright anthropocentrism. Bakunin's account of human nature, though limited, is richer than Proudhon's; in any case, what is most significant about it is that Bakunin will not sacrifice it to any form of metaphysics, be it psychological, economic, or whatever. It seems that Marx and certain Marxists, in attacking Bakunin on this point, confuse his account with Proudhon's. There is, without doubt, in any case, a tendency among Marxists (and others) to conflate different anarchisms, whether closely related (as in the case of Proudhon and Bakunin) or not (as in the case of Stirner and Bakunin [we noted Paul Thomas' conflation earlier]).

What, then, does Marx himself have to say about this issue? Most tellingly, he claims that "history is nothing but a continuous transformation of human nature".[199] This is a pivotal statement — illustrating, in the context of Marx's debate with Proudhon, how irreconcilable the Marxian and social-anarchist philosophies are. Elsewhere Marx famously asserts that "The first premise of all human history is . . . the existence of living *human individuals*", and that, therefore, "the first fact to be established is the physical organization of these individuals and their consequent relation to the rest of nature". — An interesting (liberal) emphasis on the abstract individual and the consequentiality of natural relations involving such a nondescript individual. But, regardless, Marx passes on with a helpful "Of course, we cannot here go either into the actual physical nature of man, or into the natural conditions in which man finds himself". — Merely adding that "The writing of history must always set out from these natural bases and *their modification in the course of history through the action of man*". Note the idealistic tone of the last line, according to which man can (and, as will become apparent, necessarily does) modify nature, including his own nature, by economic activity. (Again Marx insists on the priority of that which is, as we will see, accessible only as mediated; that is, on the existence (even if only historical) of the inaccessible, the in-itself.) One might well ask if man's nature is not modified more fundamentally in an evolutionary sense, and thus relatively ahistorical or given. If this is the case, we need at least a descriptive account of it. But Marx is interested in neither human nature nor Nature — not to mention matter as such — all of which are subsumed by his economic metaphysics.

More importantly, Marx goes on to assert that "Men can be distinguished from animals by consciousness, by religion, *or by anything else you like. They themselves* begin to distinguish themselves from animals as soon as they begin to *produce* their means of subsistence, a step which is conditioned by their physical organization". Is this an adequate distinction? (Don't other animals produce their means of subsistence in a qualitatively identical fashion? Isn't the distinction, rather, one of the *degree* of intelligence applied in production *or any other activity* (including the uniquely human reflective recognition of difference, which mysteriously occurs in Marx's account)? If it is, we need at least a descriptive account of the nature of animal intelligence, including human intelligence, or so-called reason.) And why simply ignore "consciousness, religion, or anything else" in favor of an imposed, that is, assumed, "they themselves" account? From Bakunin's perspective, therefore, Marx's account is in itself a groundless metaphysical alternative to a more rounded naturalistic account of human development and history (which, again, is not to deny its *relative* merit — indeed, brilliance). So much, then, for his "real premises from which abstraction can only be made in the imagination", and which can therefore "be verified in a *purely* empirical way".[200]

2.16 Bakunin and Feuerbach: On Philosophy

Feuerbach's critique is not a critique of (the theologized Christian) religion alone. It is also — as we see in *Vorläufige Thesen zur Reformation der Philosophie* (*Provisional Theses for the Reformation of Philosophy*) (1842) and *Grundsätze der Philosophie der Zukunft* (*Principles of the Philosophy of the Future*) (1843) — a critique of (speculative) philosophy. His critique of religion revealed that "The secret of *theology* is *anthropology*". His critique of philosophy, on the other hand, reveals that "the secret of *speculative philosophy* is *theology*", or that philosophy as it stands — the philosophy originated by Descartes (in "the abstraction of sensation and matter"[201]) and developed by Leibniz, Spinoza, and the German idealists — is simply "the *speculative* theology". Hence there is no real distinction between theology and speculative philosophy. (Bakunin, following Feuerbach, therefore refers to the single mode of thought that embraces both as *theologism*.) Feuerbach duly claims that the critical method is the same in the case of both philosophy and religion, so that "we need only *invert* speculative philosophy and then we have the unmasked, pure, bare truth", which is the following:

> Just as in theology the *human* being is the *truth* and *reality* of God, so in speculative philosophy the *truth* of the *infinite* is the finite.[202]

Speculative philosophy, Feuerbach argues, deriving the finite from the infinite, the determined from the undetermined, or proceeding from the abstract to the concrete, from the ideal to the real, *"never arrives at a true position of the finite and determined"* — or (to put it in philosophically unfashionable language) at the truth of reality. Feuerbach declares that "true philosophy" has the duty of inverting its procedure, and revealing that "The infinite of religion and philosophy is and never was anything other than something *finite*, something determined, yet *mystified*, i.e., a finite and determined something *with the postulate* of being *not* finite and *not* determined".[203] The objects of both religion and philosophy are therefore mystifications of the real. (We may note the shift in emphasis here from man to the finite. The emphasis will subsequently shift from the finite to the natural, but continuity is preserved and no break occurs at any stage (as I will argue further below); rather, the implicit naturalism in Feuerbach's thought becomes explicit and more coherent.)

The Hegelian philosophy is described by Feuerbach as the "culmination of modern [speculative] philosophy"; as such, the task of the "new philosophy" is to develop a critique of this philosophy, and, thereby, to realize it without contradiction. The contradiction in Hegelian philosophy is expressed by Feuerbach as follows: *"The Hegelian philosophy is the last place of refuge and the last rational support of theology"*. While "Matter is . . . posited in God [or] posited as God [that is, "taken up into the absolute being as a moment in its life, growth, and development"]", Feuerbach explains, positing "matter as God amounts to saying 'There is no God', or, what amounts to the same, it is to renounce theology and to recognize the truth of materialism. But at the same time the truth of the essence of theology is nevertheless presupposed".[204] (This compromise between theology and materialism is metaphysics by Bakunin's definition, above.)

The task of the new philosophy — being the realization of the Hegelian philosophy without contradiction — is therefore the development of the true materialist philosophy (and the negation of metaphysics). Or, in the terms of Bakunin's dialectic, *the new philosophy will consist in the fulfillment of the antithetical philosophy, materialism, not in any mediating philosophy, that is, metaphysics.* (Feuerbach, contemptuous of philosophical professionalism and its fixed terminology, identifies the new philosophy as materialism, realism, empiricism, naturalism, etc., depending on context. On the whole, I favor the suitably inclusive, and frankly more accurate, term naturalism, but, following Feuerbach's lead (for the simple reason that Bakunin does), I use the terms more or less interchangeably.)

Feuerbach's alternative formulation of the above is the following: "The recognition of the light of reality [that is, sensuous materiality] in the darkness of abstraction [that is, spiritual ideality] is a contradiction; it is the affirmation of the real in its negation [it is, that is to say, an abstract recognition of the sensuous]. The new philosophy is the philosophy that thinks of the concrete [the real] not in an abstract [or ideal], but in a concrete [or empirical] manner. It is the philosophy that recognizes the real in its reality as true, namely, in a manner corresponding to the essence of the real" — which is sensuousness. Feuerbach continues: "Only a sensuous [or material] being is a true and real being. Only through the senses, and not through thought for itself, is an object given in a true sense [i.e., immediately]". The object — the other, the "not-I" — is given to the subject — the self, the "I" — in sensation. Sensation alone explains the reciprocity of this very relation: "Only sensuous [or material] beings affect one another. I am an 'I' for myself and simultaneously a 'thou' for others. This I am, however, *only* as a sensuous being". By contrast, the "abstract mind" — that which, in Cartesian fashion, abstracts from reality in its sensuousness — "can . . . only arbitrarily connect the being-for-others [or object] with the being-for-itself [or subject]".[205]

In sense perception, therefore, there is — in principle — no contradiction between the sensuous "subject" and the sensible "object"; indeed, the sensuous "subject" is at once a sensible "object" for itself and others; and the sensible "object" is — *qua* material "object" — at once potentially a sensible "subject" itself (as Diderot's materialism implies). (Wartofsky expresses this idea in the following way: "Sensation [the "subjective" dimension of reality for Feuerbach] is a dispositional property of ["objective"] matter, once this matter has been organically absorbed, [or] transformed into living stuff, and comes *literally* to constitute the sense organs themselves as material organs".[206]) It is only by idealizing the sensible "subject" (with, say, Kant), so that the subject in effect determines the object, or by idealizing the sensible "object" (with, say, Locke), so that the idea of some nebulous object in effect determines the subject — in both cases quite mysteriously, since a qualitative contradiction, a contradiction in kind, is assumed — that the contradiction between "subject" and "object" becomes problematic, or, in fact, mysterious.

The essential interconnectedness of reality, the unity of the totality of nature in its sensuous materiality, is crucial to Feuerbach. Hence, he writes, "That of which I think without sensation I think of without and apart from all connection", that is, partially, abstractly, and falsely. The preoccupation of modern philosophy with the "immediately certain" was exposed by Hegel as partial, abstract, and false in this sense. Hegel revealed the mediacy of immediacy, while, however, *insisting on the immediacy of truth in a richer sense*. Here Feuerbach makes the pertinent point that "It is scholasticism to make mediation into a divine necessity and an essential attribute of truth", so-called. Bearing in mind the supposedly rich vein of European thought, stretching from Marx to Derrida, and excluding the less profound Feuerbach and Bakunin, the following statement by Feuerbach strikes me as being momentous: "Who can elevate mediation [implicitly or explicitly] to necessity and to a law of truth? Only he who himself is still imprisoned by that which is to be negated [i.e., the irreconcilable metaphysical conflict between "subject" and "object"] . . . in short, only he in whom truth is only a talent, a matter of special, even outstanding, ability but not genius and a matter of the whole man. Genius is immediate, sensuous knowledge. What talent has only in the head genius has in the flesh and blood; namely, that which for talent is still an object of thought is for genius an object of the senses".[207]

Feuerbach's preliminary remarks on the new philosophy are worth commenting on further in this context, given the obscurantism and scholasticism of contemporary philosophy, not least in the "Continental" tradition. He begins with the apparent truism that "Philosophy is the knowledge of *what is*" — or the pursuit of such knowledge. He adds, "To have articulated what is *such as it is*, in other words, to have *truthfully* articulated what truly is, *appears superficial*. To have articulated what is *such as it is not* [on the other hand], in other words, to have *falsely* and *distortedly* articulated what truly is, *appears profound*". The Franco-Germanic alliance might well take note. However, in case the Anglo-American alliance feels justified by Feuerbach's maxim — "*Truthfulness, simplicity*, and *determinacy* are the formal marks of the *real* philosophy" — he adds the following stipulation:

> The new and only positive philosophy is the *negation of academic philosophy* . . . the negation of philosophy *as an abstract, particular, i.e., scholastic*, quality.[208]

The task of philosophical inquiry, then, is to articulate reality or nature in its sensuous materiality, as it is. In Feuerbach's words, "All sciences must ground themselves in *nature*". By this means, and by this means alone, can inquiry progress beyond the merely speculative: hence, "A doctrine is only an *hypothesis* as long as its *natural basis* is not uncovered". Crucially, Feuerbach goes on: "This holds particularly for the *doctrine of freedom*. Only the new philosophy will succeed in *naturalizing* freedom, which formerly was an *unnatural* and *supernatural hypothesis*". (In my view, Bakunin's philosophy must be understood in light of this proposition. (Take the following example: "we have envisaged ["the human world", with its potentiality for freedom] hitherto as the manifestation of a theological, metaphysical, and juridico-political idea, [but] now we must renew the study of it, taking *nature as the point of de-*

parture and *the specific physiology of man as the guiding thread*".[209]) What is more, the project of naturalizing freedom is fundamental to anarchism as a whole, most obviously the anarchism of Bookchin.) The new philosophy is therefore materialistic and naturalistic, and, as such, best suited to a new — and mutually fulfilling — alliance, in fact, re-alliance, with science:

> *Philosophy must again combine itself with natural science and natural science with philosophy.* This combining, based on mutual need and inner necessity, will be more lasting, more successful, and more fruitful than the *previous mésalliance* between philosophy and theology [that is, more fruitful than metaphysics].[210]

Feuerbach suggests a more precise direction that the new philosophy might take, and it is the inadequacy of his sketch that demonstrates that the "new" philosophy of the *Principles* is very definitely a *philosophy of the future*. Central to Feuerbach's position is an empiricist epistemology. However, his dispute with traditional empiricism is that "it forgets that the most important and essential sense object of man is man himself [or] that only in man's glimpse into man is the light of consciousness and understanding kindled". Ideas therefore originate in man, but not man in isolation, as idealism — deriving ideas "from the 'I' without a given sensuous 'thou'" — holds. Rather, ideas — and reason — are the product of "communication and conversation between man and man". Hence, "the community of man with man is the first principle and criterion of truth and generality". Feuerbach vitiates his aforementioned critique of scholasticism at this point, arguing that "The certainty of the existence of other things apart from me is *mediated* for me through the certainty of the existence of another human being apart from me", and that "That which I alone perceive I doubt; only that which the other also perceives is certain".[211] *This,* so redolent of much twentieth-century philosophy, is scholasticism. And thus Feuerbach's materialism — of this period — collapses. Wartofsky explains: "to argue for a view very much like Kant's [—] that the objectivity of what *is* is attested to by the fact that not I alone, but others too agree on what is — [is] a rather weak position, given Feuerbach's earlier critique of Kant". Or, "Feuerbach [insists] that the senses give us *truth*, that is, the thing-in-itself, as objectively existing. But here, he argues for objectivity as intersubjectivity, in a Kantian way. How can these two alternative positions cohere?".[212] They cannot, but Feuerbach manages to overcome such incoherence by developing a stricter anti-Kantian argument in his later work.

The flaw in Feuerbach's so-called materialism (to this point) is that the object of sensuousness is conceived of as being necessarily a mystical Thou rather than a real object. Therefore, Feuerbach, in seeking to demystify the epistemological relation between the real subject and the ideal object, succeeds only in mystifying the real object that he discloses — in idealizing it once again by humanizing it. (Contemporary scholastics tend to call this humanization — which they too practice — contextualization.) That is to say, once the real object is obscured by the mystical Thou, it in fact escapes any concrete cognitive relation and becomes a mere *topic of conversation*. Clearly, this topic of conversation — as opposed to the material object as such — is hugely appealing to speculative philosophers, past and present.

Feuerbach, in spite of his earlier insight, therefore makes community *in the most abstract sense* (an *intersubjective* community of I and Thou), or the mediation of communal discourse, "a divine necessity and an essential attribute of truth". As he puts it himself, "The true dialectic is not a monologue of the solitary thinker with himself; it is a dialogue between I and thou". This is anti-materialistic scholasticism — and, importantly, an aspect of Feuerbach's thought that is replicated by Marx (since he shares the anthropocentric thrust of it). Nevertheless, Feuerbach seems to grapple with this side of his argument. He writes, "The sensuous is not, in the sense of speculative philosophy, the immediate; it is not the profane, obvious, and thoughtless that is understood by itself". Feuerbach, following Hegel, asserts the mediacy of such immediacy. However, he also insists, with Hegel, on the immediacy of truth in a richer sense: "Immediate, sensuous perception comes much later than the [primitive perception of the] imagination and the fantasy". (Thus, Feuerbach's is a "sophisticated immediacy". Sensible reality "is *not* immediately given, *tout court*, but has to be achieved *as* immediate. [The] suggestion therefore is that this sensibility, as achieved, is a *product* of scientific inquiry [or] an achievement of culture and education, and therefore of history".[213] Sensation is an acquired ability to grasp without impediment — unimpeded, that is, by theology, metaphysics, etc. [Incidentally, this notion of immediacy has the advantage of forestalling charges of subjectivism, inability to deal with error, and so on.]) Contradicting the scholastic side of his argument, then, Feuerbach continues:

> The task of philosophy and of science in general consists, therefore, not in leading away from sensuous, that is, real, objects, but rather in leading toward them, not in transforming objects into ideas and conceptions, but rather in making visible, that is, in objectifying, objects that are invisible to ordinary eyes.[214]

Feuerbach's inability to ground his materialism in the *Principles* can be explained in his own terms. His materialism is purely speculative, that is, scholastic: it is not the product of a mutually fulfilling alliance with natural science. In other words, lacking a natural basis, it is merely hypothetical. It is the task of the nature-philosopher of the future to uncover this natural basis — and not simply to sanction effective relativism speculatively (in the name of the "divine necessity" of mediation) in the manner of so much contemporary thought. (There is good reason for philosophers to refuse to undertake this task, or even to deny its meaningfulness: quite simply, to acknowledge the necessity of this task would be to render philosophers with no idea of, interest in, or capacity for scientific endeavor superfluous. Philosophy as a specialized field makes sound economic and psychological sense, and might well wish to maintain itself (even if this results in the intellectual disenchantment of humanity). The specialization of science might be criticized along the same lines, though there is a degree more justification for it practically speaking. It is incumbent on philosophers, therefore, to pursue the alliance.)

2.17 Interlude: Bakunin and Marx Revisited

Marx's critique of Feuerbach here must be commented upon. Marx, in his fifth thesis on Feuerbach, properly argues that Feuerbach's materialism — or one side of it — is merely speculative: "Feuerbach, not satisfied with *abstract thinking*, appeals to *sensuous contemplation*". However, Marx adds, decisively, that "he does not conceive sensuousness as practical, human-sensuous activity".[215] It is at this point that Marx makes his speculative leap, and at which Marx and Bakunin go their separate ways. Marx's interpretation of Feuerbach's materialism places him in the tradition of scholasticism — which Feuerbach exposed, but could not escape (as he almost admits in his appeal for philosophical revolution in §65 of the *Principles*).

While rejecting Feuerbach's abstract community of I and Thou, or the mediation of communal discourse, Marx actually proposes an abstract economic community, or the mediation of productive activity. Hence, Marx says of Feuerbach that he "does not see how the sensuous world around him is, not a thing given direct from all eternity, remaining ever the same, but the product of industry and of the state of society . . . Even the objects of the simplest 'sensuous certainty' are only given him through social development, industry, and commercial intercourse". Neither Feuerbach (at this stage) nor Marx offers a naturalistic account: both of their metaphysical theories lack a natural basis. Feuerbach, unlike Marx, though, is consciously aware of the need for such a basis. Of course, Marx, as I have pointed out above, does at least hint at the need for it. But Marx mocks Feuerbach's consciousness of this need: "Feuerbach speaks in particular of the perception of natural science; he mentions secrets which are disclosed only to the eye of the physicist and chemist; but where would natural science be without industry and commerce? Even this 'pure' natural science is provided with an aim, *as with its material*, only through trade and industry, through the sensuous activity of men".[216] This is a prime example of Marx's indulgence in the mediating principle that he has established as the basis of his metaphysical system. It is not that the principle is "untrue" — indeed it is a useful critical tool — but its status as "a divine necessity and an essential attribute of truth" is scarcely justified. But I have dealt with the metaphysicality of Marx's thought above.

Bakunin, by contrast, takes up the challenge posed by Feuerbach. Drawing on the authentically materialistic and naturalistic aspects of Feuerbach's thought (as opposed to the dubious "social epistemology", in which, remarkably, Marx sees the "establishment of true materialism and of real science"[217]), Bakunin seeks to ground his philosophy in nature, or to lay a natural foundation for it. That is, accepting Feuerbach's statement that "Only that thought which is determined and rectified by sensuous perception is real and objective thought — the thought of objective truth", Bakunin attempts to dissolve the contradiction between epistemologized subject and object, without preserving it in a new form — that is, without lapsing into scholasticism.[218] Bakunin is not inclined to absolutize the mediation of either communal discourse or productive activity: both principles of mediation are simple humanizations or idealizations, that is, abstractions: abstractions from the underlying — actually, all-embracing — reality that is nature. (Marx, as I have already argued, has no interest in or concept of nature, and can therefore speculate to his heart's content about man's economic domination of it. The political and ecological implications of Marx's abstraction have been noted above.)

Bakunin, again, attempts to dissolve the contradiction between the human subject and its ideal object by exposing the anthropocentric bias of this epistemological relation. In other words, he rejects the Kantian tendency toward the humanization of reality, insisting that there is something over and above the human which includes it and which is, in principle, accessible to it, i.e., nature. The status of man, as Bakunin views it, is that of a natural or physical "subject" of a particular — or particularly developed — kind. The "object" which is available to this "subject" is necessarily a natural or physical "object". Hence, "subject" and "object" are both natural and naturally related. The human "subject" relates *immediately* to the "object" in nature sensuously — not in the obvious sense of speculative philosophy, as Feuerbach might put it, but in a richer sense. Natural "subject" and natural "object" are indeed distinct *in themselves*, yet, at the same time, "substantially" one — and therefore "cognitively" one in the natural process of "sensuous perception" (to use Feuerbach's expression). That is to say, in sensuous perception there is no contradiction, no necessity for mediation: it is scholasticism to maintain otherwise.

Frederick M. Gordon's critique of the naturalistic aspect of Feuerbach's "epistemology" might therefore be leveled at Bakunin. Gordon summarizes the "epistemological" claim of Feuerbach as follows: "Immediacy . . . is gained only after long mediation, through philosophy and science. What at first appears as immediacy is mere 'imagination of the object' . . . Only when education has done its work can one see things as they are — as sense-immediacy". The weakness that Gordon sees here is that "once immediacy is defined as the product of mediation, the force of [Feuerbach"s] original claims is dissipated. Whatever mediated immediacy is, it is not what he had previously dramatically called sense-immediacy".[219] Is this true? And even if it is true, is it problematic? Most importantly, why the aversion to "mediated immediacy"? Mediation of this kind simply represents the historical development of knowledge of both the individual and humanity as a whole, which the philosopher traces as a phenomenology. From the naturalistic philosopher's point of view, the highest form of knowledge is scientific knowledge: it is by scientific observation, or sensuous perception as such, that one comes to know what is as it is. Hence the importance of the knowledge of scientific method, and, generally speaking, education in this method. This may all rest on "dogmatic assertion", as Wartofsky suspects.[220] But, in fact, Feuerbach and Bakunin work within a dialectical framework in which their claims must be assessed. Their claims depend on the genetic critique of idealism, and are asserted ("dogmatically" or not) on the basis that idealistic or theocentric philosophies cannot withstand this critique and that they are, in spite of themselves, turning into their antithesis.

What is apparent in the approach of both Feuerbach and Bakunin — in contrast to the essentially Kantian approach of Marx and many contemporary thinkers — is its Hegelianism. That is, their fundamental concern is to overcome the Kantian bifurcation — or to dissolve the contradiction between human subject and the object of human cognition — and to establish the immediacy of knowledge within a phenomenological context. However, both are anti-Hegelian insofar as they seek to naturalize the epistemological relation rather than to spiritualize or idealize it. Putting Spirit aside, then, both seek to articulate the natural. Feuerbach's articulation in *Das Wesen der Religion* (*The Essence of Religion*) (1845) and *Vorlesungen über das Wesen der Religion* (*Lectures on the Essence of Religion*) (delivered 1848-49; published 1851) laid the foundation for Bakunin's subsequent philosophy.

2.18 Bakunin and Feuerbach: On Naturalism

Feuerbach summarizes his thinking in *The Essence of Religion* in the following manner: "the foundation of religion is a feeling of dependency; the first object of that feeling is nature; thus nature is the first object of religion". There are, therefore, two elements in this account of religion which require further explanation: the first element is the "subjective" element; the second element is the "objective" element. Feuerbach says of the subjective element that "we find no other appropriate and all-embracing psychological explanation of religion than the feeling or consciousness of dependency". This feeling of dependency is chiefly manifest as fear. Hence primitive religions exhibit a preoccupation with "the frightening aspects of nature", while, in more developed religions, "the supreme Godhead is a personification of those natural phenomena which arouse *the highest degree* of fear in man: he is the god of storms, of thunder and lightning".[221] Feuerbach claims that this holds even for Christians, in whom the religious sentiment is most prevalent in the moment of fear.

Fear is only the negative expression of the feeling of dependency. It is the positive expression of this feeling that explains why the religious sentiment is not merely fleeting. This positive expression is simply the opposite emotion attached to the same object (of fear). Feuerbach characterizes it as "the feeling of *release* from danger, from fear and anxiety, a feeling of delight, joy, love, and gratitude", and concludes: "Fear is a feeling of dependency on an object *without which* I am nothing, which has the power to destroy me. Joy, love, [and] gratitude are feelings of dependency on an object *thanks to which* I am something, which gives me the feeling, the awareness that through it I live and am".[222]

Religion, in this fundamental sense — as the consciousness of dependency or the rudimentary expression of man's relation to nature (as "it seems to his uncultivated and inexperienced reason, [that is,] to his imagination and feeling") — is "essential to or innate in man". However, this is not religion in its entirety: it "is not the religion of theology or theism, not an actual belief in God [as] a being outside and above nature", which develops much later through "hyperphysical speculation and reflection", and obscures man's relation to nature, exalting him above it. Feuerbach attacks the "arrogant, presumptuous ecclesiastical religion" which upholds such absurdity; indeed, he recognizes that "being ecclesiastical, [it] is now represented by a *special official class*". He even voices his approval for the "*simple fundamental truth*" of nature religion in quasi-ecological terms: "man is dependent on nature . . . he should live in harmony with nature . . . even in his highest intellectual development he should not forget that he is a part and child of nature, but at all times honor nature and hold it sacred, not only as the ground and source of his existence, but also as the ground and source of his mental and physical well-being". Feuerbach insists that this "ecological" perspective is not religious, or a deification of nature, in the sense of theology or pantheism. Rather, it is based on the simple conviction that man should "make *no more*, but *also no less*" of nature than it merits. He adds: "Nature religion, pantheism, makes too much of nature, while conversely, idealism, theism, [and] Christianity make too little of it, and indeed ignore it".[223]

Feuerbach adds that the subjective or psychological element of his account can be reduced to the principle of egoism. To worship a god out of fear or, what is the same thing, gratitude — in other words, to worship something upon which one feels dependent — is in fact to feel dependent upon one's own needs. As Feuerbach puts it: "Dependency on another being is in reality a dependency on my own being, my own drives, desires, interests. Consequently, the feeling of dependency is merely an indirect, inverted or negative feeling of egoism, not an immediate egoism, however, but one mediated by and derived from the object on which I feel dependent". Hence, the strength of religious feeling — the degree of religious reverence — reflects the strength of desire. Desire, however, implies a lack. When one comes to possess what one previously lacked, therefore, the religious feeling tends to wane. In any case, Feuerbach concludes:

> . . . the feeling of dependency has led us to *egoism* as the ultimate hidden ground of religion.[224]

Feuerbach turns specifically to the objective element of his account. He distinguishes nature as the first object of religion from the object of religion at a later stage; he distinguishes, that is, between the natural object of paganism and the spiritual object of Christianity, which, as he demonstrated in *The Essence of Christianity*, is man himself, or, rather, human nature. These two objects reflect different needs: the "finite, real, and sensuous" object of paganism reflects "an immediately sensuous or physical need", whereas the "infinite, universal, merely cogitated or represented object" of Christianity reflects "a need of the soul", the desire for "eternal life". Of course, since the spiritual object has no existence apart from the natural object, and since the real physical need takes precedence over the spiritual need, the objective element in Feuerbach's mature account of religion is nature itself. In Feuerbach's words:

> [Nature] is a fundamental, first and last being which we cannot leave behind without losing ourselves in the realm of fancy and vacuous speculation . . . [We] must stay with nature and cannot derive from nature a being distinct from nature, a spirit, a thinking being whom we place between it and ourselves . . . [If] we produce nature out of spirit, the product will be a subjective, formal, intellectual abstraction and not a real, objective creation and being.[225]

Thus, in *The Essence of Religion*, Feuerbach attempts to provide a fundamental, naturalistic account of religion, such as was lacking in *The Essence of Christianity*. So what is nature? Feuerbach describes it, in effect, as the totality of causality, or as "the sum of . . . cosmic, mechanical, chemical, physical, physiological, [and] organic . . . causes" in their interaction. Hence: "Nature has no beginning and no end. Everything in it is relative, everything is at once cause and effect, acting and reacting on all sides". Unlike Bakunin, and in keeping with his earlier writings, however, Feuerbach suggests a distinction between the natural, so understood, and the human. He excludes human activity and thought from the natural realm, and implies that while man is the product of nature and is dependent on it, he is somehow distinct from it and merely enclosed by it. Hence man is natural only insofar as he "acts instinctively and unconsciously".[226] Thus, despite Feuerbach's naturalism, a certain dualism persists — a dualism Bakunin was to reject. Nevertheless, this detracts little from Feuerbach's analysis of nature in terms of causality.

The understanding of nature as the totality of interactive causality or as an "endless chain [or "infinite series"] of causes" leaves no room for the first cause. The first cause is "a mere concept, a figment of thought; it has only logical and metaphysical, but no physical significance". This theologico-metaphysical concept, which requires that we "effect a leap out of the series" of causes, is introduced by reason, almost arbitrarily, as a matter of convenience; thus, it reveals "the limitations of man's thinking [in] his taste for convenience". (This limitation is both natural and practical, since "The very nature of thought and speech [as well as] the requirements of life itself oblige us to make use of abbreviations on every hand, to substitute concepts for intuitions, signs for objects, in a word, the abstract for the concrete, the one for the many, and accordingly one cause for many causes". However, it would seem that this limitation is something that one can become conscious of and, to that extent at least, overcome.) Feuerbach continues: "*this need of mine* to break off the endless series is no proof of a real break in the series". What is more, reason, properly applied, actually confirms the infinity of this series:

> Even though reason rebels against tracing back causes *ad infini-tum* . . . such an endless series is by no means incompatible with a reason formed by observation of the world.[227]

Feuerbach describes the process by which reason makes the concrete and complex abstract and simple for the sake of convenience as follows: "Even in the area of human consciousness, even in the realm of history . . . we see how, partly out of ignorance to be sure, but partly out of the mere tendency to abbreviate and make things easy for ourselves, we break off our historical investigations and substitute One Cause, One Name for the many names, the many causes it would be too complicated, too tedious to track down, and which in fact often escape man altogether". The very idea of God is introduced by reason as a matter of convenience. It is, in the case of polytheism, a collective name, and, in the case of monotheism, a generic name that conveniently substitutes for the various natural attributes it would be too complicated and tedious to explain. As such, religion represents the lazy evasion of scientific inquiry; a means by which to explain away, for example, the infinity of temporal and spatial relations by referring to the eternal and omnipresent God, the power of nature by referring to the omnipotent God, and causality itself by referring to the First and Absolute Cause. Thus, Feuerbach concludes that while "It is a universal doctrine in our upside-down world that nature sprang from God . . . we should say the opposite, namely, that God was abstracted from nature and is merely a concept derived from it", or that God is nature "removed from physical perception".[228] Hence, religion obscures the object of sensuous perception, the object of science.

The ethical and political implications of this view of nature as the true object of religion are suggested by Feuerbach. Of the ethical implication, Feuerbach says that, contrary to popular belief, "in annulling what is Above Man theologically", such a view does not annul the "ethically Higher". In other words, the ethical subsists independently of the divine, as the *"human* ideal and aim".[229] Hence naturalism and atheism do not imply amoralism (versus Leszek Kolakowski, who supports the notion that "If Goes does not exist, then everything is permitted", a notion that leads to an utterly cynical argument for the existence of God[230]). However, while the ethical and the natural are regarded as *compatible*, Feuerbach does not seem to believe, as Bakunin does, that the ethical is the *highest development* of the natural, since he maintains a distinction between the natural and the human. As I have said, a certain dualism persists.

Feuerbach's political claim, on the other hand, is this: "Nature does not culminate in a monarchic summit; it is a republic. Those who are accustomed to a monarchy cannot conceive of human society without a prince, and likewise those who have grown up with the idea of a Father in Heaven find it hard to conceive of nature without a God, without an extranatural or supernatural being, as of a state or nation without a royal idol situated outside and above it". He goes on: "just as the republic is the historical task, the practical goal of man, so his theoretical goal is to recognize the republican constitution of nature, not to situate the governing principle of nature outside it, but to find it grounded in nature".[231] Bakunin would argue that the idea of the republican constitution of nature or society is almost as stupefying as that of the monarchic government of nature or society, since, according to him, as we have seen, all government is separate and hostile to that which is governed. There may be government of the people, but it is never by the people and for the people. As for the government of nature, it necessarily presupposes the idea of divine legislation, a patent absurdity in naturalistic terms.

Of course, Feuerbach's politics here (like those of Marx) are essentially Hegelian, that is, statist, and Bakunin has nothing but contempt for such a position. We might say of Feuerbach (and Marx), then, that he is so accustomed to the idea of the State, or so attached to Hegel's mystification of the State (whatever "inversions" he performs), that he cannot conceive of human society without political authority. (The influence of Hegel's politics on Feuerbach is made explicit, for example, toward the end of his *Provisional Theses*, where he refers to Hegel's *Grundlinien der Philosophie des Rechts* (*Elements of the Philosophy of Right*), and argues that "The state is the realized, cultivated, explicit totality of the human essence", which is little more than a restatement, in his own terms, of Hegel's claim that "The state is mind on earth . . . consciously realizing itself there". Furthermore, Marx's claim (of 1843) that "Hegel starts from the state and makes man the subjectified state [whereas] democracy starts from man and makes the state objectified man" is little more than a restatement, in his own terms, of Feuerbach's "inversion". (For that matter, lest one is inclined to defend Marx on the basis of his youth, his later claim (of 1875) that "Freedom consists in converting the state from an organ superimposed upon society into one completely subordinate to it" amounts to much the same thing.)[232] Whether the State fulfills itself in man or man fulfills himself in the

State (and whether the State is superimposed on society or the State is subordinate to society) — whatever all this means — makes little difference from the practical point of view because, in either case, the State is conceived as an abstraction, not concretely, as the *concrete* manifestation of political authority in one form or another.)

Nevertheless, Feuerbach uncovers the ground of religious authority and establishes, at least provisionally, the relation between religious authority — divine and ecclesiastical — and political authority. (His concept of the "special official class", which Bakunin re-employs, is central in this regard.) Bakunin would maintain, however, that Feuerbach — following Hegel — misunderstands or mystifies political authority in "rationalizing" it, and this mystification of political authority is something Bakunin deplores. (This mystification, again, occurs with the claim that the State exists over and above "the strictly political state" as "the actuality of the ethical Idea", that is, as an ethical community, or as "the actuality of concrete freedom".[233] The notion that the political and the ethical are in any way related, that the State is anything other than political, or that the State is the domain of concrete freedom, is unacceptable to Bakunin.)

While Feuerbach's achievement lies, therefore, in exposing the mystification of religious authority, Bakunin's lies in exposing the mystification of political authority and, by extension, scientific authority. As such his thought represents the culmination of the Left Hegelian project, which Marx defined in the following way: "It is . . . the task of philosophy, which is in the service of history [and therefore freedom], to unmask human self-alienation in its secular forms, once its sacred form has been unmasked. Thus . . . the critique of theology [is transformed] into the critique of politics".[234] However, among all the proponents of this project (such as Bruno Bauer, Ruge, and Marx) Bakunin was the only one to hold that just as the conclusion of the critique of theology is anti-theologistic, that is, naturalistic and atheistic, so the conclusion of the critique of politics is anti-political, that is, anarchistic. Bakunin, in other words, is the sole Left Hegelian to bring the project to its logical conclusion.

Apart from Bakunin, Edgar Bauer made some ground in this regard, but became disillusioned and abandoned the project. As for Stirner, whatever we might say of his anarchism (that is, regardless of his critique of the State), his thought, far from representing the culmination of Left Hegelianism, as has been widely held, in fact represents a premature rejection of it and a subversion of the naturalistic conclusion of its basic critique of religion. It represents, that is to say, a (supposed) rejection of Left Hegelianism in its anthropocentric forms, in ignorance of its naturalistic potential. Stirner's egoism presents no threat to naturalism. Indeed, Stirnerian egoism — "the assertion . . . that man is not the measure of all things, but I am this measure" — is simply *another form* of anthropocentrism; that is, another form of the prioritization of the human subject over the real or natural object (with the consequent generation of an idealized object) in the epistemological relation. (Perhaps it is the logical form of this prioritization, but what of it?) Hence Stirner's most absurd — and blatantly idealistic — statement: "Objects are to me only material that I use up".[235] The ecological implications of this view, for instance, are fairly obvious.

Feuerbach, for whom atheism and naturalism are one and the same thing, regards all forms of anthropocentrism as theistic in his later writings, and would therefore concur with the above critique of Stirner. He writes: "The difference between atheism or naturalism, the doctrine which interprets nature on the basis of nature or of a natural principle, and theism, the doctrine which derives nature from a heterogeneous, alien being distinct from nature, is merely that the theist takes man as his starting point and proceeds to draw inferences about nature, whereas the atheist or naturalist takes nature as his starting point and goes on to the study of man. The atheist takes a natural [that is, logical], the theist an unnatural [that is, illogical] course".[236] Is this not the very difference between Feuerbach's approach in *The Essence of Christianity* and his approach in *The Essence of Religion*?

Admirers of Stirner, such as Lawrence Stepelevich, sidestep the entire issue of Stirner's anthropocentrism by arguing that Stirner *re-*

duced Feuerbach to holding an "embarrassingly crude" materialism in his later, and insignificant, writings. (Thus, a break [convenient, as are all breaks posited by scholars] occurred between Feuerbach's Left Hegelian writings and his supposedly non-Left Hegelian writings as a result of Stirner's immaculate critique. This rather ignores the fact that Feuerbach was heading in the direction of naturalism some time before *Der Einzige und sein Eigentum* (*The Ego and Its Own*) (1844) was published — demanding the naturalization of philosophy and an alliance of philosophy with the natural sciences in the *Provisional Theses* and the development of a philosophy grounded on "sensuous perception" in the *Principles* (versus David McLellan's contention that "This is an aspect of Feuerbach's thought which only came to the fore in his reply to Stirner".[237]) In other words, there is no such break. Feuerbach's naturalism develops within his Left Hegelian philosophy, as a consequence of it: this is made clear by Feuerbach's critique of Hegel in the *Principles*. Therefore, naturalism is not extrinsic to Left Hegelianism. Stirner, incapable of fending off Feuerbach's naturalism, then, is incapable of concluding the Left Hegelian project.) And yet, at the same time, Stepelevich *credits* Stirner with having "positively assisted" Feuerbach in this basically sound move — the assumption being that Stirner's egoism is compatible with, or even the premise of, "naturalistic realism". (Hence Stepelevich censures Feuerbach for his "failure" to embrace "concrete individuality, a resolution in accord with his sensuous epistemology". In fact, Stirner's philosophy has little to do with "concrete individuality": it is predicated on an idealized individuality, on the completely abstract autonomous, or *potentially* autonomous, ego, which is no basis for Feuerbach's naturalism and its realistic epistemology.)[238]

2.19 Bakunin and Comte

We arrive now at the fourth major influence on Bakunin's critique of theologism: that of Auguste Comte, whom Bakunin describes as "the true father of modern scientific atheism".[239] Bakunin regards Comte as

Feuerbach's French counterpart, and credits him with an achievement which he might be said to have shared with Feuerbach: "[Hegel], true metaphysician that he was, spiritualized matter and nature, deducing them from logic, that is to say, from spirit. Auguste Comte, on the contrary, materialized [or naturalized] the spirit, grounding it solely in matter. And therein lies his great glory".[240] In fact, Comte's famous "law of the three states", which underpins the entire *Cours de philosophie positive* (*Course on Positive Philosophy*) (1830-1842), bears a striking resemblance to the tripartite division that emerges in Feuerbach's works. (We concentrate here on the exposition of the "law" in the *Course*, though it is adumbrated in Comte's 1824 *Plan of the Scientific Work Necessary for the Reorganization of Society*; we pass no judgment on its originality (that is, on the influence of Turgot, Condorcet, Saint-Simon, or anyone else); neither do we assess the relative importance of the *Système de politique positive* (*System of Positive Polity*) (1851-1854). The reason for all this is that the *Course* is the work of Comte that had the greatest impact on Bakunin. Most of his references to Comte, including those in his most sustained critique in the *Philosophical Considerations*, are to the second, 1864 edition of the *Course* and its preface by Emile Littré.)

Comte's analysis of the theological, metaphysical, and positive philosophies, then, corresponds roughly to Feuerbach's analysis of religion, speculative philosophy, and the "philosophy of the future", as outlined above. Comte also shares with Feuerbach an awareness of the relation between religio-philosophical and political forms. In other words, Comte too is aware — perhaps more acutely so than Feuerbach, who is less politicized — of the religio-philosophical basis of political authority. He had, as we will see, a considerable influence on Bakunin in this respect. (Bakunin, though, opposes the simplistic idealism of Comte — the conviction that "the world [or every aspect of it] is governed and overturned by ideas"[241] — as much as he opposes the economistic absolutism of Marx. He is uncomfortable with any theory that approaches metaphysical monocausality as opposed to naturalistic diversity. This fact accounts for the apparent contradictions or "vacillations" in his thinking that have been examined above.)

There is, as Bakunin sees it, a major difference between Comte and Feuerbach. Comte's naturalism, notwithstanding its weaknesses (see below), is scientific (therefore, as Bakunin states above, his atheism is also scientific), while Feuerbach's naturalism remains philosophical (as does his atheism). As far as Bakunin is concerned, it is Comte who concludes Feuerbach's project — provisionally, at any rate — by allying philosophy with science. He achieves this alliance: firstly, by formulating a methodological and historical *philosophy of science* (in accordance with the "general aim" of the *Course*, which is "to consider [science] under the twofold aspect of its essential methods and its principal achievements"); and secondly, by applying the method of science as it emerges — the positive method — to those natural phenomena which have tended to elude it, i.e., social phenomena, including, in a very broad sense, freedom (in accordance with the "special aim" of the *Course*, which is "to complete the system of observational sciences by the foundation of social physics").[242]

Similarly, but crucially, it is Comte who lends scientific weight to Feuerbach's conception of human nature by treating man as a biological phenomenon. Thus Comte proclaims "the fundamental law of continuous human development", which represents "the existing evolution [of mankind] as the necessary result of the gradual series of former [biological] transformations". The implication being:

> If we regard the course of human development from the highest scientific point of view, we shall perceive that it consists in educing, more and more, the characteristic faculties of humanity, in comparison with those of animality; and especially those which Man has in common with the whole organic kingdom. It is in this philosophical sense that the most eminent civilization must be pronounced to be fully accordant with nature, since it is, in fact, only a more marked manifestation of the chief properties of our species.[243]

Thus the civilization of mankind, man's emancipation from his merely animal state — this development — is to be understood as "fully accordant with nature". Freedom is, therefore, to be recognized as a natural phenomenon. In any case, Bakunin adopts Comte's fundamental law — that mankind is nothing more or less than a particular, albeit the "highest", natural development. However, this is not, strictly speaking, an evolutionary theory but merely a means of biological classification. (In this context, Mary Pickering notes that "Instead of Lamarck's transformism, Comte maintained the old doctrine of the [actual] fixity of the species", but adds: "Although he himself opposed theories of evolution, his predilection for placing animals and humans on the same continuum pointed the way toward Darwinism".[244]) However, in the words of Kenafick, Bakunin "improved . . . on Comte, by reason of the fact that he was acquainted with the theories of Darwin . . . [Thus] his ideas on biology can be said to be Comteanism, enriched by Darwinism, for, to the Comtean . . . concept of Animality developing into Humanity . . . Bakunin has added the Darwinian concept of Man developing [or *emerging*] from actual apeman, and the further concept of the struggle for [as Herbert Spencer put it] the survival of the fittest".[245]

Richard B. Saltman — quite wrongly, in my view — focuses on Lamarck as the evolutionary theorist whose influence pushed Bakunin in this general direction. (Generally, it might be said that Saltman's work is admirably conceived — as a defense of Bakunin's theoretical achievements against the "psycho-historical" reduction of them [by E. H. Carr, Edmund Wilson, Max Nomad, George Woodcock, James Joll, etc., and, we may add, Eileen Kelly and Arthur Mendel] — but poorly executed. Firstly, Saltman's ascription of intellectual influences to Bakunin is, as we will see, dubious. Secondly, Saltman's arbitrary use, if not misuse, of philosophical terminology (such as "dialectic", which features heavily in the text) is damaging, especially to his account of the debate between Marx (with his so-called "dialectical perspective") and Bakunin (with his supposed Lamarckian "evolutionary perspective", an evolutionary perspective which is, according to Saltman, irreconcilable with any element of dialectic). Thirdly, Saltman marginalizes

the critique of religion in his analysis of Bakunin's philosophy, representing religion as merely "a second ideological defense of the state"
between the "concept of public interest" and patriotism; this is, for all
the reasons outlined in this essay, a clear misrepresentation. And,
fourthly, Saltman associates Bakunin, after Feuerbach, with the anthropocentric tradition which, as we have seen, he sought to overcome;
hence Saltman claims that "From Feuerbach, Bakunin absorbed a fundamentally anthropological conception of the universe, in which the
sentient human individual [sic] was simultaneously the *center* and *purpose* of all philosophical endeavor", and that "Feuerbach and Bakunin
both understood mankind [what happened to the individual?] to be at
the *center* of a *natural* universe".[246] As a result, Saltman's book does more
harm than good to Bakunin's reputation by seeming to confirm (in
spite of itself) the "psycho-historians" view that he was theoretically
deficient.)

Saltman argues that the work of Lamarck is one of the two "most
important intellectual roots" of Bakunin's social theory (the other being
the work of Feuerbach, which I obviously do not dispute). Inevitably,
he is forced to concede that his "conclusion isn't based on Bakunin's
own statements of intellectual acknowledgement", but on "Bakunin's
conceptual approach to man's nature, and . . . the language and conceptual apparatus through which Bakunin conveyed that approach". Dubious, indeed. To begin with, Bakunin acknowledges his debt to Feuerbach frequently, and even a superficial biographical analysis confirms
this debt (Bakunin, for example, spent a large part of the 1840s writing
a book [now considered lost] on Feuerbach, entitled *Exposé et développement des idées de Feuerbach*). Saltman also writes that Bakunin "apparently
never mentioned Lamarck at all", which is also untrue; he mentions his
name very infrequently.[247] But he acknowledges his true debt to Lamarck's successor, Darwin, more frequently. Note the following example: "Human history . . . is only the continuation of the great struggle for
life which, according to Darwin [and Bakunin does not contest it], constitutes the basic law of the organic world".[248] In any case, for the rea-

sons given by Kenafick above, Darwin's influence is quite apparent. Darwin aside, though, Saltman does not even mention the broader influence of Comte, who, as Kenafick puts it, "was the chief intellectual influence of Bakunin's last decade".[249] So we ought to look at him more closely, examining here, in as much detail as is reasonable in the current context, his systematic exposition of human development with particular reference to its influence on Bakunin's critique of theologism. (We might bear in mind also that Bakunin's anarchist predecessor, Proudhon, had already made use of the law of the three states in his *De la création de l'ordre dans l'humanité* (*On the Creation of Order Among Men*) (1843); in other words, the influence of Comte's analysis on anarchism generally.)

In Comte's first stage of human development, the *theological* or *fictitious* stage, man, in pursuit of "absolute knowledge", that is, ignorant as yet of the limits of his understanding, occupies himself with "the most insoluble questions, such as the inner nature of objects, or the origin and purpose of all phenomena", and deems "all really soluble problems . . . hardly worthy of serious thought". In consequence, man is led to represent "these phenomena as being produced by the direct and continuous action of more or less numerous supernatural agents, whose arbitrary intervention explains all the apparent anomalies of the universe".[250] That is to say, in the vain effort to deal with theological questions, man is forced to postulate any number of fictions or absurdities.

Nevertheless, for all its absurdity, the theological state is the necessary point of departure for all human development, and for this reason: while positive scientific theory is, as we will see, based on observation, all meaningful observation presupposes certain theory (though not in the contemporary sense of "theory-ladeness"); without theory, observations remain isolated and unrelated, and therefore positive scientific theory can never be established. "Thus, [historically,] there were two difficulties to be overcome: the human mind had to observe in order to form real theories; and yet it had to form theories of some sort before it could apply itself to a connected series of observations. The

primitive human mind, therefore, found itself involved in a vicious circle".[251] The theological mode of thought offers a way out of this vicious
circle: by means of wild speculation on random observations, theory
arises, however absurd it may be and whatever fictitious entities it may
entail. Such theory is a starting point for more serious investigation.
Thus it is possible for Bakunin to maintain with Comte that religious
belief is simultaneously absurd and necessary to man's further development. Religion is, as Bakunin might put it, the dawning of reason in a
provisional state of unreason.

Comte specifies three forms of the theological philosophy: fetishism, polytheism, and monotheism. As Pickering demonstrates, Comte
follows both Charles de Brosses (in *Du culte des dieux fétiches,* (1760)) and
Benjamin Constant (in the first two volumes of *De la religion considérée
dans sa source, ses formes, et des développements* (1824-1825)) here. Bakunin, as
we have seen, maintains this specification.[252] Fetishism, then, is the
first form of the theological philosophy, the original manifestation of
man's speculative activity. (Like Feuerbach and Bakunin, Comte, because of his quasi-evolutionary outlook, ascribes a degree of speculative
activity to certain animals and holds, therefore, that they too can
"attain a kind of gross fetishism". Unlike Feuerbach and Bakunin, however, Comte does not develop his argument along Schleiermacherian
lines.) Fetishism is characterized by the deification of all natural phenomena that preoccupy man's nascent reason. In ignorance of particular natural laws, or even the concept of natural law itself, primitive man
"instinctively [conceives] of the production of unknown effects according to the passions and affections of the corresponding being regarded
as alive; and this is the philosophical principle of fetishism".[253] That is
to say, the fetishist regards certain natural objects which attract his
attention, because of their immediate effect on him, as *supernatural*, because he is incapable of explaining them scientifically: that is, in their
own right as natural objects, susceptible to investigation by means of
the positive method.

Comte assesses both the theoretical and the practical impact of each stage of human development. (These are worth looking at in particular detail at the theological stage because of the extent of their influence on Bakunin.) The theoretical impact of fetishism is described by Comte as follows: fetishism, notwithstanding its necessity as a point of departure, "obstructs all advance in genuine knowledge. It is in this form, above all others, that the religious spirit is most directly opposed to the scientific [since] all idea of natural laws is out of the question when every object is a divinity with a will of its own". Human reason does at least occupy itself with the external world at this stage, but the fetishist is in a state of "permanent hallucination", where "imaginary facts overwhelm real ones [and] the most absurd beliefs impair all direct observation of natural phenomena".[254]

Practically, the fetishistic stage was represented by pre-political forms of authority: the practical form of military authority (displayed by the hunters and warriors of the time) which is the basis of temporal authority; the theoretical form of gerontocracy (grounded on the knowledge of tribal tradition) which is the basis of spiritual authority; and the auxiliary domestic influence of women. But in itself fetishism had minimal actual political impact because it lacked a priesthood, or "a distinct speculative class", whose "sacerdotal authority" could serve as the basis for political authority in the proper sense. Fetishism could not give rise to a priesthood because of the individuality, the multiplicity and diversity of its gods, which therefore have "little power to unite men, *or to govern them*". Comte remarks:

> It was the subsequent polytheistic belief in gods that were invisible, more or less general, and distinct from the substances which they ruled, that originated and developed a real priesthood, enjoying high social influence, in its character of mediator between the worshipper and his deity.[255]

The second form of the theological philosophy, in fact its principal and most durable form, is polytheism. The polytheist, as we have already ascertained, conceives natural objects as being inert (rather than alive or supernatural), but subject to the *will* of divine agents, which govern objects of particular *kinds*. Thus the polytheist conceives the imaginary deities as being separate from or external to their natural objects, that is, the kind of objects they govern. Comte infers that the deities of polytheism have assumed "a more general and abstract character" than those of fetishism, since they can now govern vast orders of things from, as it were, afar. Hence there are fewer deities under this form of the theological philosophy than under the previous form, where every object could be conceived as a deity in itself since no relation between individual objects could be established. These differences reflect a definite development of reason — the capacity to compare, abstract, and generalize, or to "perceive likeness between phenomena, and observe their succession".[256]

Theoretically, polytheism is "unfavorable to science" in the sense that it "represses all scientific expansion under the weight of detailed religious explanations of all phenomena". In other words, it explains everything in terms of the will of divine agents and opposes "every idea of invariable physical laws". (The religious explanations of polytheism are more detailed than those of fetishism because the deities themselves are, once again, more abstract and more universal. The necessity for such detailed arguments gives rise to the aforementioned speculative class.) Nevertheless, polytheism, unfavorable to science as it may be, inadvertently discloses "an access to the ulterior principle of the invariableness of natural laws"; that is to say, it engages "the awakened scientific spirit in philosophical meditation, by establishing a primitive connection among human ideas, which [is] not the less infinitely valuable for being chimerical in nature".[257] The relations between the various deities of polytheism reflect the observed relations between the various orders of natural phenomena that they govern. Thus there is in polytheism a sense, albeit a perverted sense, of a complex order in a law-governed universe.

The political impact of polytheism was highly significant. Comte argues that the pre-political forms of authority, properly so-called (both temporal or practical, that is, generally militaristic, and spiritual or theoretical, that is, generally patriarchal, to say nothing of their "domestic auxiliary", the "elementary influence . . . of women"), having emerged under fetishism, were only politicized, that is, institutionalized and supposedly legitimated, with the advent of polytheism. The politicization of such authority was assured by the emergence of the speculative class (which, as we have said, was necessitated by the very nature of the polytheistic divinities, and served to create a certain fixed and authoritative body of opinion), and by the regularization of worship (which served to disseminate this body of opinion among a population sharing a common language). As Comte puts it:

> These rudiments of all succeeding establishments of authority would not have passed beyond their incipient stage, if polytheism had not attached them to the double institution of regular worship and a distinct priesthood, which afford the only means of admitting anything like a social organization among scattered families. This is the chief political destination of the theological philosophy.[258]

The essential characteristic of this socio-political organization, notwithstanding its theocratic basis, was its militarism. (Indeed, there was no contradiction between the theocratic element and the military element here. As Comte argues, the spiritual and the temporal powers were concentrated in the polytheistic system [though there was a preponderance of one or other in particular systems — the Egyptian system being preponderantly theocratic, the Roman system being preponderantly militaristic, and the Greek system being transitional].) This is so because while the polytheistic deities were sufficiently universal or inclusive to bind a population under a certain organization, they were also sufficiently national or exclusive to produce a spirit of conquest within this population. The simultaneous universality and nationality of the polytheistic deities also accounts for the characteristic institution of slavery in this socio-political organization: thus the deities were sufficiently universal to bind the conqueror and the conquered, but sufficiently national "to maintain social distance" in the established master-slave relationship. Both militarism and the institution of slavery, abhorrent as they may be to the civilized mind, were in fact vital civilizing factors at this stage: conquest "being the only means of rendering the political organism durable and progressive"; and slavery representing an advance — both moral and economic — on the mere "sacrifice of captives".[259]

The third form of the theological philosophy is monotheism: the belief in a single abstract, universal, spiritual deity. Comte says little about monotheism in general, preferring to explain the development of its truest form: Catholicism. He attributes its development to three factors: the Hellenic factor, the Judaic factor, and the Roman factor. Of the Hellenic factor, he writes: "the necessary and continuous destination of the Greek philosophy [was] to serve as the organ of the irrevocable decline of polytheism, in preparation for the advent of monotheism". Greek philosophy, in other words, is the metaphysical or negative intellectual basis of monotheism. The Jewish religion, on the other hand, combined "an intense and obstinate [sense of] nationality" and a willingness to propagate its faith (necessary for the initial success of the new theology) with a quasi-monotheistic outlook. As such, it provided the "requisite organs" or the concrete basis for the true or Catholic monotheistic philosophy. Rome's contribution was to provide the geopolitical basis for the universal propagation of the new theology, having "united the civilized world under her sway" — that is, having conquered and annexed everything in sight.[260] Bakunin's debt here is apparent, though his formulation — which I have utilized — is perhaps more coherent than Comte's original account.

The theoretical impact of Catholic monotheism was immense. Though monotheism is antithetical to science, insofar as it opposes its "conception of an arbitrary will as the universal governing power" to the "conception of the invariableness of natural laws", Catholic monotheism did much to advance the cause of science. Comte offers numerous examples — nine that I can pinpoint. First, the monotheistic concentration of "supernatural action" in a single, abstract agent, as opposed to the rampant supernaturalism of the earlier theologies, "opened a much freer access to . . . secondary studies", or to scientific inquiry into, as it were, mere natural phenomena. Second, the Catholic "disposition to admiration of divine wisdom, which has since proved a retrograde influence, was [originally] promotive of scientific inquiry"; in other words, the conjunction of wisdom and divinity, or the divinization of wisdom, stimulated the pursuit of knowledge of all things, natural as well as spiritual. Third, Catholicism's "suppression of inspiration, with all its train of oracles and prophecies, apparitions and miracles, testifies to [its] noble efforts . . . to enlarge, at the expense of the theological spirit, the as yet narrow field of human reason". Fourth, the nature of the "sacerdotal life" of Catholicism — the prerequisites for and requisites of it — contributed to the growth of "intellectual culture" in general. Fifth, the universal propagation of Catholic ideas, which was the basis of universal education (which in turn is the possible basis of universal science), aided the general "intellectual development of the multitude". Thus Comte writes:

> So far from the Catholic system having always been repressive of popular intelligence, as is now most unjustly said, it was for a long period the most efficacious promoter of it.[261]

Sixth, Catholicism's "efforts . . . to prove its superiority to former systems [enabled] the great philosophical principle of human progression [theoretical and practical] to arise . . . however inadequate in strength or quality". Seventh, the universal education of Catholicism and the discovery of intellectual or philosophical historicity and progressiveness created a "spirit of social discussion", which, aside from binding individuals and groups and thereby assisting socio-political development, created a huge potential for intellectual development. Eighth, Catholicism's receptiveness to metaphysics, especially Aristotelian metaphysics, weakened its theological aspect, and facilitated its intellectual progression. And, ninth, Catholicism's separation of social theory and social practice (which results from the separation of the spiritual and temporal powers that we will discuss below) "laid the foundation for social science, in distinction from mere Utopias".[262]

Politically, Catholicism's impact was also immense. Its major accomplishment was to bring about the separation of the spiritual and temporal powers, which Comte pronounces to be "the greatest advance ever made in the general theory of the social organism, and . . . the main cause of the superiority of the modern to the ancient polity". (Islamic monotheism failed to accomplish this, Comte adds.) Thus the sacerdotal authority that was inseparable from political authority — indeed its very basis — in the theocratic system assumed a moral, educative, and non-political character in the Catholic system; which is to say, the speculative class became precisely that, engaging in "calm and enlightened, but not indifferent observation of practical life, in which it could interpose only in an indirect manner, by its moral [and educational?] influence". Comte continues: "The grand social characteristic of Catholicism was that by constituting a moral power, wholly independent of the political, it infused morality into political government" from without.[263] The spiritual power therefore constituted a *universal* moral authority that would be particularized with the concentration of powers or its politicization. Hence the Catholic system's universality could exceed that of even the Roman system, and its empire was consequently greater in scope.

The spiritual Catholic empire, to the extent that it was militaristic, was therefore only defensive. (Comte argues that even the Crusades, for example, were defensive in nature, being "intended as a barrier against the invasion of Mohammedanism".) As such, Catholicism facilitated the decline of the military system and the emergence of the feudal system, that is, it expedited the collapse of the Roman Empire (which was by nature ultimately self-destructive) and the process of territorial and political decentralization. Hence, Catholicism also influenced the emergence of serfdom in place of slavery: with the decline of the military system, fewer slaves were available, so slave-owners became "disposed to make an hereditary property of them" in order that they would henceforth be "attached to [their] families and their lands". The serf's lot is, Comte claims, better than that of the slave because Catholicism interposed "a salutary spiritual authority between . . . the lord and his serf, an authority which is equally respected by both, and which is continually disposed to keep them up to their mutual duty". Thus, while there was — and is — an element of arbitrariness about the institution of slavery, Catholicism imposed a "new social discipline" (grounded on "the principles of obedience and protection") on the institution of serfdom.[264] Therefore, Catholicism enhanced the universality of polytheism by subverting the element of exclusivity or patriotism, which supports the institution of slavery, and replacing it with a universal morality, perverse as it was.

Comte highlights another crucial way in which the Catholic system influenced political progress — albeit indirectly, by example. Catholicism replaced the hereditary principle with an elective principle (based, in its case, on intellectual and moral merit). This transformation was brought about chiefly by means of the distinctly Catholic "institution of ecclesiastical celibacy". Furthermore, Catholicism enriched the elective principle by "admitting to choice of office the whole of society" (or at least the whole of male society), and also by "reversing the order of election, by causing the superiors to be chosen by the inferiors". Comte acclaims Catholicism's innovation in this regard as "a masterpiece of political wisdom".[265]

Monotheism, the third form of the theological philosophy, is necessarily its final form. In logical terms, the theological philosophy progresses as the number of its deities is reduced (as the as yet concealed positive spirit dictates): a theological progression beyond the single deity of monotheism therefore entails the absolute negation of the theological philosophy. The metaphysical or critical spirit is thus the immediately progressive factor in the theological stage; however, with the negation of the theological, the metaphysical spirit begins to indulge itself in its own empty abstractions (that is, the negative in itself, robbed of its vitality, as Bakunin might say, becomes merely negative). However, such a condition could only be provisional, as we will see below. Nevertheless, the concrete remnant of the theological order — the Church — assists the metaphysical spirit by its obstinate refusal to admit its necessary and self-evident defeat; by, that is, "exchanging its progressive for a stationary, or even a retrograde character, such as sadly distinguishes it at this day".[266]

The second stage of human development, then, is the *metaphysical*, *abstract*, or *critical* stage. Comte holds (like Bakunin and Feuerbach) that there is no real, qualitative distinction between the theological and the metaphysical; as he puts it, "the metaphysical state . . . is in reality only a simple general modification of the [theological] state". The difference, such as it is (though it is vitally important for Comte), is that "the supernatural agents [of theology] are replaced [in the metaphysical state] by abstract forces, real entities, or personified abstractions, inherent in the different beings of the world". Explanations of natural phenomena in terms of their imagined supernatural status or their relation to any number of imagined supernatural agents are therefore replaced by explanations in terms of abstractions from the phenomena themselves. Hence the metaphysical philosophy shares with the theological philosophy a dualistic approach to the study of natural phenomena, though the dualism is subtler; and it shares with the positive philosophy a predilection for the natural rather than the supernatural order. As such, it is the "transitional" philosophy between the theological and the positive. Comte summarizes: "By substituting, in the study of phenomena, a corresponding inseparable entity for a direct supernatural agency — although at first the former [is] only held to be an offshoot of the latter — man gradually [accustoms] himself to consider only the facts themselves . . . It is impossible to imagine by what other method our understanding could [pass] from frankly supernatural to purely natural considerations, or, in other words, from the theological to the positive regime".[267]

Comte divides the metaphysical stage of history into two periods. The first period comprises the fifteenth and sixteenth centuries in which the theological order began to self-destruct under the weight of its own theoretical and practical contradictions, as indicated above. The second period comprises the sixteenth, seventeenth, and eighteenth centuries, "during which the disorganization . . . proceeded under the growing influence of an avowedly negative doctrine [inspired, Comte tells us, by the sight of the old order's self-destruction], extended by degrees to all social ideas, and indicating the tendency of modern society to renovation, though the principle of renovation has remained undisclosed".[268] According to Comte, the principle of "renovation" or creativity is foreign to the metaphysical or destructive spirit. Bakunin disagrees, as the famous last line of *The Reaction* testifies.

The second period is sub-divided by Comte into a period of Protestantism (c. 1500-1650), which culminated, as Bakunin argues, in religious revolution, and a period of deism (c. 1650-1800), which culminated, as Bakunin argues, in political revolution. In the Protestant period, Comte writes, "the right of free inquiry, while fully admitted, was restrained within the limits of the Christian theology; and, in consequence, the spirit of discussion was chiefly employed in destroying, in the name of Christianity, the admirable system of the Catholic hierarchy, which was, in a social sense, the only thorough realization of it. In this appeared conspicuously the inconsistency which characterizes the whole of the negative philosophy, proposing . . . to reform Christianity by destroying the indispensable conditions of its existence". Such logical "inconsistency" in modern Christian thinking is critiqued at various points by Bakunin (see above). In the deist period, Comte continues, "the right of free inquiry was declared to be indefinite; but it was taken for granted that metaphysical discussion would remain within the general limits of monotheism, whose foundations were supposed to be unalterable". Bakunin highlights this "compromise" — free thought within the bounds of the assumption of God's mere existence — in modern idealism, as we have seen. Importantly, Comte adds:

> [The limits of monotheism] were in their turn . . . broken up before the end of the period, by a prolongation of the same [critical] process. The intellectual inconsistency was notably diminished by this extension of the destructive analysis; but the social dissolution appears more evident, through the absolute disposition to establish political regeneration on a series of mere negations, which can produce nothing but anarchy.[269]

This is the very tradition to which Bakunin is heir. Bakunin consistently, and from the point of view of "positive philosophy", broadly understood, extends the "destructive analysis" to metaphysics itself while demonstrating the continuity of this analysis with anarchism, with the "destructive analysis" of the political. However, anarchism is not, as Bakunin sees it, reducible to "a series of *mere* negations": there is no room in his logic for such an element. Furthermore, there is no necessity, as Bakunin sees it, for the revolutionary element, and the class that represents it, to be constrained and ordered from without. Bakunin simply rejects Comte's belief that, as Bakunin puts it, "The vast majority of men . . . are incapable of governing themselves" and must therefore be governed by those who know better — in this case, a new "sacerdotal" class, albeit "scientific" rather than "religious".[270]

Comte's interpretation of the "metaphysical" or critical moment's dialectical role here differs substantially from that of Bakunin. For Comte, progressive as the critical moment may be, it must be synthesized with an extraneous element of order if it is to achieve its dialectical fulfillment in an ultimate third. The revolutionary element represents mere chaos, contrary to the Proudhonian idea that anarchy is order or the Bakuninian idea that destruction is itself creative. Thus Comte's dialectic is tripartite. While theology and metaphysics are in some sense identical, then, they still represent two distinct dialectical moments *from* which a third moment, the "positive", emanates.

Bakunin also acknowledges an historical continuity between theology, metaphysics, and positive philosophy, but he denies any logical compatibility between theology and metaphysics, or theologism, on the one hand and positive philosophy on the other. For him, it is the "positive" state that is negative. The metaphysical, on the other hand, is negative only to the extent that it is non-metaphysical or even anti-metaphysical. In particular, what Comte designates as the "deistic" period of the metaphysical stage of history often expresses a revolutionary, if partial, anti-theologism that contributed in large part to the political, and therefore partial, revolutions of the time. It is in fact the very compromise entailed by deism that shows, to the extent that it remained genuinely metaphysical, that it was not genuinely negative. Positive philosophy, broadly conceived, alone negates the precepts of metaphysics, which in turn rest on the precepts of theology. It is the very presence of "positive" thinking within the metaphysical period that rendered it negative in some degree. (We have already discussed the relationship in Bakunin's thinking between theoretico-ontological positivity and practico-logical negativity; such a concept of the negativity of positive philosophy expresses precisely this relationship.)

When Comte describes the metaphysical stage as "the greatest revolution, intellectual and social, that the human race could undergo at any period of its career", it is apparent that this revolution, or the very *principle of revolution*, is insufficient. It must be coupled with something of what preceded it, that is, the *principle of order*, to bring about the new social order. The revolutionary "destruction of old elements" may indeed be "the very means of disclosing the new" — but not in the Bakuninian sense. Again, something extraneous, some means of *creating* order, is needed to supplement the element of destruction: destruction may "disclose", but it is not creative. Like Bakunin, Comte thinks destruction, defined in terms of the "preparation of the ground", is "indispensable" ("Without the impulsion of this critical energy, humanity would have been stationary"); unlike Bakunin, however, Comte thinks, once again, it is insufficient. Thus we proceed to the third and final state "which alone can satisfy the needs at once of order and progress, in which the former philosophies . . . have, when it became necessary to *unite* them, signally failed".[271]

The third stage of human development is the *positive* or *scientific*. Here "the human mind, recognizing the impossibility of obtaining absolute truth, gives up the search after the origin and hidden causes of the universe and a knowledge of the final causes of phenomena". Instead, it "endeavors . . . to discover, by a well-combined use of reasoning and observation, the actual laws of phenomena — that is to say, their invariable relations of succession and likeness".[272] Bakunin agrees that a "positive philosophy" must give up the search for first and final causes, that it must devote itself to the discovery of natural laws which reflect what are, to all intents and purposes, invariable relations between natural phenomena, and that the means of discovering such laws are observation and "comprehension". However, there is a major difference between Bakunin and Comte.

Comte writes: "we regard the search after what are called causes, whether first or final, as absolutely *inaccessible* and unmeaning". He even adds: "Everybody . . . knows that in our positive explanations, even when they are most complete, *we do not pretend to explain the real causes of phenomena*, as this would merely throw the difficulty further back; we try only to analyze correctly the circumstances of their production, and to connect them by normal relations of succession and similarity". Thus, all remaining questions (such as "what attraction and weight are *in themselves*, or what their [real] causes are") are viewed "as insoluble and outside the domain of the positive philosophy; we, therefore, rightly abandon them to the imagination of the theologians or the subtleties of the metaphysicians".[273]

Bakunin, responding to such sentiments, raises the question: "What does the positive philosophy do in refusing to pronounce itself on this question of the first cause? Does it [deny] its existence? Not at all. It only excludes it from the scientific domain, declaring it scientifically unverifiable; which is to say, in simple human language, that this first cause *may* exist, but that the human mind is incapable of conceiving it". Thus "the positivists open the door [or leave it open] to theologians". Indeed, this is a fundamentally Kantian procedure; hence Bakunin refers to "the completely Kantian metaphysics of positivists". Like Kant, Comte separates the accessible phenomenal, and the intelligible causes that operate therein, from the "inaccessible" noumenal, and the unintelligible causes that operate therein. For Bakunin this supposedly enlightening procedure simply vindicates the mysterious, and therefore "absurd", and encourages theologistic speculation. Put simply, then, "the system of Positive Philosophy of Auguste Comte opens the door to mysticism" in general.[274]

Bakunin, closer in this respect to Feuerbach than to Comte, willingly pronounces on these matters. Thus, through genetico-critical analysis, he arrives at the conclusion that the first cause is meaningless, a symptom of mechanistic thinking, that the final cause is a matter of rational convenience, etc. From this viewpoint, he asks the following: "Was Auguste Comte ignorant that the idea of creation and of a creator is not just inaccessible, [but] that it is absurd, ridiculous, and impossible? One would almost believe that he was not very sure himself, as the relapse into mysticism which signaled the end of his career proves". Bakunin is not only willing to pronounce on these matters himself — he believes it is imperative that all would-be "positivists" decide — *either-or* — on questions of such importance; to compromise, here as elsewhere, is effectively to choose, surreptitiously, the conservative side. He writes: "[Comte's] disciples at least, warned by [the] fall of their master, should understand all the danger in remaining, or at least leaving the public [to remain], in such incertitude on a question the solution of which, whether affirmative or negative, must exercise a great influence on the whole future of humanity".[275]

For all the differences between Bakunin and Comte that have been referred to above, Bakunin pursues at least some of the goals of positive philosophy as Comte formulates it — goals with regard to which it is thought most advantageous. First, he too believes in the necessary unification of science on the grounds that its object is, for all its diversity (including its social developments), one: "The divisions that we establish between the sciences, although not arbitrary as some people suppose, are yet essentially artificial. In reality, the subject of our researches is one". (Bakunin expresses much the same idea as follows: "One single [totality of] Being [i.e., nature], one single [totality of] knowledge [i.e., science], and, at bottom, always the same method [i.e., the realist method], which is necessarily complicated in the measure that the facts which are presented to it become more complex".[276]) Scientific progress, Comte adds, is hampered at present because "scientists are so addicted to specialization".[277] As Bakunin explains it, to abstract from the totality that is nature — by divorcing the social from it, for instance — is to understand it partially, is to render science itself abstract and false — is, in fact, to render it "metaphysical" rather than "positive" on Comte's definition.

Another goal that Bakunin and Comte share, related to the first, is, as they see it, the necessary "recasting of our educational system". "European education", as it stands, "is still essentially theological, meta-physical, and literary" rather than "positive" or suited to "the [rational] spirit of our time" and "adapted to the [regenerative] needs of modern civilization". Thus this education is characterized by "exclusive spe-cialty" and "rigid isolation", that is, by abstraction. Education in the ways of "positive" or "natural philosophy", in its true, unified form, alone facilitates the necessary "recasting". Comte writes:

> In order that natural philosophy may be able to complete the . . . regeneration of our intellectual system, it is . . . indis-pensable that the different sciences of which it is composed — regarding them as different branches of a single trunk — should first be reduced [before the introduction of further "special education"] to what constitutes their essence — that is, to their principal methods and most important results. It is in this way only that the teaching of the sciences can become the basis of a new general and really rational education for our people [including "the mass of the people"].[278]

Bakunin's enthusiastic support for this program (later toned-down by a more skeptical attitude toward Comte, but basically sus-tained by his recommendation of universal scientific education) is voiced in this way: "Positive philosophy, which has dethroned religious fables and the dreams of metaphysics in [people's] minds, already al-lows us to glimpse what scientific education should be in the future". It ought to be based, initially or prior to "special" education, on "a general knowledge of all the sciences", that is, on "a non-superficial, very real knowledge" of them in their totality.[279] It is only on the foundation of such education, rather than education founded on religious imagination and metaphysical abstraction, that reason can prevail and theologistic phantoms can finally be overcome among the mass of people.

A final goal that Bakunin and Comte share is the achievement of "the social reorganization that must terminate the crisis in which the most civilized nations have found themselves for so long".[280] For Comte, this demands the closure of revolution, the overcoming of the metaphysical, *qua* critical, state by the synthesis of it, as a progressive factor, with the organizational factor afforded by the theological order. For Bakunin, though, it calls for exactly the opposite: the *disclosure* of revolution, the liberation of the revolutionary from reaction, whether consistent or mediating. As such, the at once destructive form and crea-tive or "regenerative" content of the negative or "critical" principle is said by Bakunin to be misunderstood by Comte, who perceives it, quite literally, metaphysically. Comte thereby contributes (in the dialectical role of the reactionary "preach[ing] moderation and resignation"[281]) to the modern crisis (or "contradiction") by attempting to conceal and therefore subvert it as a meaningfully progressive opportunity.

Notes to Part Two

1. Ludwig Feuerbach, *Lectures on the Essence of Religion*, trans. Ralph Manheim (New York: Harper & Row, 1967), p. 218.

2. *Considérations philosophiques*, pp. 193-94. Emphasis in original.

3. *Ibid.*, p. 199. Emphasis in original. Or, as Bakunin put it in an earlier work: "*Tout ce qui est naturel est logique, et tout ce qui est logique est réalisé ou doit se réaliser dans le monde réel: dans la nature proprement dite, et dans son développement postérieur — dans l'histoire naturelle de l'humaine société*" [*Fédéralisme, socialisme et antithéologisme*, p. 116; emphasis in original]. Note that "*le monde réel*" becomes "*le monde naturel*", and that the notion of "*l'histoire naturelle de l'humaine société*" which is a "*développement postérieur*" of nature changes to "*le monde naturel, y compris le monde social*", in the later version — reflecting the development of a more explicit and more coherent naturalism in Bakunin's later writing.

4. *Tractatus Logico-Philosophicus*, trans. D.F. Pears and B.F. McGuinness (London: Routledge, 1974), pp. 5-8 (propositions 1.1, 2, 2.01, 2.0121, 2.04, and 2.06).

5. *Ibid.*, pp. 6-7 (propositions 2.0141 and 2.024).

6. *L'Empire knouto-germanique (Seconde livraison)*, p. 116. Emphasis added.

7. *Pis'ma M.A. Bakunina k A.I. Gersenu i N.P. Ogarevu*, p. 252. Translated by Pyziur, *op. cit.*, pp. 16-17.

8. *The Philosophy of Social Ecology: Essays on Dialectical Naturalism*, Second Edition (Montréal: Black Rose Books, 1996), pp. 14, 58.

9. *L'Empire knouto-germanique (Seconde livraison)*, p. 116. Emphasis added. Bakunin's admiration for Diderot is hinted at in, for instance, *Pis'ma M. A. Bakunina k A. I. Gertsenu i N. P. Ogarevu*, pp. 244-45; and in a draft for *L'Empire knouto-germanique*, *Archives Bakounine*, VII, p. 488.

10. "Diderot and the Development of Materialist Monism", *Diderot Studies*, II (1952), p. 295. Diderot himself writes (in October 1865): "Sensitivity is a universal property of matter, an inert property in inorganic bodies ... [a] property rendered active in these bodies by their assimilation with a living animal substance . . . The animal is the laboratory where sensitivity . . . becomes active" [quoted in *Oeuvres philosophiques de*

Diderot, ed. Paul Vernière (Paris: Editions Garnier Frères, 1964), p. 249].

11. *D'Alembert's Dream*, trans. L.W. Tancock (Harmondsworth: Penguin Books, 1966), p. 153.

12. *Op. cit.*, pp. 18, 56-60.

13. *Dieu et l'Etat* (the pamphlet, not the note), *Archives Bakounine*, VII, p. 134.

14. *Considérations philosophiques*, p. 194. Emphasis added.

15. *La Commune de Paris*, p. 301.

16. *Considérations philosophiques, pp. 194-95. Emphasis in original.*

17. *Fédéralisme, socialisme et antithéologisme, p. 115. Emphasis added.*

18. *Considérations philosophiques, pp. 199, 201.*

19. *La Commune de Paris, p. 301..*

20. *Considérations philosophiques*, p. 199, first footnote. Emphasis in original.

21. *Op. cit., p. 82.*

22. *Considérations philosophiques*, p. 201.

23. *The Essence of Christianity*, trans. George Eliot (Buffalo: Prometheus Books, 1989), pp. 189-91.

24. *Considérations philosophiques*, p. 194.

25. *Ibid.*, pp. 244-45.

26. *Ibid.*, pp. 196, 245.

27. *Ibid.*, pp. 241-44.

28. *L'Empire knouto-germanique (Seconde livraison)*, p. 94, including note.

29. *Considérations philosophiques*, pp. 242-44.

30. *What is Property?*, pp. 21, 25. See also *L'Empire knouto-germanique (Seconde livraison)*, p. 92, where Bakunin defines a "mystery" as that which is "inexplicable, that is to say ... absurd, because only the absurd admits of no explanation".

31. *Considérations philosophiques*, p. 241.

32. *Manuscrit de 25 pages qui précédait le manuscrit l'appendice de l'Empire knouto-germanique (25-Page Manuscript Preceding the Manuscript of the Appendix to The Knouto-Germanic Empire)* (1871), *Archives Bakounine*, VII, p. 359. Emphasis added.

33. Quoted (from *The Essence of Religion*) in Marx W. Wartofsky, *Feuerbach* (Cambridge: Cambridge University Press, 1977), pp. 398-99.

34. *Réponse d'un International à Mazzini* (1871), *Archives Bakounine*, I, Part One, p. 7.

35. *Considérations philosophiques*, pp. 208-09.

36. *Op. cit.*, pp. 78-79, xiii. Emphasis added.

37. *Language and Responsibility* (Brighton: Harvester Press, 1979), p. 95.

38. *Language and Problems of Knowledge: The Managua Lectures* (Cambridge: MIT Press, 1988), pp. 161, 166-67, 169-70.

39. *Op. cit.*, pp. 62, 79.

40. The integrity of Bakunin's materialism (as opposed to Marx's, as we will see) is hardly disputable. Voegelin writes: "The materialism of Bakunin is 'genuine' in the sense of Lucretian materialism as opposed to a phenomenalist materialism [or an "historical materialism"]. In its development Bakunin displays considerable critical acumen. He is careful not to deny the autonomy [within naturalistic bounds] of

moral and intellectual phenomena; he does not attempt to explain them as epiphe-
nomena of matter. He distinguishes between the *vile matière* of the idealists who
project the most important content of matter into God so that nothing remains
but a *caput mortuum* deprived of its spiritual content, and the matter of the materialist who conceives matter as containing the forces of life and intelligence, to be
manifested in the course of progressive evolution. Bakunin's matter is not matter in
opposition to mind; it is not the matter of inorganic nature; it is rather the fundamental force of the universe which manifests itself in the differentiated realms of
being — in the inorganic as well as the organic and in the moral and intellectual
realms"[*op. cit.*, pp. 237-38]. However, Voegelin argues, in a vaguely theological
manner, that there is some conflict between Bakunin's materialism and his philosophy of freedom. Let us see.

41. *L'Empire knouto-germanique (Seconde livraison)*, p. 91.

42. *Op. cit.*, pp. 28, 31.

43. *L'Empire knouto-germanique (Seconde livraison)*, p. 92.

44. *Considérations philosophiques*, pp. 195, 234. Emphasis in original. Regarding the latter
    passage, compare with the earlier version: *"L'homme formant avec toute la nature un seul
    être et n'étant que le produit matériel d'une quantité indéfinie de causes exclusivement matérielles,
    comment cette dualité . . . a-t-elle pu naître, s'établir et s'enraciner si profondément dans la con-
    science humaine?"* [*Fédéralisme, socialisme et antithéologisme*, pp. 123-24. Emphasis in
    original.] Suffice it to say the change from *"une quantité"* to *"un concours"* suggests an
    enrichment of Bakunin's naturalism in his later writings. The later version also
    tidies up some of the messier elements of the earlier version — thus the tautolo-
    gous (as Bakunin sees it) *"causes* exclusivement *matérielles"* changes to *"causes
    matérielles"*, and the careless expression *"cette dualité"* becomes *"l'idée de cette dualité"*.

45. *L'Empire knouto-germanique (Seconde livraison)*, p. 132.

46. *Considérations philosophiques*, p. 237. Emphasis added.

47. *L'Empire knouto-germanique (Seconde livraison)*, p. 97. cf. *Fédéralisme, socialisme et an-
    tithéologisme*, pp. 122-23.

48. *Manuscript de 25 pages*, p. 359.

49. *Fédéralisme, socialisme et antithéologisme*, p. 171. Bookchin exposes the socialized ego-
    ism of an outlook that is "based on the atomistic development of single-life
    forms" (as we will see, he makes a similar point regarding class analysis), and seeks
    "to explore an ecological notion of natural evolution based on the development of
    ecosystems, not merely individual species" [*The Modern Crisis* (Philadelphia: New
    Society Publishers, 1986), p. 56.]. (He says of Darwin: "Allowing for the nuances
    which appear in all great books, *The Origin of the Species* accounts for the way in
    which *individual* species originate, evolve, adapt, survive, change, or pay the penalty
    of extinction as if they were fairly isolated from their environment. In that account,
    any one species stands for the world of life as a whole, in isolation from the life-
    forms that normally interact with it and with which it is interdependent . . . [The]
    reality of truly emerging being . . . is contextual in an ecological sense. The horse
    [for example] lived not only among its predators and food but in creatively interac-

tive relationships with a great variety of plants and animals. It evolved not alone but in ever-changing ecocommunities, such that the 'rise' of *Equus caballus* occurred conjointly with that of other herbivores that shared and maintained their grasslands and even played a major role in creating them . . . One could more properly modify *The Origin of the Species* to read as the evolution of ecocommunities as well as the evolution of species. Indeed, placing the community in the foreground of evolution does not deny the integrity of the species" [*The Philosophy of Social Ecology*, pp. 80-81] — there is no conflict here, any more than there is between the individual and the species of which it is part. [See also, *Ibid.*, pp. 95-96, note 4.])

Bakunin is certainly deficient in this regard, though his emphasis on the notion of the interactive totality of all natural things carries him beyond the atomistic outlook *toward* the ecological perspective. Hence Brian Morris comments that "Bakunin's philosophical writings on Nature present *in embryonic form* an ecological approach to the world" [*op. cit.*, p. 84; emphasis added]. Nevertheless, there is — on the surface — an anti-ecological strain in Bakunin's thought. He states that "man . . . can and should conquer and master ["external nature" or the "external world" ("through science and work"), if he is to] wrest from it his own freedom and humanity" [*Considérations philosophiques*, pp. 228, 208]. This strain is of the tradition countered by Bookchin, a tradition that makes much of the "image of a demonic and hostile nature, [a] 'realm of necessity' that opposes 'man's' striving for freedom and self-realization. Here, 'man' seems to confront a hostile 'otherness' against which he must oppose his own powers of toil [work] and guile [science]. History is thus presented to us as a Promethean drama in which 'man' heroically defies and willfully asserts himself against a brutally hostile and unyielding natural world" [*The Modern Crisis*, p. 50]. (Bookchin argues, furthermore, that within this tradition "human freedom from 'the domination of man by nature' entails the domination of human by human as the earliest means of production and the use of human beings as instruments for harnessing the natural world" [quoted in *The Murray Bookchin Reader*, ed. Janet Biehl (London: Cassell, 1997), p. 76; originally in *Remaking Society* (Montréal: Black Rose Books, 1989), p. 32] This argument will be investigated below.)

Of Bakunin himself, Bookchin says: "Even so libertarian a visionary as Mikhail Bakunin, the fiery voice of nineteenth-century anarchism, echoes Marx and many radicals of his day when he militantly declares that 'Wealth [the product of the "mastery of nature by man"] has always been and still is the indispensable condition for the realization of everything human'" [*The Modern Crisis*, p. 2; Bakunin quote from *Nauka i nasushchnoe revoliutsionnoe delo*, p. 50 (as translated in *The Political Philosophy of Bakunin: Scientific Anarchism*, ed. G.P. Maximoff (Glencoe: The Free Press, 1953), p. 358)]. Hence Bookchin challenges the (quasi-Marxian or Marxian-inspired) economism of Bakunin and, in my terms, his anthropocentrism generally. (On the latter point, observe Bookchin's reduction of Bakunin's thought to "a revolutionism that is primarily rooted in a 'revolutionary instinct'", that is, a "revolutionism" rooted in the subjective or "the revolutionary act [*qua*] expression of will" ["Deep Ecology, Anarchosyndicalism, and the Future of Anarchist

Thought", *Deep Ecology and Anarchism* (London: Freedom Press, 1993), p. 56; *The Murray Bookchin Reader*, p. 153]. Bookchin obscures both the naturalistic context of Bakunin's "instinct" as well as the "objective" environmental aspect of his "revolutionism", which is as important as the "instinctive' aspect.) As the thrust of this essay thus far makes clear, Bookchin's interpretation of Bakunin is one I dispute. In my view, Bakunin is not an economistic thinker, though at times he has his reader believe otherwise; in the case cited by Bookchin, Bakunin formally endorses a Marxian-economistic outlook, though his detailed account in that work is quite opposed to such an outlook. This issue is developed below, but it may be noted in advance that one implication of this interpretation — which may disturb a few — is that Bakuninian anarchism, for all its courteous nods in Marx's direction and economistic utterances more broadly, is fundamentally at odds with anarcho-syndicalism. (Max Nettlau's opinion is similar: "I dissent from . . . efforts to revindicate Bakunin almost exclusively as a *Syndicalist*" [*Writings on Bakunin* (London: Carl Slienger, 1976), p 7].)

Bakunin is not, in fact, an anthropocentric thinker at all. The central claim in his thought is that nature precedes the human, which is entirely of the natural and incapable of escaping it or subjugating it. In the passage from which the "conquer and master" quote, above, is taken, Bakunin distinguishes nature as such from "external nature", that is, the immediate environment in which man must live and sustain himself, or the human horizon minus its fantastic trappings. Man, Bakunin says, "can neither conquer nor master" nature; he is completely determined by the greater natural processes which envelop him, and can therefore be said, in a sense, to be their "absolute slave". "But this is [in fact] no slavery [at all], since all slavery presupposes two beings existing side by side, one of them subject to the other [that is, all slavery presupposes distinct enslaver and enslaved]. Man is not apart from nature, [he is] nothing but nature [or natural]; therefore, [being one with it] he cannot be its slave" [*Considérations philosophiques*, p. 227]. From this naturalistic point of view, then, man cannot master nature and cannot be enslaved by it: there is no duality, therefore there is no conflict.

What man needs to "master", according to Bakunin, is his immediate environment; between man and this environment (and between all animals and their immediate environments), there is "constant [historically unfolding] struggle" for existence. Certainly, Bakunin's language of "mastery" and his depiction of the "struggle" are dubious (again, his naturalism, constrained by the spirit of his day, is only embryonically ecological). However, in the midst of the sort of description to rile Bookchin, Bakunin acknowledges that "mastery" may not be the right concept after all, that a rather less authoritarian concept may be more appropriate: "What all the other animal species, taken together, could not do, man alone did. He actually transformed a large part of the earth's surface, [and] made it into a place favorable to existence [and] human civilization. He mastered and conquered [external] nature. He transformed this enemy, the first terrible despot, into a useful servant, *or at least into an ally as powerful as it is faithful*" [*Ibid.*, p. 225]. For Bakunin, "master" and "mastered" are never allies; therefore, what man has achieved (or continually seeks to achieve) is not the "mastery" or domination of external nature as such, but some kind of *self-conscious* (versus "all the other animal species") alliance, some kind of harmonious relation, with this "faithful" partner, a relation which allows man to fulfill his potential for "civilization" and freedom. The quest to "conquer and master" is therefore not an attempt to dominate on man's part, but an attempt to overcome any domination on the part of his immediate environment — which presents itself as antithetical to him, as his "enemy", as a "terrible despot", as a "yoke" [*ibid.*, p. 229], as "intent on devouring him" [*ibid.*, p. 202], though, in fact, as Bakunin's naturalism requires, it is, for all the tension within the process of human development, one with him, as man, in his rationality, comes to recognize.

Man's relation to his immediate environment, whether conceived as one of "mastery" or "alliance", is never determined by an act of the arbitrary free will of metaphysics: this environment, though it is *man's* environment (shared, if you like, by all the flora and fauna which, together with man, constitute this ecosysytem), is not *for* man, any more than it is for — you name it — the pygmy shrew. (Versus Marx, who credits capitalism with "the great civilizing influence" of having brought man to the rational recognition that, in fact, "Nature [is] simply an object *for* mankind, purely a matter of utility" [*Marx's Grundrisse*, Second Edition, ed. David McLellan (London: Macmillan Press, 1980), p. 99; emphasis added].) Man, as much as the pygmy shrew, is determined, ultimately, by nature as a whole; the extent to which he can determine his relation to his environment (the extent to which he is free) and the extent to which he is determined by it (the extent to which he is determined by his natural, including social, environment) is naturally conditioned. Freedom and determination are natural factors. Man is no free agent existing outside his environment: he is enmeshed in it and can play a self-consciously active role in it only to the extent that nature permits. His vision of himself as anything different, though capable of impacting destructively on his environment, can have no other final effect than self-destruction, a prospect to which nature is, so to speak, suitably indifferent. From this point of view, then, the ecological imperative is not so much for nature's benefit as for man's (and, logically, for the benefit of the ecosystem to which he belongs): it is a rational expression of the preservative instinct.

50. *Considérations philosophiques*, pp. 235, 237. Emphasis added.

51. *Ibid.*, p. 236. Emphasis added.

52. *Foreword to Hinrich's Religion* (1822), trans. J. Michael Stewart, *G.W.F. Hegel: Theologian of the Spirit*, ed. Peter C. Hodgson (Edinburgh: T. & T. Clark, 1997), p. 166.

53. *Lectures on the Philosophy of Religion*, I, ed. Peter C. Hodgson (Berkeley: University of California Press, 1984), p. 279. The quotes I have included from Schleiermacher are taken from an editorial note in the same volume, pp. 279-80.

54. *Towards a Critique of Hegel's Philosophy* (1839), trans. Zawar Hanfi, *The Young Hegelians: An Anthology*, p. 114.

55. *Lectures on the Essence of Religion*, pp. 119-20.

56. *Considérations philosophiques*, p. 238.

57. *Principles of the Philosophy of the Future*, trans. Manfred Vogel (Indianapolis: Hackett, 1986), p. 70 (§55).

58. *Fédéralisme, socialisme et antithéologisme*, p. 140. Emphasis added, except to the word "liberty" which is emphasized in the original.

59. *The Modern Crisis*, p. 10.

60. *The Philosophy of Social Ecology*, p. xiv.

61. *Fédéralisme, socialisme et antithéologisme*, pp. 174-75.

62. *L'Empire knouto-germanique (Seconde livraison)*, p. 139.

63. Tilo Schabert, "Revolutionary Consciousness", *Philosophical Studies*, XXVII (1980), p. 131.

64. *Fédéralisme, socialisme et antithéologisme*, p. 213. Emphasis in original.

65. *L'Empire knouto-germanique (Seconde livraison)*, p. 90. Emphasis in original.

66. *Fédéralisme, socialisme et antithéologisme*, p. 143.

67. Quotes from Hegel are from *Introduction to the Philosophy of History*, trans. Leo Rauch (Indianapolis: Hackett, 1988), pp. 74, 19-22.

68. *Considérations philosophiques*, pp. 236, 238. Emphasis added, except for the phrase "imaginative reflection", which is emphasized in the original.

69. *Ibid.*, p. 239.

70. *L'Empire knouto-germanique (Seconde livraison)*, p. 132.

71. *Considérations philosophiques*, p. 239.

72. *Ibid.*, p. 240.

73. *Ibid.*, p. 240. Emphasis added.

74. *L'Empire knouto-germanique (Seconde livraison)*, p. 133. Emphasis added.

75. *Fédéralisme, socialisme et antithéologisme*, pp. 154, 156. Emphasis in original.

76. *Considérations philosophiques*, pp. 240-41.

77. *Fédéralisme, socialisme et antithéologisme*, p. 153. An almost identical passage appears in *Considérations philosophiques*, p. 241, though the phrase "invisible and extra-mundane spiritual God" is dropped and replaced with the term "*God-Universe*", as pantheistic counterpart to the objects of fetishism (the "God-thing") and sorcery (the "man-God"). It seems that the three equivocal terms which stand for the objects of these three religions are intended to illustrate the (one might say decreasing) partiality of these religious forms, and that the proper use of the term "God" is reserved in Bakunin's *later* account for the object of the consummate Christian religion. In any case, the later term brings out the transitional element of pantheism which the earlier phrase obscures; that is to say, the earlier account almost oversteps the pantheistic element in omitting to define its object (which it appears to conflate with the object of monotheism, i.e., the "invisible and extra-mundane spiritual God").

78. *Lectures on the Essence of Religion*, pp. 146-48.

79. *Considérations philosophiques*, p. 231.

80. *Fédéralisme, socialisme et antithéologisme*, pp. 164, 166.

81. *L'Empire knouto-germanique (Seconde livraison)*, p. 98. Emphasis in original.

82. *Fédéralisme, socialisme et antithéologisme*, pp. 167-69.

83. Letter of Paul to the Romans 13:1 (New English Translation).

84. *Fédéralisme, socialisme et antithéologisme*, p. 170.

85. *Réponse d'un International à Mazzini*, p. 9.

86. *Fédéralisme, socialisme et antithéologisme*, pp. 99-104. cf. *Considérations philosophiques*, pp. 232-33.

87. For helpful tables outlining this transition, and the varying status of the Jewish, Greek, and Roman elements in the 1824, 1827, and 1831 lectures, see the editorial material in *Lectures on the Philosophy of Religion*, single volume edition, ed. Peter C. Hodgson (Berkeley: University of California Press, 1988), pp. 492-93, 498-99.

88. *Dieu et l'Etat* (the pamphlet, not the note), p. 133. Biblical reference is to Exodus 20:2-5 (New English Translation).

89. *Ibid.*, p. 134. Emphasis added.

90. *Ibid.*, p. 133.

91. *L'Empire knouto-germanique (Seconde livraison)*, p. 135.

92. *Considérations philosophiques*, note on p. 277. See also, e.g., *The Confession of Mikhail Bakunin*, p. 35.

93. *L'Empire knouto-germanique (Seconde livraison)*, pp. 135-36. Emphasis added.

94. *Ibid.*, pp. 136-38.

95. *Ibid.*, pp. 138.

96. *Ibid.*, p. 98.

97. *Ibid.*, p. 99. Emphasis in original.

98. *Ibid.*, pp. 99-101. Emphasis in original. The standard English translation of the above "dilemma" (based on the translation by Benjamin Tucker — "If God is, man is a slave; now, man can and must be free; then, God does not exist") implies that Bakunin is attempting to formulate a syllogism. (Indeed, some scholars have interpreted it as such — Peter Marshall [*Demanding the Impossible: A History of Anarchism* (London: Fontana, 1993), p. 289] for one.) This is misleading, and leaves one wondering why a would-be formal, logical argument is followed by (in Tucker's translation) "I defy anyone whomsoever to avoid this circle; now, therefore, let all choose" [*God and the State*, ed. Paul Avrich (New York: Dover, 1970), p. 25]. Syllogisms are not circular or matters of choice. Bakunin, in any case, is not given to formulating supposed syllogisms. Rather, he applies his dialectical form of reasoning (as outlined earlier) throughout, presenting each "dilemma" in the form of an either-or. For example, in the 1867 version of the above "dilemma" he writes: "God exists, therefore man is a slave. Man is intelligent, just, and free — therefore God does not exist. We defy anyone to escape this circle, and now let all choose" [*Fédéralisme, socialisme et antithéologisme*, p. 101].

99. *L'Empire knouto-germanique (Seconde livraison)*, p. 129.

100. *Réponse d'un International à Mazzini*, p. 8.

101. *L'Empire knouto-germanique (Seconde livraison)*, pp. 112-13. Emphasis added.

102. *Ibid.*, p. 113.

103. *Trois Conférences faites aux Ouvriers du Val de Saint-Imier*, p. 220.

104. *L'Empire knouto-germanique (Seconde livraison)*, p. 142.

105. *Ibid.*, pp. 115-16. Emphasis added.

106. *Ibid.*, pp. 117, 131.

107. *The Essence of Christianity*, p. 274.
108. *L'Empire knouto-germanique (Seconde livraison)*, p. 115.
109. *Ibid.*, pp. 92-93.
110. *Ibid.*, pp. 97-98, 93.
111. *Gosudarstvennost' i anarkhiia*, p. 171; *Statism and Anarchy*, p. 207.
112. *L'Empire knouto-germanique (Seconde livraison)*, p. 93.
113. *Principles of the Philosophy of the Future*, p. 23 (§15).
114. *La Commune de Paris*, pp. 302-03. Emphasis added.
115. *L'Empire knouto-germanique (Seconde livraison)*, pp. 93-94.
116. *The Essence of Christianity*, p. 15.
117. *L'Empire knouto-germanique (Seconde livraison)*, p. 94.
118. *Ibid.*, p. 95. Emphasis added.
119. *Ibid.*, pp. 95-97. The last quote hardly tallies with Bakunin's supposed belief in a primitive "Golden Age" to which he would have us return (versus Kelly).
120. *Dieu et l'Etat* (the pamphlet, not the note), p. 134. It is in this passage (" . . . *Hegel, malgré même la critique . . . dans l'histoire*") that Bakunin cites the four influences.
121. *Sources of the Self: The Making of Modern Identity* (Cambridge: Cambridge University Press, 1992), p. 366.
122. *Kant's Transcendental Idealism: An Interpretation and Defense* (New Haven: Yale University Press, 1983), p. 242.
123. *Immanuel Kant's Critique of Pure Reason*, Revised Edition, trans. Norman Kemp Smith (London: Macmillan, 1933), pp. 271-72 (A254-55 / B310-11).
124. *Op. cit.*, p. 246.
125. J.N. Findlay, *Kant and the Transcendental Object: A Hermeneutic Study* (Oxford: Clarendon Press, 1981), pp. 3-4.
126. *The Ecology of Freedom*, Revised Edition (Montréal: Black Rose Books, 1991), pp. 38-39. Emphasis added.
127. *Marxism and Materialism: A Study in Marxist Theory of Knowledge* (Sussex: Harvester Press, 1977), p. 63.
128. *Considérations philosophiques*, p. 267.
129. *Principles of the Philosophy of the Future*, pp. 28-29 (§17).
130. *L'Internationale et Mazzini*, p. 42.
131. *Dieu et l'Etat* (the pamphlet, not the note), p. 134.
132. *Introduction to the Philosophy of History*, p. 20.
133. *Phenomenology of Spirit*, pp. 4, 54 (§§6, 85). I have changed Miller's translation of "*Begriff*" from "Notion" to "Concept" for reasons outlined by the editors of *The Encyclopaedia Logic* on pp. xxix, 348 of that volume.
134. *Phenomenology of Spirit*, p. 56 (§87).
135. *Reason in Religion: The Foundations of Hegel's Philosophy of Religion*, trans. J. Michael Stewart and Peter C. Hodgson (Berkeley: University of California Press, 1990), pp. 194-95, 204-05. The two quotes from the *Phenomenology* within Jaeschke's text are from pp. 417, 460 (§§684, 759).
136. *Lectures on the Philosophy of Religion*, I, pp. 130, 343. Emphasis added. The introduction

to this volume (the first of three outstanding volumes) is the source of my information on the general influence of the lectures on the Left Hegelians.

137. *Ibid.*, pp. 136-37.

138. *Ibid.*, pp. 137, 139.

139. *A Contribution to the Critique of Hegel's Philosophy of Right: Introduction* (1843), trans. Annette Jolin and Joseph O'Malley, *The Young Hegelians: An Anthology*, p. 310.

140. *La Théologie politique de Mazzini (Deuxième partie)*, p. 271.

141. *Dieu et l'Etat* (the pamphlet, not the note), p. 134.

142. *The Essence of Christianity*, p. xv.

143. *Ibid.*, pp. xiii, xxi, xx.

144. *Ibid.*, pp. 2-3, 7, 281.

145. *Ibid.*, pp. 13-14. Emphasis added to the word "altogether".

146. *Ibid.*, pp. 17, 60.

147. *Ibid.*, pp. 19-22, 26.

148. *Ibid.*, pp. 21, 278, xxiii-xxiv.

149. *Theses on Feuerbach, Collected Works*, V (London: Lawrence & Wishart, 1976), p. 4. Emphasis added.

150. *Ibid.*, p. 5.

151. *L'Empire knouto-germanique (Seconde livraison)*, p. 84. Emphasis added.

152. *Gosudarstvennost' i anarkhiia*, p. 110; *Statism and Anarchy*, p. 132.

153. *Op. cit.*, p. 79.

154. *Manifesto of the Communist Party*, p. 70: "The bourgeoisie cannot exist without constantly revolutionizing the instruments of production, and thereby the relations of production, and with them the whole relations of society". Preface to *A Contribution to the Critique of Political Economy* (London: Lawrence and Wishart, 1970), pp. 20-21: "In the social production of their existence, men inevitably enter into definite relations, which are independent of their will, namely *relations of production* appropriate to a given stage in the development of their material *forces of production*. The totality of these relations of production constitutes the *economic structure* of society, the real foundation, on which rises a legal and political *superstructure* and to which correspond definite forms of social consciousness ... At a certain stage of development, the material productive forces of society come into conflict with the existing relations of production, or — this merely expresses the same thing in legal terms — with the property relations within the framework of which they have operated hitherto. From forms of development of the productive forces these relations turn into their fetters. Then begins an era of *social revolution*" etc. [emphasis added].

155. Letter to Joseph Bloch (21-22/9/1890), *The Marx-Engels Reader*, p. 760.

156. Speech at the graveside of Marx (17/3/1883), *The Marx-Engels Reader*, p. 681.

157. *Karl Marx: His Life and Environment*, Fourth Edition (Oxford: Oxford University Press, 1978), p. 115.

158. Alan Sokal and Jean Bricmont, *Intellectual Impostures: Postmodern philosophers' abuse of science* (London: Profile Books, 1998), p. 1. Emphasis added.

159. *Capital*, III, *The Marx-Engels Reader*, p. 441.

160. *The Ecology of Freedom*, p. 65. Emphasis added.

161. *The Murray Bookchin Reader*, p. 128.

162. Quoted, *ibid.*, p. 76. Originally in *Remaking Society*, p. 32. Emphasis added. I trust that the importance of this quote justifies my reuse of it.

163. *The German Ideology, Collected Works*, V, p. 40.

164. *The Concept of Nature in Marx*, trans. Ben Fowkes (London: New Left Books, 1971), pp. 15-32, 200 (note 29).

165. Schmidt's faithful defense (I believe that it is more faithful than, for example, that of Ruben, *op. cit.*) is necessarily as absurd as that which he is trying to defend. Take the following examples:

(1) "Marx, like Feuerbach, wrote of 'the priority of external nature', although with the critical reservation that any such priority could only exist *within mediation*". I have commented on this already: it is blatant Kantian metaphysics.

(2) "What Feuerbach described as the unity of man and nature related only to the romantically transfigured fact that man arose out of nature, and not to *man's socio-historically mediated unity with nature* in industry". Marx himself may believe that "man arose *out* of nature", since this belief underpins the very dualism — man versus nature — that his thought is based on. But Feuerbach believes nothing of the kind. His emerging naturalism precludes this belief: he believes, like Bakunin, that man arose *within* nature, and is eternally "bound" to it. This is why Feuerbach and then Bakunin reject Marx's dialectic and mystical vision of resolution through productive activity (a vision that appeals to capitalists as much as to Marxists). But, as Bakunin might put it, let Marx and Schmidt choose — metaphysical duality or scientific unity.

(3) "Feuerbach's man does not emerge as an independent productive force but remains bound to pre-human nature. Physical activity does, it is true, presuppose this natural basis as a counter-block to *man's transcending consciousness.* All work is work on a fixed being which nevertheless proves transitory and penetrable under the action of living Subjects". Indeed, man is "bound", historically, to "pre-human nature", that is, nature prior to man's emergence within it. Man has a natural history in the pre-human, a fact that is effectively lost on Marx. Man is still "bound", and will always be "bound", to nature (which now embraces the human without conflict): he will never "penetrate" it because he, for all his glorious productive activity, and not nature, is "transitory". In spite of Schmidt's rider, the Marxian notion of production is a transcendent notion; Marx's subject is a transcendent subject. When "Nature becomes . . . simply an object *for* mankind [and] ceases to be recognized as a power in its own right [that is, a power independent of man]" [*Marx's Grundrisse*, p. 99; emphasis added], it has been transcended in the most mystical sense.

(4) "Nature as a whole was for Feuerbach an unhistorical, homogenous substratum, while the essence of Marx's critique was the dissolution of this homogeneity into a dialectic of Subject and Object. Nature was for Marx both an element of human practice and the totality of everything that exists. By unreflectively stressing the totality alone Feuerbach succumbed to the *naive-realist myth* of a 'pure

nature'". [All the above quotes from Schmidt, *op. cit.*, p. 27; emphasis added.] Nature is no more "unhistorical" and "homogenous" for Feuerbach (or Bakunin) than it is for any naturalist. Nature has its own history, as every natural "thing", including the human species, has a narrower history within that broader natural history. And nature is no undifferentiated whole, or a mere "substratum" for the variety of existents, but a totality in indeterminate (but, in principle, determinable) difference. This concept of nature — which has nothing to do with any concept of "pure [presumably abstract] nature" — is no "myth": it is both the object of science and that which has given rise to the scientific intelligence (or "subject"). The only myth we are concerned with here is the myth of the divine mediator, the productive agent. In any case, Schmidt can call this realism "naïve" if he wishes; but the only alternative is groundless idealism, the mystification of the human, which has always and must always precipitate political, ecological, and intellectual annihilation.

(5) A final example (though we could continue *ad infinitum*), an example which gives this philosophical farce away: "what is essential is that historically *the incompatibility of man with nature* [what?], i.e., in the last analysis the necessity of labor, triumphs over the unity of man and nature" [*Ibid.*, p. 30]. In other words, the essence of Marx's philosophy is the principle of non-identity (of the natural and the human, of the object and the subject) and the principle of mediation (by labor, by socialized subjective activity). Feuerbach and Bakunin, by contrast, adhere to the (naturalist and realist) principle of identity (of the natural and the human, the object and the subject) and the (realist) principle of (sensuous) immediacy.

Some disagree with the attribution of the principle of identity to Feuerbach, seeing in his work "a polarity of subject-object, of nature and man". [Preceding quote from Manfred Vogel's "Introduction" to *Principles of the Philosophy of the Future* (Indianapolis: Bobbs-Merrill, 1966), p. xiii. Note that while I use the same translation of this work throughout, I use the newer (Hackett) edition (which has a different introduction) of it elsewhere.] I disagree with this interpretation to the extent that, while I acknowledge that Feuerbach rejects an idealist principle of identity (in spite of its final contribution to the critique of Kantian epistemology), I believe that he holds what I characterize as an anti-epistemological realist principle of identity (as an element of his ontological naturalism). As Wartofsky explains: "Feuerbach . . . does not object to the immediate unity of subject and object in identity philosophy. Rather he objects to it as an identity *in the mind*, or in thought alone" [*Feuerbach*, p. 372]. (This principle is anti-epistemological because the denial of ontological conflict or qualitative difference renders epistemological inquiry — inquiry into the mysterious relation between some kind of subject and some other kind of object — redundant. *True* realism, that is to say, is not an epistemological position at all. This is a source of frustration for Wartofsky, who sees that Feuerbach's principle of identity leads to — or "dissolves" into — a principle of immediacy which leaves no room for scholastic / epistemological endeavor — exactly as Feuerbach intended [see, *ibid.*, p. 378]. As Wartofsky says — with a little scholarly distaste: "No [epistemological] problems of appearance, illusion, hallucination, no relativity of perception, no subjectivism, or solipsism of the senses for

Feuerbach! None of the host of typical empiricist or rationalist moves regarding the [assumed] gap between perception and reality", etc. [*ibid.*, p. 382].) Thus, while Feuerbach rejects an epistemological principle of identity (with its dubious onto-logical implications) he holds what at bottom is an ontological principle of iden-tity (with its liberating anti-epistemological implications).

Wartofsky outlines three arguments for Feuerbach's realist position. They are worth rehearsing because they are — not surprisingly — similar to Bakunin's ar-guments. The first argument is *logical* or dialectical: his realism is thought to be vindicated as the antithesis and negation of speculative idealism, "as the next stage of the dialectic". This is too "formal" an argument for Wartofsky's liking, though it might be said that championing the antithesis of something that is manifestly false is a common sense procedure. Speaking of which, the second argument is the ap-peal to *common sense*, according to which realism seems "self-evident". However, Wartofsky thinks this argument is an argument from "revelation" — that is, not philosophical (or scholastic) enough. The third argument is *practical*. Wartofsky writes: "The import of a philosophical argument [here] is . . . its consequences for praxis", so that "questions [are] to be asked in such a way that what will count as a proper answer *cannot be given by philosophy, as speculation*, but only by sense experience or empirical practice itself, and notably, by the natural sciences. This is the strong positivist strain, and also the pragmatist strain in Feuerbach's" thought [*Ibid.*, pp. 369-70]. These three arguments are employed by Bakunin. His negative dialectic is a central feature of his thought. His place in the "common sense rationalist" tradi-tion is secure as well; for example, he thinks the instincts of the oppressed masses, though uneducated, are rational. And his positivistic and pragmatic orientation is also much in evidence. (The relationship between pragmatism and anarchism will be considered in my work in progress, "The Philosophy of Anarchism".)

165. *Theses on Feuerbach*, p. 4. Emphasis added.

166. "Objectless Activity: Marx's 'Theses on Feuerbach'", *Inquiry*, XXVIII (1985), pp. 75-76.

167. *On Materialism*, trans. Lawrence Garner (London: New Left Books, 1975), pp. 34, 40-41. Emphasis added.

168. *The Open Society and Its Enemies*, II, *The High Tide of Prophecy: Hegel, Marx, and the After-math*, Fifth Edition (London: Routledge & Kegan Paul, 1966), pp. 85, 106, 82. Em-phasis added.

169. *On History* (London: Abacus, 1998), pp. 24, viii.

170. *Introduction to the Philosophy of History*, p. 12.

171. *Lettre à un français*, p. 99.

172. *The Modern Crisis*, p. 3.

173. *Anamnesis*, trans. Gerhart Niemeyer (Columbia: University of Missouri Press, 1990), pp. 3, 111.

174. Letter to Joseph Bloch (21-22/9/1890), p. 762.

175. Letter to P.V. Annenkov (28/12/1846), Appendix to *The Poverty of Philosophy*, Revised Edition (Moscow: Progress Publishers, 1975), p. 166. Emphasis added to the word "incapable" and removed from the phrase "economic development".

176. *Conspectus of Bakunin's Statism and Anarchy*, *The Marx-Engels Reader*, pp. 544-45. Emphasis added to the word "absolutely".

177. *Op. cit.*, pp. 341, 343. Emphasis added.

178. *Mikhail Bakunin*, p. 241.

179. See, especially, *Ecrit contre Marx*, pp. 195-96: "[Marxists] object [to anarchists] that the State is not at all the cause of the poverty, degradation, and servitude of the masses; that the impoverished condition of the masses [and] the despotic power of the State, are . . . the effects of a more general cause — the products of an inevitable phase in the economic development of society, of a phase which, from the historical point of view, constitutes real progress, an immense step toward what they call social revolution . . . Materialists and determinists, like Marx himself, we also recognize the fatal connection of economic and political facts in history. We too recognize the necessity and inevitable character of all events that occur, but we are not inclined to bow before them indifferently, and above all we are most careful about praising and admiring them when, by their nature, they show themselves to be in flagrant opposition to the supreme end of history [that is, "the triumph of humanity", the fulfillment of the human potential for freedom]".
    Bakunin's understanding of economic determinism is evidently that effects of economic causes (and there are other causes: Bakunin accepts that economic and political facts are "connected" here, nothing more) are inevitable, but only relatively so; as we have shown, he believes the materialist conception of history to be only relatively true. Thus we should not bow before these powerful determinants, never mind praise them in the name of their civilizing and revolutionary role. Rather, we should condemn them as appropriate and devote all our energies "to the supreme end of history" that contradicts them — that is, freedom, as secured (in part, at any rate), or as determined (likewise, only relatively), by the naturalistic revolutionary will.
    It is vital to recall here that all causes and orders of causes are, within the interactive totality of "particular" causes, relative as far as Bakunin is concerned. There is no absolute cause; theological and metaphysical causes that pretend to be such — Divine, economic, or whatever — are "phantoms". Bakunin states explicitly that natural laws (including "social laws") *"are not absolute"* [*Considérations philosophiques*, p. 196; emphasis added].

180. From *Memoirs of a Revolutionist*, *The Conquest of Bread and Other Writings*, ed. Marshall S. Shatz (Cambridge: Cambridge University Press, 1995), pp. 222, 214-15.
    Kropotkin — more scientist than philosopher himself — actually accuses Marx (as Sokal and Bricmont have accused some contemporary philosophers) of abusing science — principally "the concepts and terminology coming from mathematics and physics" — in the course of his speculations. (The criteria of abuse established by Sokal and Bricmont would doubtless be supported by Kropotkin: "The word 'abuse' here denotes one or more of the following characteristics: 1. Holding forth at length on scientific theories about which one has, at best, an exceedingly hazy idea. The most common tactic is to use scientific (or pseudo-scientific) terminology without bothering much about what the words actually *mean*. 2. Importing concepts from the natural sciences into the humanities or social sciences without

giving the slightest conceptual or empirical justification . . . 3. Displaying a superficial erudition by shamelessly throwing around technical terms in a context where they are completely irrelevant. The goal is, no doubt, to impress and, above all, to intimidate the non-scientist reader . . . 4. Manipulating phrases and sentences that are, in fact, meaningless. Some of these authors exhibit a veritable intoxication with words, combined with a superb indifference to their meaning".) Marx, like his contemporary counterparts, casts doubt on the objectivity of natural science while, one might argue, paradoxically seeking to "exploit the prestige of the natural sciences in order [perhaps] to give [his] own discourse a veneer of rigor. And [he seems] confident that no one will notice [his] misuse of scientific concepts. No one is going to cry out that the king is naked" [*Intellectual Impostures*, pp. 4-5].

In the case of this particular king, Kropotkin does just that: "I read [*Das Kapital*] when I was still in Petersburg . . . Even then I very much disliked the pretentiousness of the book as well as its unscientific character — the theory of value, for example, is not demonstrated scientifically but has to be taken on faith — and its indulgence in scientific jargon. Marx's excursions into the realm of numerical expressions and algebraic formulae were comical: they demonstrate his utter inability to think concretely, in quantitative terms, and Nicholas Tsinger (an astronomer) and I had a good laugh over his 'formulae', which he sets out so pretentiously without even suspecting how amusing they are to a mathematician accustomed to the idea of units of measurement. Highly comical as well is his penchant for expressing himself in formulae where formulae express nothing" etc. [*op. cit.* pp. 220-21].

Bakunin's attitude toward *Das Kapital* is somewhat more ambivalent; while lauding Marx's "great work" for being "positivist and realist in the highest degree, in the sense that it admits no logic but that of the facts", anticipating Kropotkin's evaluation, he notes that it is at the same time "bristling with metaphysical formulae and subtleties which render it inaccessible to the great majority of readers" [*Lettre à un français*, p. 99]. Hence Bakunin sees in Marx a conflict between the scientific and the metaphysical, and therefore the universal and the scholastic, and this explains both Bakunin's intellectual respect for Marx (which, though never reciprocated, is genuine) and his intellectual abhorrence for him (which, contrary to Marxist slander, is also genuine, and, I contend — with Kropotkin among others — well grounded).

181. See *Notes from Underground*, trans. Jessie Coulson (Harmondsworth: Penguin Books, 1972), pp. 15-46.

182. *Gosudarstvennost' i anarkhiia*, pp. 26, 24; *Statism and Anarchy*, pp. 31, 28. Emphasis added.

183. *Introduction to the Philosophy of History*, p. 26. Emphasis added.

184. "La Lutte des tendances au sein de la Première Internationale: Marx et Bakounine", *From Buonarroti to Bakunin: Studies in International Socialism* (Leiden: E.J. Brill, 1970), p. 262.

185. *Op. cit.*, p. 24. Emphasis added.

186. *Op. cit.*, pp. 106, 78.

187. *Gosudarstvennost' i anarkhiia*, p. 119; *Statism and Anarchy*, p. 142.

188. *L'Empire knouto-germanique (Seconde livraison)*, p. 87. The Tucker-based translation has "is *but* a reflection", which is a clear mistranslation and overemphasis.

189. *Ibid.*, p. 96.

190. *Op. cit.*, p. 41. Emphasis added. Pyziur contends that there are two strains or "patterns" in Bakunin's thought, which he labels "anarchist" and "Marxian". Perhaps these strains are better understood as, on the one hand, libertarian and, on the other, socialist. Pyziur wrongly depicts the libertarian strain as ahistorical and voluntaristic, but is correct in highlighting its concern with the question of "oppression" or domination. The socialist strain, by seeming contrast, is primarily concerned, as Pyziur acknowledges, with the question of "exploitation" [*ibid.*, p. 59]. Pyziur, like most of Bakunin's critics, implies that these strains are tacked together (dialectically, no doubt) rather than intrinsically interwoven. The latter is clearly Bakunin's understanding of his position and of the revolutionary principle, as I have demonstrated previously. He simply refuses to countenance any diremption of this principle. Any attempt to abstract one or other element from it, in the fashion of liberalism or socialism, results in a partial ideology tending toward exploitation or domination. To repeat the famous statement: "*liberty without socialism is privilege and injustice, and . . . socialism without liberty is slavery and brutality*" [*Fédéralisme, socialisme et antithéologisme*, p. 96; emphasis in original]. If Bakunin overstates the socialist case, and the economic factor in historical analysis, his motivation is obvious enough: socialism is the more revolutionary movement in the climate of his day, and economic analysis is the more immediately penetrating. However, within the socialist movement, to counteract its more authoritarian and metaphysical (economistic) tendencies, he clearly emphasizes the question of liberty. This position is perfectly coherent.

191. *Aux Compagnons de l'Association Internationale des Travailleurs au Locle et de la Chaux-de-Fonds* (1869), *Oeuvres*, I, p. 251. Emphasis added.

192. *Lettre à la Liberté*, p. 162.

193. *Mikhail Bakunin*, pp. 174-175.

194. *Michael Bakunin and Karl Marx* (Melbourne: A. Maller, 1948), p. 364.

195. *Beyond Capital: Towards a Theory of Transition* (London: Merlin Press, 1995), p. 473. Needless to say, Mészáros levels the standard Marxist "voluntarist" accusation at Bakunin [*Ibid.*, p. 695].

196. *What is Property?*, p. 45.

197. *Language and Responsibility*, p. 91.

198. *Gosudarstvennost' i anarkhiia*, p. 119; *Statism and Anarchy*, p. 142.

199. *The Poverty of Philosophy*, p. 135.

200. *The German Ideology*, p. 31. Emphasis added, except to the word "produce", which is emphasized in the translation.

201. *Principles of the Philosophy of the Future*, p. 13 ($10).

202. *Provisional Theses for the Reformation of Philosophy*, trans. Daniel O. Dahlstrom, *The Young Hegelians: An Anthology*, pp. 156-57, 160.

203. *Ibid.*, pp. 160-61.

204. *Principles of the Philosophy of the Future*, pp. 31-33 (§§19-21); *Provisional Theses*, p. 167.

205. *Principles of the Philosophy of the Future*, pp. 49-52 (§§31-32).

206. *Feuerbach*, p. 384.

207. *Principles of the Philosophy of the Future*, pp. 52, 55-56 (§§32, 37-38).

208. *Provisional Theses*, pp. 162, 168.

209. *Fédéralisme, socialisme et antithéologisme*, p. 110. Emphasis added.

210. *Provisional Theses*, p. 170.

211. *Principles of the Philosophy of the Future*, pp. 58-59 (§41). Emphasis added.

212. *Feuerbach*, pp. 362-63.

213. *Ibid.*, p. 374.

214. *Principles of the Philosophy of the Future*, pp. 59-60, 72 (§§43, 62).

215. *Theses on Feuerbach*, p. 4.

216. *The German Ideology*, pp. 39-40. Emphasis added.

217. *The Economic and Philosophic Manuscripts of 1844*, *Collected Works*, III (London: Lawrence and Wishart, 1975), p. 328.

218. *Principles of the Philosophy of the Future*, p. 64 (§48). Thomas E. Wartenberg refers to Feuerbach's "social epistemology" in his introduction to this edition, p. xxi.

219. "The Contradictory Nature of Feuerbachian Humanism", *Philosophical Forum*, XIII (1978), p. 38.

220. *Feuerbach*, p. 378.

221. *Lectures on the Essence of Religion*, pp. 25-27. Emphasis added.

222. *Ibid.*, pp. 29-31. Emphasis added.

223. *Ibid.*, pp. 34-38, 79. I have emphasized the words "special official class".

224. *Ibid.*, pp. 79-80. See also *The Essence of Christianity*, p. 186.

225. *Ibid.*, pp. 82-84.

226. *Ibid.*, pp. 91, 100.

227. *Ibid.*, pp. 93-95, 97.

228. *Ibid.*, pp. 95, 103-04.

229. *Ibid.*, pp. 106-07. Emphasis added.

230. See *Religion* (London: Fontana, 1982).

231. *Lectures on the Essence of Religion*, pp. 100-01.

232. *Provisional Theses*, p. 170; *Philosophy of Right*, p. 279 (addition to §258); *Contribution to the Critique of Hegel's Philosophy of Right*, *Collected Works*, III, p. 29; *Critique of the Gotha Program*, *Collected Works*, XXIV (London: Lawrence & Wishart, 1989), p. 537.

233. *Philosophy of Right*, pp. 155, 160, 163 (§§257, 260, 267).

234. *A Contribution to the Critique of Hegel's Philosophy of Right: Introduction*, p. 311.

235. *The Ego and Its Own*, ed. David Leopold (Cambridge: Cambridge University Press, 1995), pp. 311-13.

236. *Lectures on the Essence of Religion*, p. 150.

237. *The Young Hegelians and Karl Marx*, p. 131.

238. "Max Stirner and Ludwig Feuerbach", *Journal of the History of Ideas*, XXXIX (1978),

pp. 455, 462-63.

239. *L'Internationale et Mazzini*, p. 42.

240. *Fédéralisme, socialisme et antithéologisme*, p. 109.

241. Auguste Comte, *Introduction to Positive Philosophy*, ed. Frederick Ferré (Indianapolis: Hackett, 1988), p. 28. This is a complete, updated translation of the first two lessons of the *Cours de philosophie positive*. For a condensed (two-volume) translation of the entire course, I have referred to the third edition of *The Positive Philosophy of Auguste Comte*, trans. Harriet Martineau (London: Kegan Paul, Trench, Trübner, & Co., 1893).

242. *Introduction to Positive Philosophy*, pp. 13-15.

243. *The Positive Philosophy of Auguste Comte*, II, pp. 36, 124.

244. *Auguste Comte: An Intellectual Biography*, Vol. I (Cambridge: Cambridge University Press, 1993), pp. 596, 599.

245. *Op. cit.*, pp. 364-65.

246. *Op. cit.*, pp. 62-63, 23-24. Emphasis added, except to the word "natural", which is emphasized in the original.

247. *Ibid.*, p. 22.

248. *Aux Compagnons de l'Association Internationale des Travailleurs au Locle et de la Chaux-de-Fonds*, p. 251.

249. *Op. cit.*, p. 358.

250. *Introduction to Positive Philosophy*, pp. 2, 5.

251. *Ibid.*, p. 5.

252. "Auguste Comte and the Return to Primitivism", *Revue Internationale de Philosophie*, LII, No. 203 (January 1998), pp. 51-77. Bakunin refers explicitly to the three forms in, for example, *L'Empire knouto-germanique (Seconde livraison)*, pp. 132-33: *"C'est ainsi que la folie collective et historique qui s'appelle religion s'est développée depuis le fétichisme, en passant par tous les degrés du polythéisme, jusqu'au monothéisme chrétien"*, etc.

253. *The Positive Philosophy*, II, pp. 156-57.

254. *Ibid.*, p. 162.

255. *Ibid.*, p. 160. Emphasis added.

256. *Ibid.*, p. 169.

257. *Ibid.*, pp. 175-76.

258. *Ibid.*, pp. 184-85.

259. *Ibid.*, pp. 186, 188, 190.

260. *Ibid.*, pp. 208, 211, 213.

261. *Ibid.*, pp. 227, 245-47.

262. *Ibid.*, p. 246.

263. *Ibid.*, pp. 217-19.

264. *Ibid.*, pp. 233-35.

265. *Ibid.*, pp. 221, 224.

266. *Ibid.*, p. 250.

267. *Introduction to Positive Philosophy*, pp. 2, 8.

268. *The Positive Philosophy*, II, p. 256.
269. *Ibid.*, p. 260.
270. *Considérations philosophiques*, p. 249.
271. *Ibid.*, pp. 253-55, 301. Emphasis added.
272. *Introduction to Positive Philosophy*, p. 2.
273. *Ibid.*, pp. 8-9. Emphasis added.
274. *Considérations philosophiques*, pp. 257, 268, 247. Emphasis in original.
275. *Ibid.*, p. 286, note.
276. *Fédéralisme, socialisme et antithéologisme*, p. 108.
277. *Introduction to Positive Philosophy*, pp. 25-26.
278. *Ibid.*, pp. 24-25.
279. *L'Instruction Intégrale*, pp. 129-30.
280. *Introduction to Positive Philosophy*, p. 28.
281. *Considérations philosophiques*, p. 246.

Conclusion

The most that can be hoped for this book is that it goes some way to filling a significant gap in Bakunin studies: an intellectual gap, left despite the pretence of the liberal psycho-biographers and Marxist ideologues to have filled it. It makes no claim to be the last word on the matter. On the contrary, it is viewed as a preliminary effort (to outline Bakunin's basic ideas and to place them in philosophical context), and, as such, is doubtless flawed. Nevertheless, it maintains with some confidence that Bakunin has been wronged by the majority of scholars — not because they deny his greatness, but because, philosophically, they deny him anything. I affirm, on the basis of what has been presented above, his philosophical significance, both from the historical perspective and from the contemporary perspective.

Historically, Bakunin belongs to a classically rooted tradition of naturalist thinking that has come to fruition in the post-Enlightenment period. This tradition laid the foundations for modern science and has sought, subsequently, to develop insights that are in accord with it while remaining critical of its intellectual and especially its ethical lapses. Thus, subsequent to the emergence of modern science, naturalist philosophers have assumed a largely critical role characteristic of the *philosophes* of the Enlightenment itself. Some have developed historically situated socio-political analyses of its consequences and, more important, of the consequences of alternative philosophies. The former have widely been held to be emancipatory, the latter enslaving.

Bakunin is undeniably part of this tradition, and stands alongside

Diderot, Feuerbach, Comte, and others as one of its most intriguing figures. Indeed, Bakunin may stand at the pinnacle of this tradition as arguably its most consistent and radical member. Not only does his naturalist anti-theologistic critique demonstrate a number of contradictions in idealism, divine and human, but his negative dialectic rules out the possibility of compromise between philosophies which represent contradictory theoretical principles and practical ends. In an age of bogus spirituality, vacuous religion, and consumer-oriented eclecticism — to say nothing of the unyielding reaction of religious fundamentalism, including the Christian form, that is often taken to justify "liberal" compromise or "moderation" — it ought to be apparent that compromise with the frankly irrational is, in many senses, reactionary, representing, for example, intellectual primitivism and meditative indifference to practical barbarity — that is, as Bakunin argued, slavery, theoretical and practical.

Politically, we can hardly disagree either: the relentless prostitution of socialism — a tradition that once broadly stood for the value of justice — confirms Bakunin's critique of social democracy. If social democracy disgraced a sincere socialist tradition, the social democratic tradition has itself been disgraced by a "Third Way" movement that, in its immense cynicism, has fooled nobody possessed of common sense. The right of the "real" social democratic tradition to complain in a moral tone, as if it were not the result of cheap compromise itself, might be questioned, however.

The last couple of observations already place Bakunin in some contemporary perspective, underlining his very relevance and critical significance. Philosophically, the same holds. From the point of view of mainstream academic philosophy, enamored as it is of the Kierkegaards, Heideggers, and Wittgensteins of the previous hundred years or so, Bakunin represents a welcome antidote. If Bakunin stands at the pinnacle of the radical tradition in question, it was Kierkegaard who, from a dialectical standpoint at least, managed to corrupt it. Kierkegaard is the betrayer of the uncompromising dialectic, the figure who transformed rationalism into absurdism by willfully choosing, *as an act of faith*, the reactionary moment (that is, in this case, *the divine order*), thereby sacrificing all revolutionary potential. In Bakunin's terms, Kierkegaard succeeded only in re-theologizing philosophy and in bringing about a philosophical reaction that persists, in large part, to this day. Thus many contemporaries, following Kierkegaard, embrace the obscure, the suggestive, the personalistic, and so on, without a care for social concerns or any rational-scientific project which might underscore the basis of human solidarity and ecological identity. God — albeit a personalistic God, butchered to the point where he satisfies every appetite of the modern or postmodern ego — once again takes precedence over the species and nature as a whole. (Stirner, in fairness to him, had the honesty to deny God's role in such a religion of the self.) Social and ecological concerns are once again set aside in the name of subjective interests and the pursuit of some means of *creating* some artificial inter-subjective "community" of interests, some contrived pluralistic society, some "union of egos", and so forth. An assumption of social non-identity, and of inevitable inter-personal conflict, re-inspired by the Kierkegaardian reaction (which had, in fact, been anticipated by Stirner) and the predominance of a Kantian outlook, governs in spite of rationalistic-scientific conclusions of human identity. The absurd idea that human nature does not exist and even that evolution does not confirm some level of natural identity persists. Worse still, the belief in human nature, for example, is thought rather fascistic. This notion needs to be refuted: if the belief in human nature has any social corollary it is internationalism, not fascism; fascism is, in fact, a socialized form of personalism, of the belief that uniqueness (of culture) is a fact and, indeed, at some level, a fact to be cherished.

Bookchin has noted the gulf between personalistic and socialistic strains within the anarchist tradition itself. Hence he writes, in the spirit of Bakunin, about the "unbridgeable chasm" between "lifestyle anarchism", the contemporary manifestation of the Stirnerian tradition of individualist anarchism, and "social anarchism". The former is, he says, a product of "the all-pervasive Yuppie and New Age personalism that marks this decadent, bourgeoisified era". Its "ideological pedigree", he adds, "is basically liberal, grounded on the myth of the fully autono-mous individual whose claims to self-sovereignty are validated by axio-matic 'natural rights', 'intrinsic worth', or, on a more sophisticated level, an intuited Kantian transcendental ego that is generative of all knowable reality. These traditional views surface in Max Stirner's 'I' or ego, which shares with [the] existentialism [inspired by Kierkegaard] a tendency to absorb all of reality into itself, as if the universe turned on the choices of the self-oriented individual". Social anarchism, in con-trast to such effectively *reactionary personalism* (characterized by its in-dulgence in the "metaphysics of the ego and its [personal, linguistic, or cultural] 'uniqueness'), is defined in terms of its *'revolutionary social out-look...* with all its theoretical... Underpinnings". These underpinnings, examined in the case of Bakunin above, demonstrate that social anar-chism is, as Bookchin puts it, the "heir to the Enlightenment tradi-tion".[1]

With regard to left-wing thought more specifically, Bakunin represents, as has been argued throughout this essay, an alternative to the Marxist paradigm. Peter Singer, for one, has said as much. His work, *A Darwinian Left: Politics, Evolution, and Cooperation,*[2] opens with a brief account of the contrast between Marx and Bakunin. Singer sides, in principle, with Bakunin, writing: "when [Bakunin] suggests that someone who holds views like those of Marx and his followers 'know nothing at all about human nature', it is hard to disagree". Singer does not follow the reasoning of Bakunin beyond this, but his analysis of philosophy on the left, at least, up to his constructive elaboration, has much in common with Bakunin's thinking.[3] Essentially, Singer recom-mends evolutionary naturalism, rather than Marxian anthropocen-trism, as a paradigm for the left.

> The left ["as a broad body of thought, a spectrum of ideas about achieving a better world] needs a new paradigm... I want to suggest that one source of new ideas that could revi-

talize the left is an approach to human social, political, and economic behavior based firmly on a modern understanding of human nature. It is time for the left to take seriously the fact that we are evolved animals, and that we bear the evidence of our inheritance, not only in our anatomy and our DNA, but in our behavior too. In other words it is time to develop a Darwinian left.[4]

Singer's critique of Marxian thought is similar to the Bakuninian critique we have examined. Thus he writes: "The materialist theory of history implies that there is no fixed human nature. It changes with every change in the mode of production". Singer continues: "To anyone who sees a continuity between human beings and our non-human ancestors, it seems implausible that Darwinism gives us the laws of evolution for natural history but stops at the dawn of human history". In other words, the Marxist claim that there has been some dramatic rupture between natural history and social history, but that it is not a major concern since we have Darwin for the former and Marx for the latter, is absurd. The grounds for this claim — that there is a qualitative distinction between human and non-human animals — is highly dubious, as Singer observes. Saying that man, unlike any other animal, produces his own means of subsistence, that he alone is a proper economic agent, is biological nonsense: "fungus-growing ants, for example, grow and eat specialized fungi that would not have existed without their activity". Singer continues: "But even if [such a distinction] were valid, why should the difference between collecting [for example] and producing be so important as to suspend the laws of evolution? Why should productive capacities not also be susceptible to evolutionary pressures?"[5] Indeed.

Singer, like Bakunin, acknowledges the achievements of Marx, but refuses to see them in absolute terms. As he puts it: "We should not abandon Marx's insight, but we should make it part of a much larger picture". The economic factor — the effect of *"changes* in the mode of production" — is important, but there are much more fundamental factors in social development, factors that are, to all intents and purposes, "*constant*". Thus Singer states: "It is time to recognize that the way in which the mode of production influences our ideas, our politics, and our consciousness is *through* the specific features of our biological inheritance", that is, "through" human nature.[6]

The similarity between these aspects of Singer's account and core elements of Bakunin's naturalism shows that the much needed "new paradigm" for the left has been prepared already — and not just by Bakunin. Outside the confines of the academy, a naturalist tradition has engaged with issues of justice and "the achievement of a better society" for more than a century. This tradition is still maturing and offers much hope for the contemporary left, attuned as it is to pressing issues, ecological as well as social. Certain of these issues, not least the ecological, are simply beyond the Marxian frame of mind. I do not for a moment claim that Bakunin's writings fully comprehend these matters or offer all the solutions. However, the limited insights of Bakunin that have paved the way for a vital contemporary movement against the injustices and idiocies of our world deserve to be represented and understood.

Notes to Conclusion

1.   *Social Anarchism or Lifestyle Anarchism: An Unbridgeable Chasm* (Edinburgh: A.K. Press, 1995), pp. 1, 11, 7, 3, 56. Emphasis added.

2.   London: Weidenfeld & Nicolson, 1999.

3.   There is a major difference when Singer offers the following as an example of an aspect of human nature because it displays "little variation across cultures": "More controversially, I would claim that the existence of a hierarchy or system of rank is a near-universal human tendency", is, indeed, "inherent in human beings" [ibid., pp. 37, 39]. He does say that "because something like hierarchy . . . is characteristic of almost all human societies [does not mean] it is good, or acceptable, or that we should not attempt to change it" [ibid., p. 38]. If something really is part of a scientifically determined human nature, it is difficult, short of some imaginable form of genetic engineering (and therefore by some exceedingly authoritative behavior), to see how we could alter it. Singer's account of human nature seems rather arbitrary, and this is likely to encourage precisely those arguments against human nature that he attacks in the case of Marx. Again: "To say that human beings under a wide range of conditions have a tendency to form hierarchies is not to say that it is right for our society to be hierarchical ["My point is not about deducing an 'ought' from an 'is'"]; but it is also to issue a warning that we should not expect to abolish hierarchy by eliminating the particular hierarchy we have in our society" [ibid., p. 38]. Singer uses "the rapid departure from equality in the Soviet Union" as an example to justify this point [ibid., p. 39]. However, there are many explanations of this (including Bakunin's prescient one) that do not require any assumptions about human nature. As important as it is to acknowledge human nature, it should not be used as a convenient explanation for any cultural phenomenon, however widespread. From the naturalistic perspective, this seems like a wild overestimate of the capabilities of the non-natural sciences, an overestimate which, I think, Bakunin was guilty of at times.

4.   Ibid., pp. 4-6.

5.   Ibid., pp. 23-24.

6.   Ibid., p. 32. Emphasis added.

SELECT BIBLIOGRAPHY

PRIMARY WORKS

Oeuvres Complètes CD-ROM (Amsterdam: International Institute of Social History, 2000). [The definitive collection of Bakunin's writings. Includes and supplements the excellent *Archives Bakounine* collection.]

Archives Bakounine, I-VII, ed. Arthur Lehning (Leiden: E.J. Brill, 1961-1981).

Oeuvres Complètes, I-VIII, ed. Arthur Lehning (Paris: Editions Champs Libres, 1973-1982). [Less expensive version of the above series. The volume numbers differ because *Archives Bakounine*, I is published in two parts which correspond to volumes I and II in *Oeuvres Complètes*.]

Oeuvres, I-VI, ed. Max Nettlau and James Guillaume (Paris: P.V. Stock, 1895-1913). [The standard edition of Bakunin's later writings before *Archives Bakounine* appeared. Includes some writings not published in that series. Volume I has been republished twice, relatively recently (Paris: P.V. Stock, 1972 and 1980).]

Sobranie sochinenii i pisem, I-IV, ed. Iurii Mikhailovich Steklov (Moscow: Izdatel'stvo vsesoiuznogo obshchestva politkatorzhan i ssyl'no-poselentsev, 1934-1936). [The standard edition of Bakunin's early writings. Another incomplete series.]

Izbrannye sochineniia, I-V (Petrograd-Moscow: Golos Truda, 1919-1921). [Another major Russian-language series.]

Pis'ma M.A. Bakunina k A.I. Gertsenu i N.P. Ogarevu, ed. Mikhail Petrovich Dragomanov (Geneva: Ukrainskaia Tipografiia, 1896). [Another volume of importance.]

English Translations Consulted

Michael Bakunin: Selected Writings, ed. Arthur Lehning, trans. Steven Cox and Olive Stevens (London: Jonathan Cape, 1973). [The best English-language anthology.]

The Political Philosophy of Bakunin: Scientific Anarchism, ed. G.P. Maximoff (Glencoe: Free Press of Glencoe, 1953). [Quantitatively, the best English-language anthology, but poorly edited.]

The Basic Bakunin: Writings 1869-1871, ed. Robert M. Cutler (Buffalo: Prometheus, 1992). [A useful anthology, well edited and translated (by the editor) with an excellent bibliography. There is an earlier edition: *From Out of the Dustbin* (Ann Arbor: Ardis, 1985).]

Statism and Anarchy, ed. Marshall M. Shatz (Cambridge: Cambridge University Press, 1991). [Excellent edition.]

The Confession of Mikhail Bakunin: With the Marginal Comments of Tsar Nicholas I, ed. Lawrence D. Orton (Ithaca: Cornell University Press, 1977). [Again, an excellent edition.]

Marxism, Freedom, and the State, ed. K.J. Kenafick (London: Freedom Press, 1990). [Quite useful, but too short and poorly edited. Originally published by the same publisher in 1950.]

Bakunin on Anarchy, ed. Sam Dolgoff, Revised Edition (Montréal: Black Rose Books, 1980). [Disappointing anthology. Badly edited and translated. The original edition appeared some years earlier (New York: Alfred A. Knopf, 1971).]

God and the State, ed. Paul Avrich (New York: Dover, 1970).

SECONDARY WORKS

Aldred, Guy. *Bakunin, Communist* (Glasgow: Spur, 1920).

Aldred, Guy. *Bakunin* (Glasgow: Strickland Press, 1940).

Anderson, Thornton. *Russian Political Thought: An Introduction* (Ithaca: Cornell University Press, 1967).

Arvon, Henri. *L'anarchisme*, Ninth Edition (Paris: Presses universitaires de France, 1987).

Arvon, Henri. *Bakounine: absolu et révolution* (Paris: Editions du Cerf, 1972).

Arvon, Henri. "Bakounine (Michel)", *Encyclopaedia Universalis*, II (Paris, 1980).

Arvon, Henri. *Michel Bakounine, ou la vie contre science* (Paris: Seghers, 1966).

Avrich, Paul. "Anarchism and Anti-Intellectualism in Russia", *Journal of the History of Ideas*, XXVII (1966), pp. 381-90.

Avrich, Paul. "Bakunin and His Writings", *Canadian-American Slavic Studies*, X (1976), pp. 591-96.

Avrich, Paul. *Anarchist Portraits* (Princeton: Princeton University Press, 1988).

Barer, Shlomo. *The Doctors of Revolution* (London: Thames and Hudson, 2000).

Berdyaev, Nicolas. *The Origin of Russian Communism*, trans. R.M. French (Ann Arbor: University of Michigan, 1960).

Berlin, Isaiah. *Russian Thinkers*, ed. Henry Hardy and Aileen Kelly (Harmondsworth: Penguin Books, 1978).

Bookchin, Murray. *Social Anarchism or Lifestyle Anarchism: An Unbridgeable Chasm* (Edinburgh: A.K. Press, 1995).

Camus, Albert. *The Rebel*, trans. Anthony Bower (Harmondsworth: Penguin Books, 1971).

Carr, E.H. *Michael Bakunin* (New York: Octagon Books, 1975).

Carr, E.H. "Bakunin, Mikhail Aleksandrovich", *Collier's Encyclopedia*, III (New York: P. F. Collier, 1993), pp. 471-72.

Carr, E.H. "Bakunin, Mikhail Aleksandrovich", *Encyclopaedia Britannica*, Fifteenth Edition, I (Chicago, 1997), pp. 817-18.

Carter, April. *The Political Theory of Anarchism* (London: Routledge & Kegan Paul, 1971).

Carter, Alan B. *Marx: A Radical Critique* (Brighton: Wheatsheaf, 1988).

Catteau, Jacques, ed. *Bakounine: Combats et débats* (Paris: Institut d'études slaves, 1979).

Chomsky, Noam. *For Reasons of State* (London: Fontana, 1973).

Clark, John. "Marx, Bakunin, and the Problem of Social Transformation", *Telos*, XLII (1979), pp. 80-97.

Confino, Michael. "Varieties of Anarchism", *The Russian Review*, XLVIII (1989), pp. 403-12.

Cole, G.D.H. *A History of Socialist Thought*, II, *Marxism and Anarchism: 1850-1890* (London: Macmillan, 1954).

Cranston, Maurice. *Political Dialogues* (London: B.B.C., 1968).

Crowder, George. *Classical Anarchism: The Political Thought of Godwin, Proudhon, Bakunin, and Kropotkin* (Oxford: Oxford University Press, 1991).

Del Giudice, Martine. "Bakunin's 'Preface to Hegel's *Gymnasial Lectures*': The Problem of Alienation and the Reconciliation with Reality", *Canadian-American Slavic Studies*, XVI (1982), pp. 161-89.

Drachkovitch, Milorad M., ed. *The Revolutionary Internationals: 1864-1943* (Stanford: Stanford University Press, 1966).

Dubois, Félix. *The Anarchist Peril*, ed. Ralph Derechef (London: T. Fisher Unwin, 1894).

Duclos, Jacques. *Bakounine et Marx: ombre et lumière* (Paris: Plon, 1974).

Eaton, Henry. "Marx and the Russians", *Journal of the History of Ideas*, XLI (1980), pp. 89-112.

Fleming, Marie. *The Geography of Freedom: The Odyssey of Elisée Reclus* (Montréal: Black Rose Books, 1988).

Fowler, R.B. "The Anarchist Tradition of Political Thought", *Western Political Quarterly*, XXV (1972), pp. 738-52.

Gay, Kathlyn and Martin K. Gay. *Encyclopedia of Political Anarchy* (Santa Barbara: ABC-CLIO, 1999).

Grawitz, Madeleine. *Michel Bakounine* (Paris: Plon, 1990).

Gray, Alexander. *The Socialist Tradition: Moses to Lenin* (London: Longmans, Green and Co., 1946).

Guérin, Daniel. *Anarchism: From Theory to Practice*, trans. Mary Klopper (New York: Monthly Review Press, 1970).

Hare, Richard. *Portraits of Russian Personalities Between Reform and Revolution* (Oxford: Oxford University Press, 1959).

Heider, Ulrike. *Anarchism: Left, Right, and Green*, trans. Danny Lewis and Ulrike Bode (San Francisco: City Lights Books, 1994).

Herzen, Alexander. *My Past and Thoughts*, III, trans. Constance Garnett, revised by Humphrey Higgins (London: Chatto & Windus, 1968).

Joll, James. *The Anarchists* (London: Eyre & Spottiswoode, 1964).

Kaminski, Hanns Erich. *Bakounine: la vie d'un révolutionnaire* (Paris: Bélibaste, 1971).

Kelly, Aileen. *Mikhail Bakunin: A Study in the Psychology and Politics of Utopianism* (Oxford: Clarendon Press, 1982).

Kelly, Aileen. "Bakunin, Mikhail Aleksandrovich", *Routledge Encyclopedia of Philosophy*, I, ed. Edward Craig (London: Routledge, 1998), pp. 645-47.

Kenafick, K.J. *Michael Bakunin and Karl Marx* (Melbourne: A. Maller, 1948).

Kofman, M. "The Reaction of Two Anarchists to Nationalism: Proudhon and Bakunin on the Polish Question", *Labour History*, XIV (1968), pp. 34-45.

Kolakowski, Leszek. *Main Currents of Marxism: Its Rise, Growth, and Dissolution*, I, trans. P.S. Falla (Oxford: Clarendon Press, 1978).

Kropotkin, Peter. *Two Essays: Anarchism and Anarchist Communism* (London: Freedom Press, 1993).

Lampert, E. *Studies in Rebellion* (London: Routledge & Kegan Paul, 1957).

Lehning, Arthur. "Bakunin", *New Society*, XVI (1970), pp. 450-52.

Lehning, Arthur. *From Buonarroti to Bakunin: Studies in International Socialism* (Leiden: E.J. Brill, 1970).

Lehning, Arthur. "Michel Bakounine: Théorie et Practique du Fédéralisme Anti-étatique en 1870-1871", *International Review of Social History*, XVII (1972), pp. 455-73.

Lehning, Arthur. "Bakunin's Conceptions of Revolutionary Organizations and Their Role: A Study of His 'Secret Societies'", *Essays in Honour of E.H. Carr*, ed. C. Abramsky (London: Macmillan, 1974).

Lehning, Arthur, ed. *Michel Bakounine et les autres* (Paris: Union générale d'éditions, 1976).

Lichtheim, George. *A Short History of Socialism* (London: Weidenfield & Nicolson, 1970).

Marshall, Peter. *Demanding the Impossible: A History of Anarchism* (London: Fontana Press, 1993).

Masaryk, Thomas Garrigue. *The Spirit of Russia*, I, Second Edition, trans. Eden and Cedar Paul (London: Allen & Unwin, 1955).

Masters, Anthony. *Bakunin: The Father of Anarchism* (London: Sidgwick and Jackson, 1974).

Mendel, Arthur P. "Bakunin: A View from Within", *Canadian-American Slavic Studies*, X (1976), pp. 466-88.

Mendel, Arthur P. *Michael Bakunin: Roots of Apocalypse* (New York: Praeger, 1981).

Miller, David. *Anarchism* (London: J.M. Dent & Sons, 1984).

Morland, David. *Demanding the Impossible? Human Nature and Politics in Nineteenth-Century Social Anarchism* (London: Cassell, 1998).

Morris, Brian. *Bakunin: The Philosophy of Freedom* (Montréal: Black Rose Books, 1993).

Nettlau, Max. *Michael Bakunin. Eine Biographie*, 3 vols (London: n.p., 1896-1900).

Nettlau, Max. "Bakunin, Michael", *Encyclopeadia of the Social Sciences*, II (New York: Macmillan, 1935), pp. 393-94.

Nettlau, Max. *Writings on Bakunin* (London: Carl Slienger, 1976).

Nettlau, Max. *A Short History of Anarchism*, trans. Ida Pilat Isca (London: Freedom Press, 1996).

Nomad, Max. *Apostles of Revolution* (New York: Collier, 1933).

Nursey-Bray, Paul, Jim Jose, and Robyn Williams. *Anarchist Thinkers and Thought: An Annotated Bibliography* (Westport: Greenwood Press, 1992).

Pirumova, Natal'ia. "Bakunin and Herzen: An Analysis of Their Ideological Disagreements at the End of the 1860s", *Canadian-American Slavic Studies*, X (1976), pp. 552-69.

Plechanoff, George. *Anarchism and Socialism*, trans. Eleanor Marx-Aveling (Chicago: Charles H. Kerr & Co., 1909).

Pyziur, Eugene. *The Doctrine of Anarchism of Michael A. Bakunin* (Milwaukee: Marquette University Press, 1955).

Ravindranathan, T.R. "Bakunin in Naples: An Assessment", *Journal of Modern History*, LIII (1981), pp. 189-212.

Ravindranathan, T.R. "The Paris Commune and the First International in Italy:

Republicanism versus Socialism, 1871-1872", *International History Review*, III (1981), pp. 482-516.

Ravindranathan, T.R. *Bakunin and the Italians* (Kingston and Montréal: McGill-Queen's University Press, 1988).

Reszler, André. "An Essay on Political Myths: Anarchist Myths of Revolt", *Diogenes*, XCIV (1976), pp. 34-52.

Ritter, Alan. *Anarchism: A Theoretical Analysis* (Cambridge: Cambridge University Press, 1980).

Rude, Fernand. "Bakounine en 1870-1871", *Cahiers d'Histoire*, XXIV (1979), pp. 75-85.

Rude, Fernand. "Le 'Testament Spirituel' de Bakounine", *Cahiers d'Histoire*, XXXI (1986), pp. 157-69.

Russell, Bertrand. *Roads to Freedom: Socialism, Anarchism, and Syndicalism* (London: George Allen and Unwin, 1918).

Saltman, Richard B. *The Social and Political Thought of Michael Bakunin* (Westport: Greenwood Press, 1983).

Steklov, Yuri. *History of the First International*, trans. Eden and Cedar Paul (New York: Russell & Russell, 1968).

Strub, Hélène. *Anarchism: Catologue of XIXth and XXth Centuries: Books and Pamplets from Different Countries* (Munich: K.G. Saur, 1993).

Thomas, Paul. *Karl Marx and the Anarchists* (London: Routledge, 1980).

Ulam, Adam B. *Ideologies and Illusions: Revolutionary Thought from Herzen to Solzhenitsyn* (Cambridge: Harvard University Press, 1976).

Utechin, S.V. *Russian Political Thought: A Concise History* (London: J.M. Dent & Sons, 1964).

Varlamov, Volodymyr. *Bakunin and the Russian Jacobins and Blanquists as Evaluated by Soviet Historiography*, trans. Lois Weinert (New York: Research Program on the USSR, 1955).

Venturi, Franco. *Roots of Revolution: A History of the Populist and Socialist Movements in Nineteenth Century Russia*, trans. Francis Haskell (London: Weidenfeld, 1960).

Voegelin, Eric. "Bakunin's Confession", *Journal of Politics*, VIII (1946), pp. 24-43.

Voegelin, Eric. *From Enlightenment to Revolution*, ed. John H. Hallowell (Durham: Duke University Press, 1975).

Walicki, Andrzej. *A History of Russian Thought: From the Enlightenment to Marx*, trans. Hilda Andrews-Rusiecka (Stanford: Stanford University Press, 1979).

Watt, A.J. "Illich and Anarchism", *Educational Philosophy and Theory*, XIII (1981), pp. 1-15.

Wilson, Edmund. *To the Finland Station* (London: Fontana, 1972).

Woodcock, George. "Bakunin, Michael", *The Encyclopedia of Philosophy*, I & II, ed. Paul Edwards (New York: Macmillan, 1967), pp. 244-46.

Woodcock, George. *Anarchism: A History of Libertarian Ideas and Movements* (Harmondsworth: Penguin Books, 1975).

Woodcock, George, ed. *Anarchism and Anarchists* (Kingston: Quarry Press, 1992).

Yemel'ian Mikhailovic Iaroslavskii, *History of Anarchism in Russia* (New York: International Publishers, 1937).

Zenkovsky, V.V. *A History of Russian Philosophy*, I, trans. George L. Kline (New York: Columbia University Press, 1953).

ADDITIONAL READING

In general (though exceptions have been made), studies of seven kinds have been excluded: (1) studies which are, by any standards, bad and/or unoriginal; (2) studies which are nationally-oriented (which deal, for instance, with Bakunin and Italy or Poland); (3) studies of the Nechaev affair; (4) studies of the First International; (5) studies of Bakunin's relations with specific individuals (e.g., Herzen or Mazzini); (6) studies of specific events or periods in Bakunin's life (e.g., his stays in Scandinavia or Japan); and (7) studies of particular "peculiarities" of Bakunin's character (e.g., incestuous desire). The grounds for such exclusion are that (a) such studies are, by and large, irrelevant to philosophical analysis of Bakunin, and (b) in certain cases (especially in the case of studies of the seventh and, obviously, the first kinds) too poor to justify inclusion. General biographies are included (in a number of cases, reluctantly) for the simple reason that they constitute almost the entire field and are, in any event, occasionally (but only occasionally) illuminating.

Studies in French:

Amédée Dunois and René Berthier, *Michel Bakounine* (Paris: Editions du Monde libertaire, 1998) [see Dunois, 1909, below].

Gaston Leval, *Bakounine: fondateur du syndicalisme révolutionnaire* (Paris: C.N.T. Région parisienne, 1998) [originally published in the early 1970s].

René Berthier, *Bakounine politique: révolution et contre-révolution en Europe centrale* (Paris: Editions du Monde libertaire, 1991).

Madeleine Grawitz, *Bakounine* (Paris: Plon, 1990) [recently translated into German: *Bakunin: Ein Leben für die Freiheit*, trans. Andreas Löhrer (Hamburg: Nautilus, 1999)].

Gaston Leval, *Michel Bakounine* (Le Havre: Groupe Etienne de la Boetie, 1989).

Tanguy L'Aminot, "Bakounine: Critique de Rousseau", *Dix-Huitième Siècle*, IXX (1987), pp. 351-65.

Miklós Kun, "Un tournant décisif dans la vie de Bakounine: données inédites sur son évolution idéologique et sur son activité conspiratrice", *Acta Historica*, XXVI (1980), pp. 27-75.

Jacques Catteau, ed., *Bakounine: Combats et débats* (Paris: Institut d'études slaves, 1979).

Philippe Oyhamburu, *La revanche de Bakounine, ou De l'anarchisme a l'autogestion* (Paris: Entente, 1975) [Spanish: *La revancha de Bakunin* (Madrid: Campo Abierto, 1977)].

Arthur Lehning, ed., *Michel Bakounine et les autres: esquisses et portraits contemporains d'un révolutionnaire* (Paris: Union générale d'éditions, 1976).

Gaston Leval, *La pensée constructive de Bakounine* (Paris: René Lefeuvre, 1976).

Jeanne-Marie V., *Michel Bakounine: une vie d'homme* (Geneva: Association Noir, 1976).

Jacques Duclos, *Bakounine et Marx: ombre et lumière* (Paris: Plon, 1974).

Henri Arvon, *Bakounine: absolu et révolution* (Paris: Editions du Cerf, 1972).

Arthur Lehning, "Michel Bakounine: Théorie et Practique du Fédéralisme Anti-étatique en 1870-1871", *International Review of Social History*, XVII (1972), pp. 455-73.

Henri Arvon, *Michel Bakounine, ou la Vie contre la science* (Paris: Seghers, 1966).

Hem Day, *Michel Bakounine: aspects de son oeuvre* (Paris: Pensée et action, 1966).

Arthur Lehning, introductions and notes to *Archives Bakounine*, I - VII (Leiden: E. J. Brill, 1961-1981) [reprinted as the introductions and notes to *Oeuvres Complètes*, I - VIII (Paris: Editions Champ Libre, 1973-1982)].

Benoît P. Hepner, *Bakounine et la panslavisme révolutionnaire; cinq essais sur l'histoire des idées en Russie et en Europe* (Paris: Marcel Riviere, 1950).

Etienne Porgès, *Bakounine* (Paris: Editions des Portes de France, 1946).

Hanns-Erich Kaminski, *Bakounine: la vie d'un révolutionnaire* (Paris: Aubier, 1938) [there is also a reprint (Paris: Bélibaste, 1971)].

Elena Aleksandrovna Izvol'skaya (Hélene Iswolsky), *La vie de Bakounine* (Paris: Librairie Gallimard, 1930).

Amédée Dunois, "Michel Bakounine", *Portraits d'hier*, VI (1909), pp. 163-91.

Victor Dave, "Michel Bakounine et Karl Marx", *L'Humanité Nouvelle*, XXXIII (1900), pp. 257-80 [various translations].

Albert François, *Michel Bakounine et la philosophie de l'anarchie* (Brussels: H. Lamertin, 1900).

Emile de Laveleye, "L'apôtre de la destruction universelle", *Revue des Deux Mondes*, 1880, pp. 546-82.

Studies in German:

Markus Heinlein, *Klassicher Anarchismus und Erziehung. Libertäre Pädogogik bei William Godwin, Michael Bakunin und Peter Kropotkin* (Würzburg: Ergon, 1998).

Irene Lawen, *Konzeptionen der Freiheit. Zum Stellenwert der Freiheitsidee in der Sozialethik John Stuart Mills und Michail A. Bakunins* (Saarbrücken: Saarbrücken Verlag für Entwicklungspolitik, 1996).

Herbert Berger, *Negative Kausalität. Soziale Welt bei Hume und Bakunin* (Cuxhaven: Trande Junghans, 1995).

Wolfgang Eckhardt, *Michail A. Bakunin (1814-1876). Bibliographie der Primär- und Sekundärliteratur in deutscher Sprache* (Cologne: Libertad, 1994).

Arthur Lehning, ed., *Unterhaltungen mit Bakunin*, trans. Rolf Binner and Gerd Müller (Nördlingen: Greno, 1987) [there is a newer edition (Leipzig: Reclam-Verlag, 1991)].

Wim van Dooren, *Bakunin zur Einfürung* (Hamburg: Junius-Verlag, 1985).

Gerd Koch, *Marx und Bakunin zur Pariser Kommune. Zerstört den Staat* (Hamburg: Association, 1974).

Justus Franz Wittkop, *Michail A. Bakunin. Mit Selbstzeugnissen und Bilddokumenten* (Reinbek: Rowohlt, 1974) [republished by the same publisher in 1987 and 1994].

G. Bartsch, *Kommunismus, Sozialismus, Anarchismus und Karl Marx* (Bonn: Bundeszentrale für politische Bildung, 1971).

Horst Bienek, *Bakunin. Eine Invention* (Munich: C. Hanser, 1970) [republished (Frankfurt am Main: Suhrkamp, 1982)].

Peter Scheibert, *Von Bakunin zu Lenin. Geschichte der russischen revolutionären Ideologien 1840-1895*, I (Leiden: E.J. Brill, 1956).

Joseph Pfitzner, *Bakuninstudien* (Prague: Verlag der Deutschen Gesellschaft der Wissenschaften und Künste für die Tschechoslowakische Republik, 1932) [republished (Berlin: Karin Kramer, 1977)].

Joseph Billig, "Der Zusammenbruch des deutschen Idealismus bei den russischen Romantikern (Bjelinski, Bakunin)", *Archiv für systematische Philosophie und Soziologie*, XXXIV (1930).

Fritz Brupbacher, *Michael Bakunin, der Satan der Revolte* (Zürich: Neuer deutscher Verlag, 1929) [republished (Berlin: Libertad-Verlag, 1979)].

Max Nettlau, *Der Anarchismus von Proudhon zu Kropotkin: seine historische Entwicklung in den Jahren 1859-1880* (Berlin: Der Syndikalist, 1927) [republished (Vaduz: Topos, 1984)].

Ricarda Huch, *Michael Bakunin und die Anarchie* (Leipzig: Insel-Verlag, 1923) [republished recently (Frankfurt am Main: Suhrkamp, 1988), having been republished twice already by this publisher (1972 and 1980)].

Hans Müller, *Michael Bakunin. Der revolutionäre Anarchismus* (Zurich: Sozialistische Verlagsgenossenschaft, 1919).

Fritz Brupbacher, *Marx und Bakunin* (Munich: G. Birk & Co., 1913) [republications (from Berlin: Verlag Die Aktion, 1922, to Berlin: Karin Kramer, 1976)].

Iurii Mikhailovich Steklov, *Mikhail Aleksandrovich Bakunin. Ein Lebensbild* (Stuttgart: Dietz, 1913) [republished by the same publisher in 1920].

Max Nettlau, *Michael Bakunin. Eine biographische Skizze* (Berlin: P. Pawlowitsch, 1901).

Max Nettlau, *Michael Bakunin. Eine Biographie*, I-III (London: n.p., 1896-1900).

Studies in Russian:

Natal'ia Mikhailovna Pirumova, *Sotsial'naia doktrina M.A. Bakunina* (Moscow: Nauka, 1990).

V.F. Pustarnakova, ed., *Filosofiia, sotsiologiia, politika* (Moscow: Izdatel'stvo Pravda, 1989 [an anthology of Bakunin's writings rather than a secondary work, but interesting for its timing if nothing else].

Vladimir Georgievich Grafskii, *Bakunin* (Moscow: Iuridicheskaia literatura, 1985).

Pavel Innokent'evich Moiseev, *Kritika filosofii M. Bakunina i sovremennost'* (Irkutsk: Vostochno-Sibirskoe knizhnoe izd-vo, 1981).

Vladimir Gurgenovich Dzhangirian, *Kritika anglo-amerikanskoi burzhuaznoi istriografii M.A. Bakunina i bakunizma* (Moscow: Mysl', 1978).

Fedor Iakovlevich Polianskii, *Kritika ekonomicheskikh anarkhizma* (Izdatel'stvo Moskovskogo universiteta, 1976).

Mikhail Ivanovich Mikhailov, *Bor'ba protiv bakunizma v I Internationale* (Moscow: Nauka, 1976).

Natal'ia Mikhailovna Pirumova, *Bakunin* (Moscow: Molodaia gvardiia, 1970).

Isaak Borisovich Zil'berman, *Politicheskaia teoriia anarkhizma M.A. Bakunina* (Leningrad: Izdatel'stvo Leningradskogo univeriteta, 1969).

R.N. Blium, "Vzgliady M.A. Bakunina na revoliutsiiu", *Uchenye zapiski Tartuskogo gosudarstvennogo universiteta*, 225 (1969).

Natal'ia Mikhailovna Pirumova, *Mikhail Bakunin: zhizn' i deiatel'nost'* (Moscow: Nauka, 1966).

Valentina A. Tvardovskaia and N. Iu. Kolpinskii, "Bakunin v russkom i mezhdunarodom osvoboditel'nom dvizhenii", *Voprosy istorii*, X (1964), pp. 69-95.

Iurii Mikhailovich Steklov, *Mikhail Aleksandrovich Bakunin. Ego zhizn' i deiatel'nost'*, *1814-1876*, Second Edition, I-IV (Moscow: Izd-vo Kommunisticeskoi

Akademii, 1926-27).

Aleksandr Aleksandrovich Kornilov, *Gody stranstvii Mikhaila Bakunina* (Leningrad-Moscow: Gosudarstvennoe Izdatel'stvo, 1925).

Viacheslav Pavlovich Polonskii, *Mikhail Aleksandrovich Bakunin. Zhizn', deiatel'nost', myshlenie* (Moscow-Leningrad: Gosudarstvennoe Izdatel'stvo, 1925).

Viacheslav Pavlovich Polonskii, *Materialy dlia biografii M. Bakunina*, I-III (Moscow-Leningrad: Gosudarstvennoe Izdatel'stvo, 1923-33).

Aleksandr Aleksandrovich Kornilov, *Molodye gody Mikhaila Bakunina* (Moscow: Izd. M. i S. Sabashnikovykh, 1915).

Studies in other languages:

Roberto Giulianelli, *Bakunin e la rivoluzione anarchica* (Salerno: Galzerano, 1998).

Giuseppe Turco Liveri, *Il cane di fuoco e l'aristocratico da letamaio: dispute nello spazio tra Marx, Nietzsche ed altri* (Rome: A. Armando, 1998).

Ramón Liarte, *Bakunin: la emancipación del pueblo* (Barcelona: Editorial Salud, 1995).

Wlodzimierz Rydzewski, *Powrót Bakunina: szkice o 'rosyjskiej idei' i mitach lewicy* (Krakow: Wydawnictwo BUS, 1993).

Demetrio Velasco Criado, *Etica y poder politico en M. Bakunin* (Bilbao: Universidad de Deusto, 1993).

Dimitur Ivanov, *Ot Platon do Bakunin: osnovni politicheski idei* (Sofia: Universitetsko izd-vo Sv. Kliment Okhridski, 1991).

Renato Pernice, *L'etica della rivoluzione in M. Bakunin* (Rome: Lo Faro, 1987).

Bergljot Hobt Haff, *Jeg, Bakunin: bruddstykker av en urostifters liv og levned* (Oslo: Gyldendal, 1983).

Miklós Kun, *Útban az anarchizmus felé: Mihail Bakunyin politikai pályaképe és eszmei fejlodése az 1860-as évek közepén* (Budapest: Akadémiai Kiadó, 1982).

Ange J. Cappelletti, "Materialismo Y Dialectica En Bakunin", *Pensamiento*, XXXVII (1982), pp. 207-10.

Tomás Cano Ruiz, *Miguel Bakunin: su vida y su obra* (Naucalpan de Júarez: Ideas, 1980).

Arthur Lehning, ed., *Bakoenin: een biographie in tijdsdocumenten* (Baarn: Wereldvenster, 1977).

Aulo Casamayor, ed., *Bakunin, Marx: al margen de una polémica* (Paris: Ruedo Ibérico, 1977).

Bakunin cent'anni dopo: atti del convergo internazionale di studi bakuniniani (Milan: Edizioni Antistato, 1977).

Giuseppe Rose, *Bibliografia di Bakunin* (Catania: Edizioni della Rivista 'Anarchismo', 1976).

Victor Garcia, *Bakunin, hoy* (Rosario: Grupo ed. de estudios sociales, 1974).

Willy Hoffman, *Analyse van de politieke filosofie van de anarchist Michael Bakunin* (Ghent: Rijksuniversiteit, 1973).

Vladimir Kasik, *M.A. Bakunin* (Prague: Svoboda, 1969).

Hanna Temkinowa, *Bakunin i antynomie wolnosci* (Warsaw: Ksiazka i Wiedza, 1964).

Anton L. Constandse, *Michael Bakoenin. Russisch rebel* (Amsterdam: Holdert, 1948) [republished (Groningen: St. Pamflet, 1976)].

Jaroslav Vozka, *Michal Bakunin: vecný revolucionár* (Prague: Delnické nakl., 1947).

C.J. Björklund, *Mickael Bakunin. Tänkaren och kämpen* (Stockholm: Holmström, 1915).

Ferdinand Domela Nieuwenhuis, *Michaël Bakunine, 1814-1876* (Blaricum: Storch, 1909).

Rudolf Rocker, *Mikhayl Bakunin: a biyografishe skitse* (Leeds: Lidzer Anarkhistische Gruppe, 1902).

Index of Names

Printed in Great Britain
by Amazon